Hogan Personality Inventory Manual

Third Edition

Robert Hogan, Ph.D.
Joyce Hogan, Ph.D.

Hogan Assessment Systems
Tulsa, OK 74114, USA

2007

Hogan Personality Inventory™

Hogan Development Survey™

Motives, Values, Preferences Inventory™

Hogan Business Reasoning Inventory™

are the exclusive registered trademarks of Hogan Assessment Systems, Inc.

www.hoganassessments.com

ISBN 978-0-9840969-5-4

Contents

1. Introduction — 8

1.1 *Applying Socioanalytic Theory to Performance at Work* — 8
1.2 *Measurement: Personality Assessment and the Five-Factor Model* — 10
1.3 *Measurement: Assessing Job Performance using Multidimensional Models* — 11
1.4 *A Viewpoint on Measurement* — 12
1.5 *What to Measure* — 13

2. Inventory Construction, Reliability, And Confirmation — 15

2.1 *Early Development* — 15
2.2 *Later Development* — 16
2.3 *Most Recent Technical Developments* — 17
2.4 *Definitions of the Scales* — 19
2.5 *Composition of the Personality Scales; The 1992 Factor Analysis* — 20
2.6 *Composition of the Personality Scales: The 2007 Confirmatory Factor Analysis* — 26
2.7 *HPI Scale Distributions and Reliability* — 31
2.8 *HPI Test-Retest Reliability* — 37

3. Validity — 42

3.1 *Correlations With Other Tests* — 43
3.2 *Interpretive Summaries of the HPI Scale Correlations with Other Tests* — 64
3.3 *HPI Correlates of Organizational Behavior* — 69
3.4 *HPI Validity for Personnel Selection in Seven Job Families* — 78
3.41 *Managers & Executives Job Family* — 83
3.42 *Professionals Job Family* — 88
3.43 *Technicians & Specialists Job Family* — 91
3.44 *Operations & Trades Job Family* — 94
3.45 *Sales & Customer Support Job Family* — 97
3.46 *Administrative & Clerical Job Family* — 101
3.47 *Service & Support Job Family* — 103

4. Interpretation — 107

4.1 *Adjustment* — 108
4.2 *Ambition* — 109
4.3 *Sociability* — 110
4.4 *Interpersonal Sensitivity* — 111
4.5 *Prudence* — 112
4.6 *Inquisitive* — 113
4.7 *Learning Approach* — 114
4.8 *Adjectival Correlates of HPI Scale Scores* — 115

5. Administering the HPI   121

    5.1 Key Features of the Web-Based Platform   121

    5.2 Completing the HPI Using the Online Internet System   122

    5.3 Participant's Informed Consent   125

    5.4 Using International Translations of the HPI   127

    5.5 Accommodating Individuals with Disabilities   130

    5.6 Frequently Asked Questions   130

    5.7 Alternative Testing Solutions   131

6. Compilation Of Norms   132

    6.1 Characteristics of the 2005 HPI Norming Sample   132

    6.2 Demographics of the Norming Sample   137

    6.3 Descriptive Statistics of the Norming Sample   138

7. References   143

    Appendix A: 2005 HPI Norming Sample Scale Scores   157

    Appendix B: 1995 HPI Norms (N=21,573)   166

    Appendix C: References For Transportability Of Validity Within Job Families   167

    Appendix D: Correlations of HPI Scales With Adjectival Descriptions By Observers   175

Tables & Figures

Table 1.1	Components of the Five-Factor Model	9
Table 2.1	Varimax Rotated Factor Matrix for HPI HIC	22
Table 2.2	The Constituent HICs for the Seven HPI Scales	25
Table 2.3	Intercorrelations Between HPI Observed Scale Scores and Latent Factor Scores	27
Figure 2.1	HIC-Level Confirmatory Factor Model for the HPI	28
Figure 2.2	Histogram of Standardized Residuals for the Oblique Factor Model with Maximum Likelihood Parameter Estimation	29
Table 2.4	CFA factor Loadings for the HPI HICs	30
Table 2.5	Classical Item and Scale Statistics for the HPI	35
Table 2.6	Composite Alphas and Standard Errors of Measurement for the Seven HPI Scales	36
Table 2.7	Hypothetical Scores on a Personality Scale Over Two Test Occasions	37
Figure 2.3	Hypothetical Scores and Test-Retest Reliabilities for a Personality Scale Over Two Test Occasions	38
Table 2.8	Short-Term (14-21 day interval) Test-Retest Stability Indices for the HPI	40
Table 2.9	Long-Term (8 years interval) Test-Retest Stability Indices for the HPI	41
Table 3.1	Correlations Between the ASVAB Composites and the HPI Scales	44
Table 3.2	Correlations Between the PSI Basic Skills Tests and the HPI Scales	44
Table 3.3	Correlations Between GATB (Form E) and the HPI Scales	45
Table 3.4	Correlations Between WGCTA (Form B) and the HPI Scales	46
Table 3.5	Correlations Between BMCT and the HPI Scales	46
Table 3.6	Correlations Between HBRI and the HPI Scales	46
Table 3.7	Correlations Between the MBTI and the HPI Scales	48
Table 3.8	Correlations Between the SDS and the HPI Scales	48
Table 3.9	Correlations Between the MVPI the HPI Scales	48
Table 3.10	Correlations Between the IAS and the HPI Scales	50
Table 3.11	Correlations Between Goldberg's Big-Five Markers and the HPI Scales	50
Table 3.12	Correlations Between 16PF and the HPI Scales	51
Table 3.13	Correlations Between CPI and the HPI Scales	52
Table 3.14	Correlations Between JPI-R and the HPI Scales	53
Table 3.15	Correlations Between MPQ the HPI Scales	53
Table 3.16	Correlations Between the NEO-PI-R and the HPI Scales	54
Table 3.17	Correlations Between the PCI Primary Scales and the HPI Scales	54
Table 3.18	Correlations Between the Inventario de Personalidad de Cinco Factores and the HPI Scales	54
Figure 3.1	Relations Between FFM Inventories and the HPI Scales	55
Table 3.19	Correlations Between the HDS and the HPI Scales	57
Table 3.20	Characteristics of Rated Personality Description Scales	66
Table 3.21	Scale Correlates of Rated Personality Descriptions	67
Table 3.22	Adjectival Correlates of the HPI Scales	68
Figure 3.2	Example Criteria Representing Getting Along, Getting Ahead, and HPI Personality Scales	70

Table 3.23	Distribution of Studies Based on Holland Code and Job Title	72
Table 3.24	Meta-Analysis Results Across Getting Along and Getting Ahead Criteria Combined	74
Table 3.25	Meta-Analysis Results for Getting Along and Getting Ahead Criteria Separated	74
Table 3.26	Meta-Analysis Results for Criteria Aligned by Personality Construct	77
Table 3.27	US Department of Labor Job Categories and SOC Codes Categorized by Job Family	83
Table 3.28	Managers & Executives Jobs with Criterion-Related Data for Meta-Analysis	84
Table 3.29	Meta-Analytic Correlations Between HPI Scales and Performance Criteria for Managers & Executives Jobs	85
Table 3.30	HPI Synthetic Validity/Job Component Validity for Managers & Executives Job Family Competencies	87
Table 3.31	Professionals Jobs with Criterion-Related Data for Meta-Analysis	89
Table 3.32	Meta-Analytic Correlations Between HPI Scales and Performance Criteria for Professionals Jobs	89
Table 3.33	HPI Scale Synthetic Validity/Job Component Validity for Professionals Job Family Competencies	90
Table 3.34	Technicians & Specialists Jobs with Criterion-Related Data for Meta-Analysis	92
Table 3.35	Meta-Analytic Correlations Between HPI Scales and Performance Criteria for Technicians & Specialists Jobs	92
Table 3.36	HPI Scale Synthetic Validity/Job Component Validity for Technicians & Specialists Job Family Competencies	93
Table 3.37	Operations & Trade Jobs with Criterion-Related Data for Meta-Analysis	95
Table 3.38	Meta-Analytic Correlations Between HPI Scales and Performance Criteria for Operations & Trades Jobs	95
Table 3.39	HPI Synthetic Validity/Job Component Validity for Operations & Trades Job Family Competencies	96
Table 3.40	Sales & Customer Support Jobs with Criterion-Related Data for Meta-Analysis	98
Table 3.41	Meta-Analytic Correlations Between HPI Scales and Performance Criteria for Sales & Customer Support Jobs	99
Table 3.42	HPI Synthetic Validity/Job Component Validity for Sales & Customer Support Job Family Competencies	100
Table 3.43	Administrative & Clerical Jobs with Criterion-Related Data for Meta-Analysis	101
Table 3 44	Meta-Analytic Correlations Between HPI Scales and Performance Criteria for Administrative & Clerical Jobs	102
Table 3.45	HPI Synthetic Validity/Job Component Validity for Administrative & Clerical Job Family Competencies	103
Table 3.46	Service & Support Jobs with Criterion-Related Data for Transportability of Validity	104
Table 3.47	Meta-Analytic Correlations Between HPI Scales and Performance Criteria for Service & Support Jobs	104
Table 3.48	HPI Synthetic Validity/Job Component Validity for Service & Support Job Family Competencies	105
Table 4.1	Adjustment Correlations with CQS and ACL Items	116
Table 4.2	Ambition Correlations with CQS and ACL Items	117
Table 4.3	Sociability Correlations with CQS and ACL Items	117

Table 4.4	Interpersonal Sensitivity Correlations with CQS and ACL Items	118
Table 4.5	Prudence Correlations with CQS and ACL Items	119
Table 4.6	Inquisitive Correlations with CQS and ACL Items	119
Table 4.7	Learning Approach Correlations with CQS and ACL Items	120
Figure 5.1	Hogan Assessment Systems Participant Login Web Page	122
Figure 5.2	Hogan Assessment Systems Participant Information Web Page	123
Figure 5.3	Hogan Assessment Systems Participant Menu Web Page	124
Figure 5.4	Hogan Assessment Systems Questionnaire Assessment Web Page	125
Table 5.1	HPI Language Translations	127
Figure 5.5	Hogan Assessment Systems Report Language Selection	128
Figure 5.6	Hogan Assessment Systems Language Translation Flags	129
Table 6.1	HPI Database Classified by DoL Occupations	134
Table 6.2	HPI Norming Sample Distribution by Occupation Using Applicants in Selection Contexts	135
Table 6.3	Final Norming Sample Distribution by Test Purpose	136
Table 6.4	Final Norming Sample Distribution by Occupation	136
Table 6.5	Gender Distribution of Final Norming Sample	137
Table 6.6	Race/Ethnicity Distribution of Final Norming Sample	137
Table 6.7	Norming Sample Ethnic Composition by Age and Gender	137
Table 6.8	Norming Sample Scale Means and Standard Deviations	138
Table 6.9	Norming Sample Scale Means and Standard Deviations by Age	139
Table 6.10	Norming Sample Scale Means and Standard Deviations by Gender	140
Table 6.11	Norming Sample Scale Means and Standard Deviations by Age and Gender	141
Table A.1	Norms for the Total Sample	157
Table A.2	Stratified Norms of Validity Scale	158
Table A.3	Stratified Norms of Adjustment Scale	159
Table A.4	Stratified Norms of Ambition Scale	160
Table A.5	Stratified Norms of Sociability Scale	162
Table A.6	Stratified Norms of Interpersonal Sensitivity Scale	162
Table A.7	Stratified Norms of Prudence Scale	163
Table A.8	Stratified Norms of Inquisitive Scale	164
Table A.9	Stratified Norms of Learning Approach Scale	165
Table C.1	Research References Contributing HPI Validity Data for Seven Job Families	167
Table D.1	HPI Scale Correlations with Adjective Checklist Items	175
Table D.2	HPI Scale Correlations with Adjective Checklist Items	183

1. Introduction

The Hogan Personality Inventory (HPI) is a measure of normal personality. That statement raises two questions. First, what is personality? And second, how can it be measured? Regarding nature, personality concerns two big things: (a) generalizations about human nature—what people are like way down deep; and (b) systematic accounts of individual differences—which differences among people are important and how do they arise?

1.1 Applying Socioanalytic Theory to Performance at Work

With regard to generalizations about human nature, the early pioneers of personality psychology (e.g., Freud, Jung, Adler, Horney, Erikson) argued that the most important generalization made is that everyone is neurotic—which means that the most important psychological problem in life is to overcome one's neurosis. However, that generalization is empirically false—for example, the base rate of neuroticism is too low to be a general characteristic (*Kessler, Berglund, Demler, Jin, Merikangas, & Walters, 2005; Renaud & Estes, 1961*).

Socioanalytic theory *(Hogan, 1983, 1991, 1996)* is intended to explain individual differences in interpersonal effectiveness, and is rooted in the long tradition of interpersonal psychology (*Carson, 1969; Leary, 1957; Sullivan, 1953; Wiggins, 1979*). The theory is based on the following five assumptions: personality is best understood in terms of human evolution; people evolved as group-living and culture-using animals; the most important human motives facilitate group living and enhance individual survival; social interaction involves negotiating for acceptance and status; and, finally, some people are more effective at this than others *(Hogan, 1996; Hogan, Jones, & Cheek, 1985)*. The theory is based on two generalizations relevant to organizational behavior: people always live (work) in groups, and groups are always structured in terms of status hierarchies. These generalizations suggest the presence of two broad motive patterns that translate into behavior designed to "get along" with other members of the group, and to "get ahead" or achieve status vis á vis other members of the group. Getting along and getting ahead are familiar themes in personality psychology *(cf. Adler, 1939; Bakan, 1966; Rank, 1945; Wiggins & Trapnell, 1996)*. Their importance is justified in Darwinian terms: people who cannot get along with others and who lack status and power have reduced opportunities for reproductive success.

> Socioanalytic theory is rooted in the long tradition of interpersonal psychology.

Socioanalytic theory specifies that personality should be defined from the perspectives of the actor and the observer. Personality from the actor's view is a person's identity, which is manifested in terms of the strategies a person uses to pursue acceptance and status. Identity controls an actor's social behavior. Personality from the observer's view is a person's reputation and is defined in terms of trait evaluations—conforming, helpful, talkative, competitive, calm, curious, and so forth. Reputation reflects an observer's view of the actor's characteristic ways of behaving in public. Reputation is the link between the actor's efforts to achieve acceptance and status and how those efforts are evaluated by observers. Reputation describes a person's behavior; identity explains it.

From the lexical perspective (Goldberg, 1981), the development of the Five-Factor Model (FFM) (cf. Digman, 1990; Goldberg, 1992; John, 1990, p. 72; McCrae & Costa, 1987) is based on 75 years of factor analytic research on the structure of trait terms and peer ratings (cf. Thurstone, 1934; Tupes & Christal, 1961; Norman, 1963). The FFM suggests that we think about and describe one another in terms of five broad trait-based themes (see Table 1.1).

Table 1.1

Components of the Five-Factor Model

Factor	Definition	ACL Marker Items*
I. Extraversion/Surgency	The degree to which a person needs attention and social interaction.	Quiet, Reserved, Shy vs. Talkative, Assertive, Active
II. Agreeableness	The degree to which a person needs pleasant and harmonious relations with others.	Fault-finding, Cold, Unfriendly vs. Sympathetic, Kind, Friendly
III. Conscientiousness	The degree to which a person is willing to comply with conventional rules, norms, and standards.	Careless, Disorderly, Frivolous vs. Organized, Thorough, Precise
IV. Emotional Stability	The degree to which a person experiences the world as threatening and beyond his/her control.	Tense, Anxious, Nervous vs. Stable, Calm, Contented
V. Intellect/Openness to Experience	The degree to which a person needs intellectual stimulation, change, and variety.	Commonplace, Narrow- interest, Simple- vs. Wide- interest, Imaginative, Intelligent

*The adjectives listed here were taken from John's (1990, Table 3.2) listing of factor loadings for selected Adjective Check List (Gough & Heilbrun, 1983) items.

These factors are a taxonomy of reputation (cf. Digman, 1990; John, 1990; Saucier & Goldberg, 1996), and are labeled as follows: Factor I, Extraversion or Surgency; Factor II, Agreeableness; Factor III, Conscientiousness; Factor IV, Emotional Stability; and Factor V, Intellect/Openness to Experience (John, 1990). Because reputations are a rough index of the amount of acceptance and status a person enjoys (Foa & Foa, 1974, 1980; Wiggins, 1979), and because reputations are encoded in FFM terms (Saucier & Goldberg, 1996), it follows that the five factors are also evaluations of acceptance and status (Digman, 1997). Digman (1997) concluded that two higher-order factors organize the FFM; he notes that these two broad factors precisely parallel earlier dichotomies such as social interests versus superiority striving (Adler, 1939), communion versus agency (Bakan, 1966; Wiggins, 1991), union versus individualism (Rank, 1945), status versus popularity (Hogan, 1983), and intimacy versus power (McAdams, 1985).

Occupational life consists of episodes *(Motowidlo, Borman, & Schmit, 1997)* organized according to agendas and roles—what will be done and who will do it. Efforts to get along and get ahead take place during these episodes. Although most people try to get along and get ahead at work, there are substantial individual differences in how their efforts are evaluated by others. To get along, people must cooperate and seem compliant, friendly, and positive. When successful, they are evaluated by others as good team players, organizational citizens, and service providers *(Mount, Barrick, & Stewart, 1998; Moon, 2001)*. On the other hand, to get ahead, people must take initiative, seek responsibility, compete, and try to be recognized. When successful, they are described by others as achieving results, providing leadership, communicating a vision, and motivating others toward goals *(Conway, 1999)*.

The foregoing discussion suggests a model for understanding motivation and for assessing individual differences in performance at work. People seek acceptance and status in the workgroup, and their behavior reflects these efforts. Individual differences in performance criteria can be organized in terms of the themes of getting along and getting ahead. The FFM also can be interpreted in terms of efforts to gain approval and status *(cf. Digman, 1997; Wiggins & Trapnell, 1996)*.

1.2 Measurement: Personality Assessment and the Five-Factor Model

Socioanalytic theory maintains that the process of responding to questionnaire items is similar to social interaction more generally. People use their answers to tell others how they want to be regarded—e.g., calm, ambitious, hardworking, flexible, or enthusiastic. That is, these responses are self-presentations. The responses are then interpreted by the anonymous observer behind the questionnaire (i.e., the scoring key) who codes or rates self-presentations using, minimally, the FFM categories of evaluation *(J. Hogan & Hogan, 1998, p. 39)*. Reputations are the result of how self-presentations were evaluated by others; consequently, profiles on well-developed personality inventories predict reputation, with varying degrees of accuracy *(cf. Costa & McCrae, 1992; Watson, Hubbard, & Wiese, 2000)*.

The FFM provides a useful starting point for developing a personality inventory. It is useful because it provides a systematic method for classifying individual differences in reputation. The evidence is quite clear: all multidimensional personality inventories can be reconfigured in terms of these five dimensions *(De Raad & Perugini, 2002)*. Consequently, the FFM has become, in a sense, the starting point for modern personality research.

> The FFM provides a useful starting point for developing a personality inventory.

Although the FFM provides a structure for inventory construction, the model has some significant limitations. For example, it doesn't include some important dimensions of personality—such as masculinity-femininity *(Hough, 1992)*. Furthermore, the FFM concerns the structure of observer ratings; the structure of self ratings is necessarily more complex *(J. Hogan & Hogan, 1991)*. Finally, although we can describe ourselves in terms of the FFM—using trait words such as honest and confident—that is not how we normally think about ourselves. We think about and describe other people using trait terms (the FFM is a taxonomy of trait terms); we think about ourselves in terms of our hopes, dreams, fears, aversions, aspirations, and long term goals—in short, in terms of our identities.

1.3 Measurement: Assessing Job Performance using Multidimensional Models

The metaconcepts of getting along and getting ahead are latent in such phrases as "instrumental and expressive roles," "initiating structure and providing consideration," "task and socioemotional inputs," "production-oriented versus service-oriented groups," and "task performance versus contextual performance." Consider the following job performance models and how they reflect, in part, the themes of getting along and getting ahead. Campbell, McHenry, and Wise (1990) proposed that performance in entry level jobs in the U.S. Army could be evaluated in terms of five dimensions: core proficiency, general soldier proficiency, effort and leadership, personal discipline, and physical fitness/military bearing. Campbell, McCloy, Oppler, and Sager (1993) subsequently expanded this taxonomy into a general model of job performance consisting of eight factors for job-specific task proficiency and non-job-specific task proficiency. These factors are written and oral communication task proficiency, demonstrating effort, maintaining personal discipline, facilitating peer and team performance, supervision/leadership, and management/administration. In these models, proficiency and leadership concern getting ahead, whereas personal discipline and facilitating peer and team performance concern getting along.

Borman and Motowidlo (1993) distinguished between task performance and contextual performance – non-task performance that is important in all jobs. Task performance corresponds to getting ahead, and contextual performance corresponds to getting along with others. Similarly, Hunt (1996) proposed a nine-factor model of entry-level job performance, with the factors differentially appropriate for a variety of jobs. Hunt's model highlights the importance of technical proficiency for job success (getting ahead), but it also emphasizes contextual performance, organizational citizenship, and pro-social behavior. These three dimensions are indices of getting along at work. Finally, Tett, Guterman, Bleier, and Murphy (2000) synthesized 12 models of managerial performance including both published and practitioner models. Tett et al. (2000) identifies 53 dimensions of performance in managerial jobs. An inspection of these dimensions suggests the presence of the ubiquitous factors of initiating structure and consideration (Bass, 1990; Fiedler, 1967; Fleishman, 1953). Initiating structure concerns trying to help the group get ahead; being considerate of others is the prerequisite for getting along.

Next, consider the dynamics of performance appraisal, which typically take the form of a rating on certain job performance dimensions. The rating is influenced, in part, by the incumbent's personality (Hogan & Shelton, 1998). For example, ratings for attention to detail will be affected, in part, by an incumbent's conscientiousness. Several researchers provide support for the interpretation that conscientiousness influences performance through motivational variables (cf. Barrick, Mount, & Strauss, 1993; Moon, 2001). Implicit in performance appraisal is an evaluation of the personal attributes that contribute to performance effectiveness. To predict job performance using personality measures, it is critical to link the predictor variables with the personality characteristics that underlie job performance. This makes clear why Campbell's *(1990)* strategy for aligning predictors and criteria using the underlying construct should yield optimal predictive results. This is the approach we use to organize our research.

1.4 A Viewpoint on Measurement

Modern discussions of the structure of personality in general, and the FFM in particular, often concern the precise number and meaning of the various dimensions of personality. These discussions often have little to do with the primary goal of personality assessment. We would like to make five points about this goal that distinguish our perspective from that of most other test authors.

> **The goal of assessment is to predict non-test behavior.**

First, assessment has a job to do. The goal of assessment is to predict non-test behavior, meaning that the most important criterion for evaluating an assessment device is the degree to which it predicts significant non-test behaviors.

Second, the goal of assessment is not to measure dimensions, qualities, or factors that exist inside people. Personality measurement does this by sampling from a range of a person's characteristic interpersonal behavior—most often by means of a person's responses to inventory items. When people respond to items on a personality inventory, they are responding to questions from an anonymous interviewer. They are not providing self-reports, they are trying to manage the impression that the interviewer might form of them—they are trying to control their reputations *(cf., Johnson, 1981)*. In our view, this is why the issue of faking personality measures is a non-issue *(J. Hogan, Barrett, & Hogan 2007)*.

Third, the scoring key for an inventory scale allows us to identify common themes in a set of items across a group of respondents, which we then use to make predictions. Assume, for example, that a group of people give the same answers to a set of items that concern submissiveness. We then discover, empirically, that their peers describe this group of people as wimpy, anxious, and indecisive. This does not mean that we have measured, in this group, a trait of submissiveness; it means only that we have devised a statistical procedure for identifying people who will be described by their peers as abject and unassertive.

Fourth, personality assessment is formally identical to measurement in petroleum geology. We know that certain critical signs co-vary with the presence or absence of certain desired characteristics. The signs are assessed at a great distance from the researcher—under the ground or in the mind of another person. The presence of the critical signs means that there is some probability, but no certainty, that the desired characteristics are really there. In both kinds of measurement, we are dealing with probabilities, not certainties, and it is always possible that we will reach a wrong conclusion. Nonetheless, some data are always better than no data.

Finally, the fact that a person gets a high score on a valid measure of, for example, submissiveness means that there is some possibility that the person's peers will describe him or her as timid and unassertive. But the score does not explain why the person behaves so as to be described as timid. Assessment is about prediction, not explanation. The explanation for a person's timidity must be determined by additional research. That research only makes sense if the person has a high score on a scale, and peers describe high scorers on that scale as submissive, which brings us back to our first point.

1.5 What to Measure

> Only recently has the question of what to measure been answered systematically.

All personality assessment begins with the question, "What should we measure?" Until recently, in the history of personality assessment, this question has never been answered in a systematic manner. Typically the question has been answered idiosyncratically, based either on certain practical concerns or a test author's personal interests. For example, the Woodworth Personal Data Sheet came from efforts to screen soldiers in World War I for stress proneness. The Personal Data Sheet is the prototype of all modern psychiatric screening inventories, including the Minnesota Multiphasic Personality Inventory *(MMPI; Hathaway & McKinley, 1943)*. The MMPI is the most widely used personality inventory in the world, and unfortunately in the popular mind, the MMPI is a metaphor for all personality measurement.

On the other hand, personal interests led to the development of such widely used measures as the Locus of Control Scale *(Rotter, 1966)*, the Self-Efficacy scale *(Bandura, 1977)*, the Authoritarian personality syndrome *(Adorno, Frenkl-Brunswik, Levinson, & Sanford, 1950)*, the Self-Monitoring scale *(Snyder & Gangestad, 1986)*, and thousands of other special-purpose measures appearing in the research literature.

Sometimes the "what should we measure" question is answered in a more theory-driven way. Reflecting the continuing influence of Allport, "trait theory" has been the overwhelming model of choice for inventory construction. The well-known personality inventories developed by Cattell *(Cattell, Eber, & Tatsuoka, 1970)*, Comrey *(1995)*, Eysenck *(Eysenck & Eysenck, 1976)*, Guilford *(Guilford, Zimmerman, & Guilford, 1976)*, and Costa and McCrae *(1985)* are all based on trait theory—cf. Matthews, Deary, and Whiteman *(2003)*.

Trait theory is based on four major assumptions. First, traits are enduring "neuro-psychic entities" that exist somewhere inside people; these traits are real, and they motivate and direct each individual's characteristic behavioral signature. Second, people's behavior can be explained in terms of their traits. Third, the strength or potency of the various traits can be "measured" using questionnaire items. That is, there is a point-for-point, monotonic relationship between the strength or potency of an underlying trait and a person's score on a personality scale for that trait. Fourth, the goal of personality assessment is to measure these traits and determine the relationships that exist among them.

In our view, trait theory has been a major disaster for personality psychology, and we say this for four reasons. First, defining personality in terms of neuro-psychic structures means the agenda for personality psychology is the same as that for neuro-psychology—to find the neuro-psychic structures using the methods of modern neuro-science. That is a reductionist model that is not necessarily valid, and in any case, there are useful things for personality researchers to do in addition to hunting for neuro-psychic structures. Second, to date, no such structures have been discovered, which raises the possibility that they are convenient fictions rather than neuro-scientific realities. Third, trait terms are used both to describe behavior (Fred is aggressive) and to explain it (Fred is aggressive because he has a trait for aggressiveness), and this is a patent tautology. Fourth, it is sheer metaphysics to claim that there is a monotonic relationship between the strength or potency of a hypothetical neuro-psychic structure and answers to items on a personality questionnaire. The causal chain linking neuro-psychic activity and item endorsement is too long to be credible. And finally, trait theory defines the goals of assessment as measuring traits, and we think the goal is to predict outcomes.

> For the HPI, the question of "what to measure?" is based in socioanalytic theory

For the HPI, the question of "what to measure?" is based in socioanalytic theory and is structured by the FFM. The theory postulates two universal human motives (needs for social acceptance and status), distinguishes between the actor's and the observer's views of personality, and suggests that, because we only see an actor's behavior, our measurement efforts should focus on reputation. Modern research indicates that reputations can be described in terms of the FFM's five broad dimensions. When people respond to items on a personality inventory, they provide self-presentations rather than self-reports. Self-presentations produce or cause reputations. Scoring keys allow us to aggregate aspects of self-presentations that are associated with dimensions of reputations. Profiles on well-developed inventories of personality tell us about a person's reputation; the profiles do not tell us what the person is like "way down deep." These profiles can be used to evaluate the manner in which a person is perceived by others. How a person is perceived has important consequences for his or her social acceptance and career success.

2. Inventory Construction, Reliability, And Confirmation

2.1 Early Development

The original model for the HPI is the California Psychological Inventory *(CPI; Gough, 1975)*. We worked with the CPI for over 25 years because we agree with its measurement goals. In brief, the CPI is designed to assess folk concepts – – aspects of social behavior that are cross-culturally significant, and that non-psychologists intuitively understand. In addition, the CPI is not designed to measure traits. The most important feature of the CPI, we believe, is that it is designed to predict important social outcomes; consequently, in the development of the CPI (and in the development of the HPI), formal psychometric considerations were used to facilitate prediction; they were not ends in themselves.

The HPI began in the late 1970's as a project in a graduate class in personality assessment. As noted in the previous chapter, the two fundamental questions in personality assessment concern what to measure and how to measure it. We believed the literature on the FFM provided an answer to the first question.

With regard to the second question, we believed that Hase and Goldberg *(1967)* were correct when they argued that there is little to choose among the various methods of scale construction as long as the end product is evaluated in terms of empirical validity. Similarly, Harrison Gough *(Gough, 1996)* believed firmly that the value of a scale is in its external predictions. We agree.

We suggested to our graduate class that, if the FFM is correct, and if the Hase and Goldberg argument is correct, then we have solid guidelines for constructing an inventory of normal personality; that is, we know what to measure and how to measure it. As for the test items themselves, socioanalytic theory provided a guide for item writing: taking each of the major dimensions of reputation in turn, one should ask what sorts of self-presentational behaviors might lead to high or low standing on that dimension–as evaluated by others. Consider Factor V of the FFM–Intellect/Openness to Experience. Persons with high scores on this factor seem bright, sophisticated, and aesthetically oriented. This suggests that an Intellect scale should contain items about the degree to which a person enjoys chess, opera, and trendy cuisine.

From a socioanalytic perspective, we wrote items to reflect the standard FFM dimensions *(cf. Goldberg, 1992)* using the foregoing algorithm. In the process, we made three discoveries. First, the standard FFM dimension called Surgency has two components that are conceptually unrelated. One component is Sociability, which concerns impulsivity and the need for social interaction–or a lack of shyness. The other component is Ambition, which concerns a desire for status, power, recognition, and achievement. Clearly, there are shy people who are ambitious – Warren Buffet – and sociable people who are lazy – Falstaff. Second, we found that the FFM dimension called Intellect/Openness to Experience has two components; one component concerns an interest in culture and ideas, and the other concerns interest in acquiring new knowledge. Our third discovery was that each of the primary scales breaks down into a group of related sub-themes. For example, the Adjustment scale contains themes about worry, regret, complaints, patience, irritability, and so forth. Because the items in these sub-themes clustered together, we called them Homogenous Item Composites *(Zonderman, 1980)* or HICs.

We wrote items for HICs within each dimension, and pilot tested them using undergraduate samples. We retained items that correlated highly with the other items on a HIC and discarded items that did not. We continued this process until we arrived at a reasonably coherent set of 45 HICs containing 420 items distributed across six scales.

Between 1979 and 1984 we tested over 1700 people, including students, hospital workers, U. S. Navy enlisted personnel, clerical workers, truck drivers, sales representatives, police officers, hourly and professional staff in a large insurance corporation, school administrators, and incarcerated felons. The ages in these samples ranged from 18 to 60. There were 470 women and 1159 men, 726 whites and 232 blacks. Some demographic data were missing. About 20% of the sample was college educated. In our view, every valid case was valuable. Test administration consisted of paper booklets of items and paper answer sheets. Items responses were entered by keyboard into a data file that was scored according to Fortran statements programmed into a mainframe computer.

> Between 1979 and 1984, we tested over 1700 people. In our view, every valid case was valuable.

2.2 Later Development

In the spring of 1984, with the assistance of Stephen R. Briggs, we carefully refined the internal consistency of each HIC. In the process, we shortened the inventory to 225 items on 43 HICs; we retained 85 unscored items for research purposes, so that the HPI paper test booklet contained 310 items.

Between 1984 and 1992 we tested over 11,000 people, primarily employed adults in organizations around the country. In this sample, the ages ranged from 18 to 67 years. There were 7061 men and 3465 women, 5610 whites, 1036 blacks, 348 Hispanics, 231 Aasian Americans/Pacific Iislanders, and 253 American Indians/Alaskan Natives. Some demographic data were missing. About 20% of this sample was college educated. We conducted over 50 validity studies in various organizations, and we gathered HPI matched sets of data with other tests, inventories, observer descriptions, and job performance criteria. During this time, we administered the assessments using paper booklets and optically scanned answer sheets. We developed PC-based software to score inventories locally and to archive the data files. One obvious limitation of PC-based software is the inability to accumulate data across users; we pursued our clients to share their data with us.

In 1990, we developed a scale called Unlikely Virtues; this scale was designed to identify persons who try to create an excessively favorable impression on the HPI by manipulating their responses. After working with this scale for two years, we decided to delete it; three reasons prompted this decision. First, the scale rarely disqualified a profile because the base rate for faking in the general population is low. The base rate for impression management is unknown, and is difficult to judge because the socialization process begins early in life. Second, in those cases where a score on Unlikely Virtues raised a question about faking, the respondent was found to be the kind of person who in fact would get a high score on Unlikely Virtues–he or she was cautious, conforming, and moralistic. Finally, our clients–the persons in organizations who use the test to make personnel decisions–never understood the point of the scale. As a result, it created more problems in individualized assessment than it solved. The core of the Unlikely Virtues scale now appears on the Prudence scale in the form of a HIC called Virtuous. There is now a body of research that suggests social desirability corrections may not be effective *(Ellingson, Sackett, & Hough, 1999).*

In the spring of 1992, using all our archival data, we conducted a number of factor analyses of the HIC correlation matrix; we concluded that there are seven factors underlying the matrix (see Table 2.1). These factors formed the basis of the present HPI scales. A few HICs had substantial loadings on two factors; we used this information to balance the number of items on each scale, i.e., if a HIC had nearly the same loading on two factors, and one scale was defined by fewer HICs than the other, we assigned the HIC to the smaller factor so as to balance the scale length.

The 1992 HPI *(published in the R. Hogan and Hogan [1995] revised edition manual)* contains seven primary scales and a validity scale. These scales contain a total of 206 items arranged in 41 HICs. No items overlap on HICs and no HICs overlap on scales.

2.3 Most Recent Technical Developments

Over the last ten years, we focused on HPI validity research, using the technical and methodological processes needed to promote evaluation of test validity. It seemed clear that we needed more work on personality-based job analysis, and although we developed a methodology to evaluate personal requirements as "abilities" in the conventional KSA vernacular *(R. Hogan & Hogan, 1995, p. 75)*, we considered the possibility that a direct approach could be more efficient. We developed the Performance Improvement Characteristics (PIC) job analysis that asked subject matter experts to evaluate personality characteristics that improve performance in a job *(Hogan & Rybicki, 1998)*. Now, we have a reliable and valid job analysis tool for evaluating and documenting the personality-based requirements of jobs.

Similarly, we began paying attention to the criterion problem and tried to conceptualize performance data in terms of models that were consistent with socioanalytic theory. That is, if the veracity of the motivational premises "getting along" and "getting ahead" is useful, then we ought to be able to recover and evaluate these themes in job performance. We developed the Competency Evaluation Tool (CET) as a performance taxonomy organized conceptually around socioanalytic theory and developmentally around the domain model of skills *(R. Hogan & Warrenfeltz, 2003; J. Hogan, Davies, & Hogan, 2007; Warrenfeltz, 1995)*. The CET is the basis for our validity generalization research and is an organizing feature of the HPI archives.

Also during this decade, we applied a systematic focus on local validation research. The technology solution relies on a web-based assessment platform that can be accessed from any device with an internet
connection. The systems are monitored 24/7; the data are encrypted
and stored on redundant servers, ensuring high availability and reliability. The platform was designed with our clients' requirements in mind,
providing flexible solutions and timely implementation while maintain-

> The platform provides flexible solutions and timely implementation while maintaining the highest security.

ing the highest security. We built a data warehouse and a research archive on a foundation of criterion-related validity studies, with the HPI as the primary predictor. We conducted over 200 empirical studies with
client organizations across jobs that represent 95% of the US economy. These are both private and public
sector organizations. Our data base is almost exclusively samples of job applicants or working adults. Of
those who are working, these individuals have completed tests either for selection research or for professional development. Internet online testing facilitated rapid accumulation of data and the ability to process
validation studies efficiently.

With sufficient validity evidence accumulated for the HPI, we began aggregating results and generalizing
validity inferences. We use the strategies of transportability of validity, synthetic/job component validity,
and meta-analysis. In 2003, we published a comprehensive HPI-based meta-analysis which showed that
when predictors and criteria are aligned using socioanalytic theory, the meta-analytic validity exceeds that
of atheoretical approaches *(J. Hogan & Holland, 2003)*. Subsequently, we published a demonstration project
of validity generalization methods for personality measures *(J. Hogan, Davies, & Hogan, 2007)*. Most recently,
we published a technical manual documenting the validity of the HPI for personnel selection into seven job
families, which incorporates the O*NET job families as well as the Standard Occupational Classification
system and the EEOC's job classifications. We attempt to provide a valid and fair selection solution with
the HPI that can generalize to many jobs in the US economy.

In 2005, we updated the norms for the HPI. These now appear in this manual, along with the description of how the norming population was identified. The score distributions for all scales on the HPI have
changed slightly since 1995. Specifically, the scale means increased over time, resulting in a somewhat
skewed distribution of scores. Consequently, for clients who use the HPI for selection, cutoff scores based
on the 1995 norms no longer result in the same pass rates that they did in earlier years. We believe that
our 2005 norming process, based upon 156,614 respondent records, meets the highest professional
standards and is representative of the US workforce. This sample was drawn from the Hogan Archive data
warehouse consisting of adult employees or job applicants who completed the HPI during a two-year period
prior to June 2005. Characteristics of the sample are provided in Chapter 6 and Appendix A.

Since we began large-scale assessment work with the US government, it is necessary to begin to develop parallel forms of the HPI. Although equivalent forms of cognitive ability and achievement tests are available from commercial test publishers, parallel forms of personality measures are typically unavailable. A notable exception is SHL's OPQ32 *(SHL Group, 2006)*. Current research is now devoted to developing multiple parallel forms for the HPI.

Finally, we should acknowledge the number of language translations we completed in the last ten years. Although the translation process is continual, the translations have come about reactively in response to client needs. Our US domestic clients who have global businesses have driven our efforts to undertake translations. This strategy has hidden advantages in that there is a premium on accurate and equivalent translations because, in many cases, organizations want to compare people from around the world for corporate jobs across the globe. Sixteen language versions of the HPI are available for administration and at least one reporting option can be produced from each translation. Of key importance in this work is the investigation of score equivalence and construct/predictive validity for each translated test. This is a multifaceted process which, in part, depends on using straightforward psychometric measurement invariance analyses alongside procedures for demonstrating predictive equivalence *(e.g., Millsap, 1997)*.

2.4 Definitions of the Scales

The seven primary scales of the inventory are:

Adjustment - *the degree to which a person appears calm and self-accepting or, conversely, self-critical and tense.*

Ambition - *the degree to which a person seems socially self-confident, leader-like, competitive, and energetic.*

Sociability - *the degree to which a person seems to need and/or enjoy interacting with others.*

Interpersonal Sensitivity - *the degree to which a person is seen as perceptive, tactful, and socially sensitive.*

Prudence - *the degree to which a person seems conscientious, conforming, and dependable.*

Inquisitive - *the degree to which a person is perceived as bright, creative, and interested in intellectual matters.*

Learning Approach - *the degree to which a person seems to enjoy academic activities and to value educational achievement for its own sake.*

In addition to the seven primary scales, the inventory contains a validity key. This scale, consisting of 14 items, is designed to detect careless or random responding. The scale was constructed rationally using items endorsed consistently "yes" or "no" by respondents (n = 1,700). For each Validity item, 99% of the research sample answered the same way. Therefore, an incorrect response to one of these items is an infrequent occurrence; an incorrect response to nine of these items (validity cutoff score) would place a person in the 5.7th percentile of a large representative sample (N = 65,535). Slightly under two-thirds (64.3%) of this sample (N = 65,535) obtained a perfect score on this scale.

Overall, HPI scales demonstrate adequate psychometric qualities *(Lobello, 1996)*. Items retained in the final battery were selected based on their demonstrated ability to predict significant non-test behavior. There is no item overlap among the primary scales and the validity scale. Items were screened repeatedly for content that might seem offensive or to invade privacy. In 2005, 28 items were replaced with equivalent items based on client requests following the 2005 Karraker v. Rent-A-Center, Inc. Seventh U. S. Circuit Court of Appeals decision, which involved the inappropriate use of the MMPI. There are no items concerning sexual preference, religious beliefs, criminal offenses, drug and alcohol incidents, or racial/ethnic attitudes. Readability statistics conducted on the 206 items indicated an average sentence length of 8.3 words, an average word length of 4.1 letters, and an average of 1.44 syllables per word. The Flesch-Kincaid reading level analysis shows that the inventory is written at the 4.6 grade level. Finally, there are no items concerning physical or mental disabilities. Empirical validation research conducted over the last 20 years provides a firm understanding of construct validity and the nature and range of job performance prediction. The HPI is a well-validated instrument that predicts job performance across occupations and organizations *(Axford, 1996; J. Hogan & Holland, 2003)*.

The HPI is intended to be used with adults, not children nor adolescents. It is intended for a normal population, not clinical, psychiatric, nor psychopathological samples. Although the HPI is used widely in occupational contexts for personnel selection and professional development, it is also appropriate for use with adults in peer, family, community, and friendship relations research and counseling. The HPI is neither a medical examination, nor can it be used to evaluate medical conditions, mental illness, mental disabilities, or physical disabilities. In addition, unintended assessment uses would also include forecasting or evaluating neuropsychological behavior, suicidal thoughts/behavior, specific criminal actions, cognitive ability, cognitive deficits, dementia, non-verbal reasoning, academic skills, learning disabilities, visual/motor abilities, hyperactivity, perceptual abilities, and/or information obtained from polygraph/biofeedback instruments.

2.5 Composition of the Personality Scales; The 1992 Factor Analysis

Factor analysis is a statistical methodology designed to account for the relationships between many variables using a fewer number of "factor" variables. That is, a factor represents something shared "in common" by the items; it is a linear combination of items which together measure a single construct. Thus, when using this technique to analyze questionnaire responses on personality inventories like the HPI, we are able to examine whether these responses seem to cluster together into distinct factors, thus allowing us to make sense of the many thousands of relationships between individual questionnaire items.

When conducting a factor analysis, it is common to express the relationship between questionnaire items as correlations, and so construct a correlation matrix. Then, a factor analysis algorithm is deployed, which generally extracts common "components" or "factors" from this matrix, such that each factor extracted accounts for as much variance as possible within the correlation matrix. In this way, a series of factors is extracted from a matrix, each factor accounting for as much variance as possible using a linear combination of items, after the preceding factor has extracted its share of the common variance from these correlations. The technical terminology for the parameter indicating how much variance is extracted by a factor is "eigenvalue." Each factor so extracted maximizes the variance accounted for, and each factor vector (containing the "loadings" or correlations of each item with that factor) is orthogonal (statistically independent) to every other factor. Of course, one of the tasks for the factor analyst is to determine how many components or factors to extract from a matrix of correlations. That is, at what point might a factor be accounting for so little variance that it is considered a "specific" factor? The factor only really accounts for either error or what is left after all the common variance has been extracted from the items. Several methods have been put forward; one of the most popular is the scree test *(Cattell, 1966)*, which is a method of determining a discontinuity in a 2-dimensional plot of each eigenvalue by the extraction order of that eigenvalue.

However, although the factor solution might maximize the variance extracted by each factor, the patterns of item loadings on each factor are in many cases difficult to interpret. By mathematically rotating the factor vectors against one another in geometric space, it is possible to obtain more "simple" factor structures, which maintain the overall amount of variance accounted for by the factors, but maximize the simplicity of the solution by trying to ensure that a questionnaire item is only associated with one factor (a high "loading") and not associated with any other factors (a loading near zero on the other factors). This is the purpose of what is called "simple structure" *(Thurstone, 1935)*. It is generally obtained using Varimax rotation for orthogonal factors (the factor vectors are constrained to be at right angles to each other throughout the rotation process) or using a method like Direct Oblimin *(Jennrich & Sampson, 1966)* to produce oblique simple structure, where factor vectors are allowed to be correlated with one another.

The 1992 analyses that led to the seven HPI scales proceeded in several steps. First, we intercorrelated the scores on the original 43 HICs, plus 8 experimental HICs using a sample of 2500 employed adults. An exploratory principal component factor analysis (PCA) was then undertaken. We chose the number of components to be extracted from the matrix based on the size of the eigenvalues, a scree test *(Cattell, 1966)*, and an examination of the comprehensiveness and comprehensibility of several alternative solutions. Finally, after deciding on the number of components to be extracted, we refined the components using orthogonal varimax rotation. Table 2.1 presents the results of this initial exploratory analysis.

These data provided initial support for the primary scale and HIC structure for the HPI. However, a few HICs (i.e., five) are seen to "load" on more than one scale. This is possibly due to the factors being constrained to be independent from one another (i.e., the varimax rotation). As we shall see in Section 2.6, when we relax this constraint and model the data more formally, we do achieve good simple structure for these data.

Table 2.1

Varimax Rotated Factor Matrix for HPI HICs

Scales	Factor						
HICs	I	II	III	IV	V	VI	VII
Adjustment							
Empathy	.72						
Not Anxious	.71						
No Guilt	.66						
Calmness	.64						
Even Tempered	.63						
No Complaints	.51						
Trusting	.46						
Good Attachment	.44						
Ambition							
Competitive		.68					
Self Confidence		.60					
Accomplishment		.54					
Leadership		.52					
Identity		.49					
No Social Anxiety	.43	.42					
Sociability							
Likes Parties			.75				
Likes Crowds			.75				
Experience Seeking			.47				
Exhibitionistic			.38		-.41		
Entertaining			.31				
Interpersonal Sensitivity							
Easy to Live With				.66			
Sensitive				.62			
Caring				.59			
Likes People			.47	.43			
No Hostility	.55			.36			
Prudence							
Moralistic					.75		
Mastery					.67		
Virtuous					.54		
Not Autonomous					.71		
Not Spontaneous					.61		
Impulse Control					.41		
Avoids Trouble					.36		
Inquisitive							
Science Ability						.70	
Curiosity						.68	
Thrill Seeking						.62	
Intellectual Games						.33	.37
Generates Ideas						.27	
Culture						.22	
Learning Approach							
Education							.74
Math Ability							.67
Good Memory							.67
Reading							.31

The HICs with the highest loadings on factor I are Empathy and Not Anxious. These HICs reflect maturity, equanimity, and concern for others. The factor also is defined by significant loadings for No Guilt, Calmness, Even-Tempered, and No Complaints; these HICs suggest an absence of moodiness, irritability, and tendencies to worry. The moderate loadings for Trusting and Attachment expand the factor definition to include a lack of suspiciousness and positive attitudes toward authority. Overall, this factor appears to be a highly coherent syndrome of psychological maturity broadly defined. Based on this analysis alone, people with high scores on the first factor might be described by their peers as mature, self-confident, and stable. Conversely, persons with low scores might be described as anxious, insecure, moody, and hostile. We label this factor "Adjustment."

The HICs with the highest loadings on factor II are Competitive and Confident. These reflect achievement orientation, self-assurance, and desire for success. Loadings for Accomplishment, Identity, and No Social Anxiety suggest a sense of direction and a positive interaction style. Finally, the single HIC, Leadership, adds an element of desire to direct and influence others. Overall, two themes seem implicit in this factor--ascendence and social self-confidence. Based on this analysis only, people with high scores on factor II should seem ambitious, leader-like, forceful, and confident of their abilities. Conversely, people with low scores on this factor should seem unconcerned with personal advancement, happy to abide with the decisions of others, and uncomfortable making public presentations. We label this factor "Ambition."

The HICs with the highest loadings on factor III are Likes Parties and Likes Crowds. These HICs reflect energy and the need for intensive social interaction. Loadings for Experience Seeking and Exhibitionistic suggest a need for stimulation and a desire to be the center of attention. Finally, the loading for the Entertaining HIC reinforces the theme of wanting attention. Overall, this factor appears to combine the needs and tendencies that we associate with extraversion. Based on this analysis alone, people with high scores on the third factor might be described by their peers as sociable, energetic, and perhaps compulsively interactive. Their exhibitionism will lead them to create a vivid social impression. Conversely, people with low scores on this factor will be seen as anergic, shy, and reserved. We label this factor "Sociability."

The HICs with the highest loadings on factor IV are Easy-to-Live-With, Sensitive, and Caring. These HICs reflect themes of kindness, tactfulness, and interpersonal sensitivity. The HICs, Likes People and No Hostility, which have secondary loadings on this factor, extend the factor definition to include warmth and congeniality. Overall, this factor seems to be a coherent syndrome involving agreeableness. Based on this analysis only, people with high scores on the fourth factor will be seen by their peers as easy going and concerned about the feelings of others. Conversely people with low scores will be seen as interpersonally insensitive, abrasive, and hostile. We label this factor "Interpersonal Sensitivity."

The HIC with the highest loading on factor V is Moralistic. This HIC reflects self-righteousness, rigidity, and public adherence to convention/prissiness. Moderate loadings for the Mastery and Virtuous HICs suggest a cautious concern for social appropriateness and traditional values. When these themes are combined with the four remaining HICs–Not Autonomous, Not Spontaneous, Impulse Control, and Avoids Trouble–the themes of conformity, self-control, and responsiveness to authority emerge. Overall, this factor appears to be a two-component syndrome: one component involves conscientiousness, conventional values, and a degree of self-righteousness; the other component involves caution, control, and conformity. Based on this analysis only, persons with high scores on this factor can be described as rule abiding and virtuous. Conversely, persons with low scores on this combined factor should be described as impulsive and non-conforming. We label this factor "Prudence."

The 1986 version of the HPI contained a scale labeled Intellectance, and it included themes of cultural interests and educational achievement. However, the results of earlier analyses indicate that the original Intellectance factor is somewhat complex and probably contains at least two components. The HICs with the highest loadings on factor VI are Science Ability and Curiosity. These HICs concern interest in how the world works. The moderate loading for Thrill Seeking reflects a desire for challenge, stimulation, and ex-citement. The modest loading for Intellectual Games along with loadings for Generates Ideas and Culture suggest interest in intellectual matters. Overall, this factor appears to concern intellectual curiosity. Based on this analysis alone, people who have high scores on this factor should seem bright, creative, and well-educated. Conversely, people with low scores on this factor should seem conventional, unimaginative, and narrow. We label this factor "Inquisitive."

The HICs with the highest loadings on factor VII are Education and Math Ability. These HICs concern beliefs about one's academic ability and academic achievement. The moderate loading for Good Memory further enhances the theme of academic achievement. Finally, the loading for Reading adds an element of bookishness to the meaning of this factor. Overall, this factor concerns beliefs about educational perfor-mance. Based on this analysis alone, people with high scores on this factor should seem to enjoy aca-demic pursuits and will push for learning and training opportunities. Conversely, people with low scores on this factor should seem uninterested in traditional venues of education. They may prefer learning through application and hands-on training. We label this factor "Learning Approach."

Table 2.2 presents the HPI scales, their constituent HICs, definitions of each HIC, and sample items. The largest scale is Adjustment, with 37 items distributed across 8 HICs; the smallest scale is Learning Ap-proach, with 14 items distributed across 4 HICs. The 7 primary scales contain a total of 41 HICs.

Table 2.2

The Constituent HICs for the Seven HPI Scales

Scale Name	Description	
Adjustment	Measures the degree to which a person appears calm and self-accepting.	

HICs	Description	Sample Item
Empathy	Concern for others	I dislike criticizing people, even when they need it.
Not Anxious	Absence of worry	Deadlines don't bother me.
No Guilt	Absence of regret	I rarely feel guilty about the things I have done.
Calmness	Not volatile	I keep calm in a crisis.
Even Tempered	Patience	I hate to be interrupted.
No Complaints	Complacence	I almost never receive bad service.
Trusting	Belief in others	People really care about one another.
Good Attachment	Good relations with authority	In school, teachers liked me.

Scale Name	Description	
Ambition	Measures the degree to which a person is leader-like, competitive, energetic, and socially self-confident.	

HICs	Description	Sample Item
Competitive	Desire to win	I want to be a success in life.
Self Confident	Self-assurance	I expect to succeed at everything.
Accomplishment	Personal effectiveness	I am known as someone who gets things done.
Leadership	Leadership tendencies	In a group I like to take charge of things.
Identity	Satisfaction with one's life	I know what I want to be.
No Social Anxiety	Social self confidence	I don't mind talking in front of a group of people.

Scale Name	Description	
Sociability	Measures the degree to which a person seems to need and/or enjoy interactions with others.	

HICs	Description	Sample Item
Likes Parties	Affability	I would go to a party every night if I could.
Likes Crowds	Affiliativeness	Being part of a large crowd is exciting.
Experience Seeking	Needs variety	I like a lot of variety in my life.
Exhibitionistic	Showing-off	I like to be the center of attention.
Entertaining	Being witty and engaging	I am often the life of the party.

Scale Name	Description	
Interpersonal Sensitivity	Measures the degree to which a person is seen as perceptive, tactful, and socially sensitive.	

HICs	Description	Sample Item
Easy to Live With	Being easy-going	I work well with other people.
Sensitive	Being considerate	I always try to see the other person's point of view.
HICs	Description	Sample Item
Caring	Social sensitivity	I am sensitive to other people's moods.
Likes People	Companionable	I enjoy just being with other people.
No Hostility	Tolerant	I would rather not criticize people, even when they need it.

Scale Name	Description	
Prudence	Measures the degree to which a person is conscientious, conforming, and dependable.	

HICs	Description	Sample Item
Moralistic	Self-righteousness	I always practice what I preach.
Mastery	Diligent	I do my job as well as I possibly can.
Virtuous	Perfectionism	I strive for perfection in everything I do.
Not Autonomous	Conformity	Other people's opinions of me are important.
Not Spontaneous	Planful	I always know what I will do tomorrow.
Impulse Control	Self-discipline	I rarely do things on impulse.
Avoids Trouble	Professed probity	When I was in school, I rarely gave the teachers any trouble.

Scale Name	Description	
Inquisitive	Measures the degree to which a person is perceived as bright, creative, and interested in intellectual matters.	

HICs	Description	Sample Item
Science	Analytical	I am interested in science.
Curiosity	Investigative	I have taken things apart just to see how they work.
Thrill Seeking	Stimulus seeking	I would like to be a race car driver.
Intellectual Games	Playful cognition	I enjoy solving riddles.
Generates Ideas	Ideational fluency	I am known for having good ideas.
Culture	Cultural interests	I like classical music.

Scale Name	Description	
Learning Approach	Measures the degree to which a person enjoys academic activities and values educational achievement for its own sake.	

HICs	Description	Sample Item
Good Memory	Powers of recall	I have a large vocabulary.
Education	Academic talent	As a child, school was easy for me.
Math Ability	Numerical talent	I can multiply large numbers quickly.
Reading	Verbal talent	I would rather read than watch TV.

2.6 Composition of the Personality Scales: The 2007 Confirmatory Factor Analysis

Although the exploratory factor analysis procedure described in section 2.5 indicates a substantive factor structure, modern psychometrics has now developed procedures to allow data to be fitted to a predetermined factor model, and to be tested for acceptable statistical fit to the data. The general model-fitting process is known as structural equation modeling. In the particular case of fitting factor models to data, it is known as confirmatory factor analysis (CFA). Essentially, the procedure requires that we fit the ideal simple structure HPI model to data, where HIC scores are accounted for by a single HPI factor and no HIC loads on any other factor other than its designated HPI factor. In CFA, we set to zero all non-keyed HIC loadings, and estimate values only for keyed HIC-factor loadings. Also, we can fit models where the factors are expected to be correlated, or where we force the factors to be independent from one another.

Therefore, the key difference between the analysis reported in section 2.5 and this one in section 2.6 is that the former is an exploratory analysis, where a set of dimension reducing and coordinate rotation procedures are used to discover the HPI factor structure (albeit some expectations were obviously present from the design of the questionnaire itself). In the analysis reported below, we present the current expected idealized factor model as a "target," then fit this to the data using the structural equation modeling procedure. This fit process confirms (or disconfirmsnot) the expected factor structure, which is why it is called Confirmatory Factor Analysis. Using the theory-based conceptualization of the HPI along with the evidence of the 7 factor structure in Table 2.1, we calculated a CFA using the 2005 normative sample dataset, including all 156,614 respondent records.

Figure 2.1 presents a graphic schematic of the final HPI model fitted to the data. The lines between boxes and ovals represent two kinds of parameters (or paths as they are sometimes known) to be estimated. The arrows from the latent HPI factors (ovals) to the HIC variables (rectangles) represent the factor loadings to be estimated; it is hypothesized that the latent unobserved factors "cause" the observed HIC cluster scores. The curved lines between each latent factor represent factor correlations to be estimated. However, although previous investigations indicated that a better fit to the HPI model was found by modeling oblique factors, we also computed an orthogonal HPI model and compared the relative fit of the two models via a statistical chi-square test.

Prior to the modeling analyses, we tested one of the main assumptions of structural equation modeling and CFA which uses maximum likelihood parameter estimation. The assumption is that data are multivariate normally distributed. To investigate the validity of this assumption, we used Mardia's *(1970, 1974)* test for multivariate kurtosis using the EQS 6.1 Structural Equation modeling software *(Bentler & Wu, 2005)*. The test result indicated that the data were not distributed as multivariate normal with a normalized estimate of 1377.0481. Values larger than about 5 or 6 indicate substantive positive kurtosis and non-normality. Thus, all modeling proceeded using the Robust option in EQS, which computes robust residual test statistics, standard error parameters, and the Satorra-Bentler *(1994)* adjusted chi-square and related model fit indices.

The initial comparison of an orthogonal factor HPI model to an oblique model was computed using the Satorra-Bentler (2002) scaled difference chi-square test (as the conventional chi-square model difference test is invalid when using adjusted chi-squares). The oblique model fit statistically and significantly better than the orthogonal model SBdiff c2 = 146788.2005, df = 21, p< 0.0001. This is to be expected because most personality psychological variables are all statistically correlated with each other to some small degree, even, when for all practical purposes, they can be treated as independent.

As seen in Figure 2.1, we fit the oblique factor model to the normative sample of 156,614 respondents, using EQS 6.1. to implement maximum likelihood estimation on covariances between HICs, with robust adjustment of the chi-square statistic. The Satorra-Bentler chi-square was 418824.1731 with 758 df, and p < 0.0001. As expected with such a huge sample, the chi-square exact test of fit indicated statistically significant departures (residual error) from the observed and model implied covariance matrices. Under these conditions, we examined the standardized residual matrix to ascertain the extent to which residuals are substantively discrepant. We used a custom residual matrix analysis computer program RDEVAL. The mean absolute residual discrepancy was 0.0534, with the mean standardized residual -0.0013, and the root-mean-square-residual of 0.0739. Ninety percent of all standardized residuals were found between -0.1207 and 0.1164, with 95% found between -0.163 and 0.1498, and the largest positive and negative standardized residuals being 0.4103 and -0.3247, respectively. Figure 2.2 shows the histogram of standardized residuals for this solution. Taking these results together with the robust RMSEA of 0.59 (with 90% confidence intervals also at 0.59 due to the huge sample size), we concluded that, for all practical purposes, the model provided a reasonable fit to the data, although not perfect.

Table 2.3 shows the correlations estimated between the 7 latent factors, alongside the observed scale score correlations. As seen, the latent factor correlations are always larger than their observed score counterparts. This is because the CFA modeling estimates latent factor correlations which are free from measurement error (which is accounted for in the modeling process), unlike observed data correlations which do contain measurement error (and are normally corrected using a standard disattenuation formula if the theoretical maximum correlations are required).

Table 2.3

Intercorrelations Between HPI Observed Scale Scores and Latent Factor Scores

Scales	1	2	3	4	5	6
1) Adjustment						
2) Ambition	.42 (.64)					
3) Sociability	.04 (.07)	.41 (.58)				
4) Interpersonal Sensitivity	.40 (.62)	.23 (.55)	.19 (.45)			
5) Prudence	.54 (.81)	.16 (.32)	-.19 (-.21)	.34 (.54)		
6) Inquisitive	.19 (.28)	.36 (.54)	.47 (.69)	.16 (.32)	.04 (.15)	
7) Learning Approach	.34 (.48)	.35 (.58)	.20 (.35)	.21 (.39)	.28 (.44)	.40 (.60)
Note. Figures in ( ) are the latent variable correlations from the CFA.						

Figure 2.1

HIC-Level Confirmatory Factor Model for the HPI

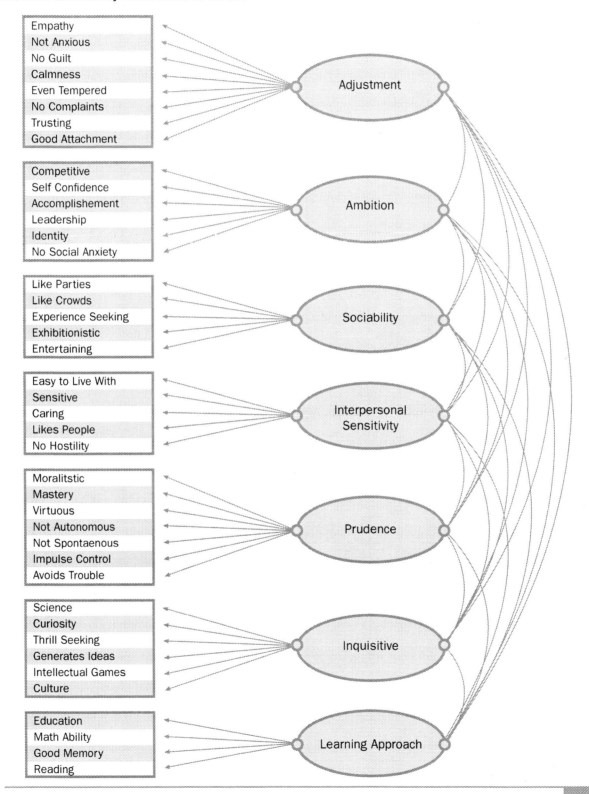

Figure 2.2

Histogram of Standardized Residuals for the Oblique Factor Model with Maximum Likelihood Parameter Estimation

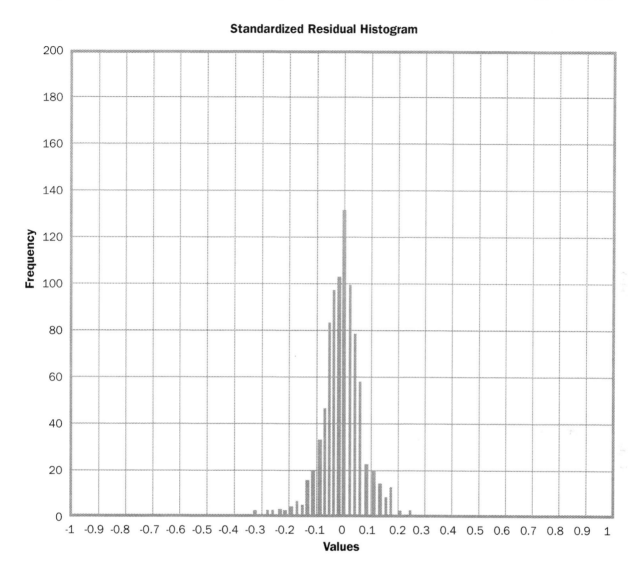

Table 2.4 shows the factor loadings for the HPI HICs estimated from the CFA analysis. Note that there are no cross-loadings. In CFA, non-keyed item loadings are constrained to zero by default, thus, this is the best possible simple structure for the HPI for this dataset. In comparison to the loadings in Table 2.1, the Principal Component Analysis (PCA) and Varimax solution, the loadings in Table 2.4 are slightly lower. This is because PCA differs from maximum likelihood common factor analysis in that it analyzes all the variance available in a matrix including measurement error and variance specific only to an individual HIC variable. However, common factor analysis methods partial out measurement and unique variable variance, and only extract factors that account for the remaining common variance. Hence, these loadings always tend to be smaller than PCA component loadings[1].

---

[1]Although it is tempting to treat these loadings as "precise" real-valued numbers, for practical purposes, it matters little to the scale scores whether we use the exact weights (the factor loadings) to construct weighted scale scores or simply sum the HIC scores to produce a scale score. Grice and Harris (1998) and Grice (2001a,b) show this statement is false unless the factor pattern is a perfect, simple structure with zero complexity (cross-loadings), but this is exactly what the CFA model represents. Further, given the unknown quantitative structure of the item responses and HIC cluster scores we are dealing with (Michell, 1997, Barrett, 2003), it is justifiable to treat the numbers as pragmatically useful magnitudes, rather than precise multi-decimal place estimates of magnitudes as with estimates of length or weight.

Table 2.4
CFA factor Loadings for the HPI HICs

Scales	Factor						
HICs	I	II	III	IV	V	VI	VII
Adjustment							
Empathy	.61						
Not Anxious	.53						
No Guilt	.63						
Calmness	.41						
Even Tempered	.63						
No Complaints	.44						
Trusting	.39						
Good Attachment	.49						
Ambition							
Competitive		.45					
Self Confidence		.47					
Accomplishment		.38					
Leadership		.49					
Identity		.35					
No Social Anxiety		.69					
Sociability							
Likes Parties			.56				
Likes Crowds			.53				
Experience Seeking			.60				
Exhibitionistic			.54				
Entertaining			.64				
Interpersonal Sensitivity							
Easy to Live With				.40			
Sensitive				.30			
Caring				.37			
Likes People				.63			
No Hostility				.31			
Prudence							
Moralistic					.59		
Mastery					.39		
Virtuous					.61		
Not Autonomous					.08		
Not Spontaneous					.31		
Impulse Control					.51		
Avoids Trouble					.41		
Inquisitive							
ScienceAbility						.62	
Curiosity						.44	
Thrill Seeking						.47	
Intellectual Games						.49	
Generates Ideas						.63	
Culture						.46	
Learning Approach							
Education							.61
Math Ability							.47
Good Memory							.71
Reading							.51

However, the data in Table 2.4 represent the current best picture of the structure of the HPI. All except one of the 41 HIC factor loadings, "Not Autonomous" on the Prudence factor V, meet or exceed the conventional 0.30 lower bound for substantive factor loadings. And all HICs are constrained to be exactly zero on all non-keyed factors. This is a zero-complexity factor solution.

2.7 HPI Scale Distributions and Reliability

Having identified and generated the empirical evidence supporting the structure of the seven HPI scales, the next step is to produce descriptive, itemmetric, and scale-score based statistics required for practitioners and researchers who might wish to use the test in applied practice. Probably the two most important indices associated with a test score (whether main scale or HIC) are the estimates of reliability and the standard error associated with a test score. The two most popular estimates of score reliability are one estimating the internal consistency of a set of items, and one estimating the reproducibility/stability of a score for an individual over two or more test occasions.

Internal consistency reliability is an estimate of how well all the constituent components of a sum scale score (whether items or HICs) estimate the same common construct or attribute. If all the components of a scale score measure the same construct, then internal consistency reliability will be high (near 1.0). However, if the components of a sum score are measuring different things, then internal consistency will be near zero. The most substantive practical consequence of low internal consistency is that individuals can attain the same scale score on a particular scale by acquiring scores on constituent components of the scale which measure completely different attributes. This affects predictive accuracy of those scores, because the link between a scale score and some outcome is diluted by the fact that the scores are merely estimates of different attributes, although they might be equivalent between individuals. So, the aim in scale design is to ensure that the components of a coherent scale score all measure the same attribute to some non-trivial degree.

If we were to ask a slightly reworded item 10 times, and use the summed responses to these items as a scale score, we would find the internal consistency coefficient for the scale might be as high as 0.98 and thus tempt us to report our scale as highly reliable. The obvious response to this is that the scale also is very narrow in meaning, as it is confined to the content of a single item. Our desire is to widen the breadth of meaning using the constituent items, while preserving the desired common meaning of the attribute to be assessed. The trade-off is that too much breadth can lead to items that are measuring different attributes; with too little breadth we are back to single-item rewords of a common item. This is a test design issue where the hypothesized breadth of attribute meaning guides the development of the constituent items; sections 2.1 through 2.4 of this chapter detail such a design process for the HPI. Sections 2.5 and 2.6 provide support for the desired dimensionality of the seven scale inventory structure. In this section, we report results for the reliability of these scales and their components.

Estimating internal consistency reliability for the seven HPI scale scores is not straightforward, because there are two kinds of constituent components of the seven HPI scale scores; these components are inventory items and HICs. First, if we compute the internal consistency of a scale using item responses as components of the sum score, we have to assume that all the items in our scale are drawn from a single hypothetical universe of items measuring the attribute in question. Using statistical sampling theory applied to the items as a sample from a universe of such items, it is possible to estimate the average correlation between our inventory scale and the hypothetical universe of all possible scales constructed from all possible items measuring the single attribute. That estimated average correlation is the internal consistency reliability of the scale and is known as coefficient alpha *(Cronbach, 1951)*. However, when we use HICs to form a scale score, the HICs become the constituent components of our attribute, but each "composite" component is now assumed to be constructed from items drawn from its own discrete universe of items. So, the estimation of the "composite reliability" of a linear combination of HIC scores for an HPI scale needs to take into account both the reliability of each component HIC score as well the size of relationships between these HICs. These considerations are discussed more comprehensively by Nunnally and Bernstein *(1994)*.

The respective formulae for Cronbach's alpha and composite reliability appear below:

$$\alpha = \frac{k}{k-1}\left(1 - \frac{\sum_{i=1}^{k} s_i^2}{s_T^2}\right)$$

where

$k =$ the number of items in the scale

$s_i^2 =$ the sample varience of item *i* of *k* items

$s_T^2 =$ the sample variance of the scale scores

which also can be expressed as:

$$\alpha = \frac{k}{k-1}\left(\frac{\bar{\bar{R}} - k}{\bar{\bar{R}}}\right)$$

where

$\bar{\bar{R}} =$ the sum of all the pairwise correlations between all *k* items in the scale including the diagonal values of the correlation matrix, k^2 correlations in total

Composite reliability for an HPI scale is calculated as:

$$r_c = 1 - \frac{k - \sum_{i=1}^{k} \alpha_i}{\bar{R}}$$

where

$k =$ the number of component scales

$r_c =$ the composite reliability of the test scale

$\alpha_i =$ the alpha reliability of HIC cluster i of k clusters

$\bar{R} =$ the sum of all the pairwise correlations between all k items in the scale

including the diagonal values of the correlation matrix, k^2 correlations in total

From the logic of domain sampling theory (true score theory on which coefficient alpha is based), it appears that the most appropriate reliability coefficient to be used in the future for each of the seven HPI scale scores is in fact the composite reliability estimate, as each HIC cluster score is considered a sample of items from a discrete attribute universe. When dealing with hypotheticals such as "item universes" and "infinite domains", what matters is the pragmatic consequence of such a decision. This consequence is reflected in parameters or procedures which rely upon the use of a reliability estimate. The most important one for practitioners is the standard error of measurement associated with a test score. Therefore, in tables 2.5 and 2.6 below, both reliability estimates for the seven HPI scales are included for comparative purposes, along with the standard error of measurement computed using each reliability estimate.

Another misconception prevalent in many test manuals is the use of an inappropriate estimate of the standard error of measurement for an observed test score. We use the equation provided by Dudek *(1979)*, specifically for the case where the aim is to compute the standard deviation of observed scores if the observed score is held constant:

$$sem_3 = s_T \sqrt{(1 - r_{xx}^2)}$$

where

$s_T =$ the standard deviation of the scale scores

$r_{xx} =$ the reliability of the test

As Nunnally and Bernstein *(1994, pp 259-260)* indicate, this is the optimal formula to be used when requiring an estimate of the standard error of measurement of observed rather than true scores, using observed scores rather than estimated true scores as the initial score estimates. The conventional formula used is:

$$sem_1 = s_T \sqrt{(1 - r_{xx})}$$

where

$s_T =$ the standard deviation of the scale scores

$r_{xx} =$ the reliability of the test

This formula is applicable for estimating a range of observed scores for a fixed true score, and not an observed score. That is, to express the likely error around an observed test score, one should more correctly use sem_3 rather than sem_1.

For example, if we observe a score on Adjustment of 26, given the scale mean, standard deviation and Cronbach alpha in Table 2.5, then if we wished to use sem_1 as our estimate of the standard error of measurement, we would first need to compute the estimate of the true score (for an observed score of 26), using the formula given below:

$$t' = \left(r_{xx} \left(x - \bar{x} \right) \right) + \bar{x}$$

where

$t' =$ the estimated true score

$r_{xx} =$ the reliability of the test scale

$x =$ the observed scale score

$\bar{x} =$ the global normative scale score

So, for our observed score of 26 on Adjustment, we would calculate t' as:

$t' =$ (0.82(26-31.18)) + 31.18

$t' =$ 26.93

Then we apply sem1 (2.00) as our estimate of the standard error of measurement to this value of 26.93 to estimate a confidence interval of observed scores for this fixed true score. Given this sem_1, an interval within which we might expect to find 68% of all observed scores for the individual who scored 26 would extend from 25 through to 29.

If we had applied this sem_1 to the observed score of 26, we would have computed the interval as between 24 and 28.

Alternatively, if we applied sem3 (2.70) to the observed score (which is the more correct method to estimate the likely range of observed scores from an initial, fixed, observed score), we would obtain the same 68% confidence interval as between 23 and 29. So, the choice of an appropriate formula can have a substantive impact on the confidence interval estimation for an individual's score.

For the sake of completeness, we provide both sem_3 and sem_1 estimates in Tables 2.5 and 2.6, based on item alphas and composite reliability estimates.

Table 2.5

Classical Item and Scale Statistics for the HPI

Scale HICs	Number of Items	Mean	SD	Cronbach Alpha (a)	Mean inter-item correlation	sem$_1$ a	sem$_3$ a
Adjustment	**37**	**31.18**	**4.72**	**.82**	**.12**	**2.00**	**2.70**
Empathy	5	4.36	1.01	.57	.21	.66	.83
Not Anxious	4	2.97	1.15	.59	.27	.74	.93
No Guilt	6	4.92	1.30	.64	.24	.78	1.00
Calmness	4	3.42	0.70	.25	.11	.61	.68
Even Tempered	5	4.51	0.82	.48	.17	.59	.72
No Complaints	5	4.67	0.69	.44	.14	.52	.62
Trusting	3	2.28	0.83	.41	.21	.64	.76
Good Attachment	5	4.05	1.26	.68	.32	.71	.92
Ambition	**29**	**25.95**	**3.36**	**.80**	**.12**	**1.50**	**2.02**
Competitive	5	4.72	0.58	.31	.11	.48	.55
Self Confidence	3	2.86	0.41	.34	.14	.33	.39
Accomplishment	6	5.84	0.58	.66	.29	.34	.44
Leadership	6	4.75	1.62	.76	.36	.79	1.05
Identity	3	2.69	0.72	.71	.45	.39	.51
No Social Anxiety	6	5.08	1.38	.72	.31	.73	.96
Sociability	**24**	**14.24**	**4.68**	**.83**	**.17**	**1.93**	**2.61**
Likes Parties	5	2.47	1.26	.62	.24	.78	.99
Likes Crowds	4	2.74	1.40	.76	.45	.69	.91
Experience Seeking	6	4.67	1.37	.57	.19	.90	1.13
Exhibitionistic	5	2.06	1.55	.71	.33	.83	1.09
Entertaining	4	2.30	1.29	.64	.33	.77	.99
Interpersonal Sensitivity	**22**	**20.43**	**1.70**	**.57**	**.08**	**1.11**	**1.40**
Easy to Live With	5	4.87	0.41	.30	.11	.34	.39
Sensitive	4	3.63	0.63	.23	.07	.55	.61
Caring	4	3.85	0.41	.22	.11	.36	.40
Likes People	6	5.64	0.78	.56	.23	.52	.65
No Hostility	3	2.44	0.68	.26	.13	.58	.66
Prudence	**31**	**23.27**	**3.91**	**.71**	**.08**	**2.11**	**2.75**
Moralistic	5	3.25	1.25	.53	.19	.86	1.06
Mastery	4	3.62	0.66	.34	.13	.54	.62
Virtuous	5	4.07	0.94	.37	.11	.75	.87
Not Autonomous	3	2.03	1.08	.67	.40	.62	.80
Not Spontaneous	4	2.82	0.95	.32	.12	.78	.90
Impulse Control	5	3.40	1.30	.56	.21	.86	1.08
Avoids Trouble	5	4.08	0.99	.38	.13	.78	.92
Inquisitive	**25**	**16.55**	**4.52**	**.80**	**.13**	**2.02**	**2.71**
Science Ability	5	3.45	1.36	.56	.21	.90	1.13
Curiosity	3	2.57	0.71	.50	.26	.50	.61
Thrill Seeking	5	2.35	1.65	.72	.34	.87	1.15
Intellectual Games	3	2.27	0.88	.48	.24	.63	.77
Generates Ideas	5	3.59	1.21	.56	.21	.80	1.00
Culture	4	2.31	1.31	.58	.26	.85	1.07
Learning Approach	**14**	**10.21**	**3.00**	**.78**	**.21**	**1.41**	**1.88**
Education	3	2.48	0.82	.60	.35	.52	.66
Math Ability	3	2.08	1.11	.74	.51	.57	.75
Good Memory	4	3.35	0.95	.56	.26	.63	.79
Reading	4	2.29	1.40	.69	.36	.78	1.01

Note. sem$_1$ a = the standard error of measurement to be applied to the estimated true score for an individual given their observed score. sem$_3$ a = the standard error of measurement to be applied to the observed score for an individual.

35

Table 2.6

Composite Alphas and Standard Errors of Measurement for the Seven HPI Scales

Scale	a	r_c	$sem_1 a$	$sem_1 r_c$	$sem_3 a$	$sem_3 r_c$
Adjustment	.82	.83	2.00	1.95	2.70	2.63
Ambition	.80	.80	1.50	1.50	2.02	2.02
Sociability	.83	.85	1.93	1.81	2.61	2.47
Interpersonal Sensitivity	.57	.59	1.11	1.09	1.40	1.37
Prudence	.71	.73	2.11	2.03	2.75	2.67
Inquisitive	.80	.82	2.02	1.92	2.71	2.59
Learning Approach	.78	.82	1.41	1.27	1.88	1.72

Note. r_c = estimate of composite reliability; a = coefficient alpha

For comparative purposes, although the sets of indices presented in Tables 2.5 and 2.6 are exhaustive, for operational purposes we would recommend the use/interpretation of composite alpha reliabilities (rc) for the HPI scales, and the use of sem_3 estimates for the standard errors of measurement for both HICs and main scales. This latter recommendation is specifically relevant for the situation where the aim is to use the standard deviation of observed scores, given that an individual's observed score is held constant. This has particular relevance for computing a confidence interval around an observed score.

Chapter 6 and Appendix A provide detailed tables of score frequency distributions, normative percentile tables, and descriptive statistics for the total normative sample and the sample subdivided by age, gender, and ethnicity.

2.8 HPI Test-Retest Reliability

Two studies form the basis of evidence for short and long-term test-retest stability for the HPI HIC clusters and the seven HPI scales. In reporting the results, two kinds of stability coefficients are utilized, a Pearson correlation and the Shrout and Fleiss *(1979)* Model 2 intraclass correlation coefficient. Both coefficients are measures of agreement, but the most popular coefficient used to index test-retest reliability, Pearson correlation, is sensitive only to monotonic differences in variable magnitudes, whilst the Model 2 intraclass is highly sensitive to differences in both monotonicity and magnitude.

Examining test-retest stability is akin to person-target profiling, where the magnitude discrepancy between scores is of paramount importance. As Barrett *(2005)* shows, the choice of agreement coefficient is critical to the correct expression of agreement where both monotonic and magnitude differences are of importance to the investigator. For example, look at the set of test-retest data below in Table 2.7 and their graphical depiction in Figure 2.3. These show scores that are highly related in terms of monotonicity but discrepant in terms of magnitudes; that is, in the language of test-retest reliability *(Stemler, 2004)* the data for occasion 2 show consistency (monotonicity) but little consensus (magnitude equivalence).

Table 2.7

Hypothetical Scores on a Personality Scale Over Two Test Occasions

Person	Occasion 1	Occasion 2
1	10	15
2	12	22
3	11	12
4	9	19
5	7	17
6	5	15
7	14	24
8	13	23
9	18	28
10	23	33
11	14	24
12	10	20
13	11	21
14	16	26
15	13	23
16	12	22
17	12	22
18	9	8
19	5	4
20	20	30

Figure 2.3

Hypothetical Scores and Test-Retest Reliabilities for a Personality Scale Over Two Test Occasions

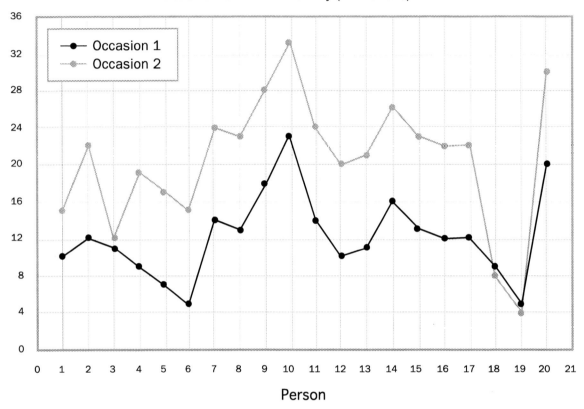

Personality scale scores over two occasions for the same individuals
Pearson correlation test-retest reliability (consistency) = 0.87
Model 2 Intraclass reliability (concensus) = 0.41

What this example demonstrates is that the Model 2 intraclass coefficient is sensitive to magnitude discrepancies between the occasion scores. The Pearson correlation of 0.87 would seem to indicate excellent test-retest stability, yet what we see "by eye" is not reflected at all in this index. In contrast, the Model 2 intraclass coefficient of 0.41 does seem to better reflect the real discrepancies between scores. Sometimes, it is sufficient to simply know scores are related, which is why the Pearson correlation is a convenient and useful index of any such relationship. However, where the magnitude differences in scores are critical (as in test-retest or person-target profiling/cut-score analyses), then the Pearson correlation coefficient can sometimes mislead the investigator into concluding that the scores are nearly equivalent (as in the example above), even when they are clearly discrepant. Thus, when we report upon test-retest stability below, we provide the conventional Pearson correlation for "familiarity reasons" along with the preferred Model 2 intraclass coefficient and the mean absolute difference between occasion scores. This provides a more comprehensive and informative approach to estimating test-retest stability.

Short-Term Stability. A sample of 87 undergraduates enrolled in junior- or senior- level business courses at a public Midwestern university were twice administered the HPI. Administration format (computer or paper-and-pencil) was randomized across students, with each student being administered the test twice using the same administration format. The sample consisted of 40 males and 47 females, with mean ages of 24.92 and 26.48 years, and standard deviations of 5.09 and 7.69 years, respectively. Sample ethnicity was 72% White, 14% Black, 13% Asian, and 1% Hispanic. Test administration was proctored for both types of administration conditions, with test-sessions lasting up to one hour. The duration of test-retest interval varied across students, within the range 14 to 21 days. The test-retest stability indices for the seven HPI scales and HICs are provided in Table 2.8.

As indicated in Table 2.8 by the mean absolute differences between occasion 1 and 2 test scores, there are only small magnitude discrepancies between these two sets of scores. This is reflected in the almost identical Pearson and Intraclass reliability coefficients. The majority of reliability indices are above 0.70, with many exceeding 0.80. Overall, the mean intraclass reliability across all 48 indices is 0.72.

Long-Term Stability. These data were drawn from a study examining the stability of HPI test scores from 141 adult job applicants over an 8 year test-retest interval. The sample was opportunistic, in that these individuals happened to be applying for jobs with a nationwide US employer with whom they had previously applied 8 years earlier. The sample consisted of 93 males and 48 females, with mean ages of 35.55 and 28.96 years, and standard deviations of 10.1 and 8.52 years, respectively. Sample ethnicity was 28% White, 36% Black, 11% Asian, and 6% Hispanic, with 19% of applicants not reporting their ethnicity. Test administration was proctored for both administration conditions. The test-retest stability indices for the seven HPI scales and HICs are provided in Table 2.9.

As can be seen in this table by the mean absolute differences between occasion 1 and 2 test scores, there are only relatively small magnitude discrepancies between these two sets of scores except for the HPI scale of Ambition. Here there is a mean absolute difference of 4.39, which is associated with a much reduced intraclass reliability estimate of 0.27 instead of the Pearson correlation of 0.49. Overall, the mean intraclass reliability across all 48 indices is 0.43, much lower than the 14-21 day interval estimate. But, this is what would be expected given such a long duration between test occasions; notably the mean absolute discrepancies between scores remain low.

This chapter has described how the scales of the HPI and its subsequent revisions were developed. The next chapter concerns the validity of these scales.

Table 2.8

Short-Term (14-21 day interval) Test-Retest Stability Indices for the HPI

Scale	Pearson Correlation	Model 2 Intraclass Correlation	Mean Absolute Score Difference
Adjustment	**0.87**	**0.87**	**2.69**
Empathy	0.75	0.75	0.74
Not Anxious	0.68	0.68	0.74
No Guilt	0.76	0.76	0.89
Calmness	0.68	0.68	0.57
Even Tempered	0.69	0.69	0.69
No Complaints	0.71	0.70	0.59
Trusting	0.63	0.63	0.57
Good Attachment	0.79	0.80	0.67
Ambition	**0.83**	**0.83**	**2.00**
Competitive	0.69	0.69	0.44
Self Confidence	0.62	0.62	0.36
Accomplishment	0.81	0.77	0.52
Leadership	0.81	0.81	0.71
Identity	0.78	0.78	0.48
No Social Anxiety	0.77	0.77	0.87
Sociability	**0.86**	**0.85**	**1.78**
Likes Parties	0.79	0.79	0.54
Likes Crowds	0.79	0.77	0.59
Experience Seeking	0.62	0.62	0.84
Exhibitionistic	0.71	0.71	0.75
Entertaining	0.82	0.82	0.52
Interpersonal Sensitivity	**0.70**	**0.70**	**1.41**
Easy to Live With	0.40	0.39	0.43
Sensitive	0.59	0.59	0.38
Caring	0.56	0.56	0.21
Likes People	0.75	0.75	0.52
No Hostility	0.59	0.58	0.60
Prudence	**0.69**	**0.69**	**2.64**
Moralistic	0.50	0.50	0.95
Mastery	0.60	0.60	0.54
Virtuous	0.71	0.71	0.57
Not Autonomous	0.64	0.63	0.57
Not Spontaneous	0.59	0.59	0.63
Impulse Control	0.66	0.66	0.86
Avoids Trouble	0.68	0.68	0.60
Inquisitive	**0.84**	**0.84**	**1.99**
Science Ability	0.79	0.79	0.61
Curiosity	0.73	0.72	0.39
Thrill Seeking	0.83	0.83	0.62
Intellectual Games	0.62	0.62	0.51
Generates Ideas	0.71	0.71	0.72
Culture	0.84	0.84	0.47
Learning Approach	**0.85**	**0.85**	**1.14**
Education	0.80	0.80	0.33
Math Ability	0.85	0.86	0.31
Good Memory	0.78	0.77	0.47
Reading	0.82	0.81	0.39

Table 2.9

Long-Term (8 years interval) Test-Retest Stability Indices for the HPI

Scale	Pearson Correlation	Model 2 Intraclass Correlation	Mean Absolute Score Difference
Adjustment	**0.43**	**0.44**	**2.57**
Empathy	0.24	0.24	0.77
Not Anxious	0.04	0.02	1.50
No Guilt	0.46	0.46	1.16
Calmness	0.11	0.11	0.69
Even Tempered	0.34	0.29	1.05
No Complaints	0.01	0.00	2.24
Trusting	0.50	0.50	0.66
Good Attachment	0.46	0.46	0.91
Ambition	**0.49**	**0.27**	**4.39**
Competitive	0.39	0.39	0.42
Self Confidence	0.27	0.26	0.30
Accomplishment	0.02	0.01	1.73
Leadership	0.50	0.50	1.18
Identity	0.27	0.27	0.48
No Social Anxiety	0.59	0.59	1.01
Sociability	**0.63**	**0.63**	**2.92**
Likes Parties	0.51	0.51	0.92
Likes Crowds	0.51	0.50	1.04
Experience Seeking	0.57	0.56	0.95
Exhibitionistic	0.52	0.52	0.97
Entertaining	0.55	0.54	0.85
Interpersonal Sensitivity	**0.30**	**0.29**	**1.54**
Easy to Live With	0.39	0.36	0.21
Sensitive	0.29	0.29	0.48
Caring	0.12	0.12	0.29
Likes People	0.40	0.40	0.70
No Hostility	0.49	0.49	0.40
Prudence	**0.46**	**0.44**	**3.23**
Moralistic	0.50	0.50	1.01
Mastery	0.35	0.35	0.42
Virtuous	0.39	0.38	0.74
Not Autonomous	0.53	0.53	0.79
Not Spontaneous	0.38	0.36	0.82
Impulse Control	0.54	0.53	0.79
Avoids Trouble	0.28	0.28	0.79
Inquisitive	**0.73**	**0.72**	**2.52**
Science Ability	0.58	0.58	0.84
Curiosity	0.46	0.46	0.39
Thrill Seeking	0.65	0.65	0.89
Intellectual Games	0.55	0.54	0.52
Generates Ideas	0.61	0.61	0.79
Culture	0.57	0.56	0.82
Learning Approach	**0.65**	**0.65**	**1.97**
Education	0.42	0.42	0.63
Math Ability	0.65	0.65	0.59
Good Memory	0.60	0.60	0.62
Reading	0.66	0.66	0.77

3. Validity

How do we know what a test score means? We discover the meaning of a test score through the process of test validation. Evidence regarding the meaning of a scale can be developed in many ways, using a variety of methods. Historically, however, validity has been defined in terms of correlations between test scores and relevant criterion ratings. For example, we might validate the HPI Ambition scale by: (a) asking a group of people to complete the Ambition scale; (b) asking other people who know these people well, e.g., their friends or coworkers to rate them for ambition; and (c) computing correlations between scores on the Ambition scale and others' ratings for ambition.

Correlations between scale scores and peer ratings for the same construct are important sources of validity information, but they are insufficient by themselves. For example, in the present case it turns out that people have trouble rating their peers for ambition; they seem unable to agree about what the defining behaviors are. Whatever the dimension or construct, however, there will be some kind of a problem with the rating. Actually, the problem is more general than that; whatever the criterion measure, whether it is a rating or some other score, there will be a question as to whether that criterion is "really" the right one. To answer this question, we must "validate" the rating data or other criteria that we want to use to "validate" our scale. And this process leads to an infinite regress as we try to validate the data that we are using to validate our scale, and so on.

The correlation between scale scores and scores on any single criterion measure is insufficient to evaluate the validity of that scale. Consequently, to understand the meaning of a test score, we must investigate as many non-test correlates of that score as we can find. Ideally, when we do this we will have a theory regarding the latent structure underlying both test scores and criterion measures *(Campbell, 1990; Hogan & Holland, 2003; Hogan & Nicholson, 1988)*. That is, we don't simply generate correlations between scores on a scale and scores on any quantitative index we can find. Rather, using our theory of what a scale measures, we predict to what the scale is and is not related, and then gather data to evaluate our predictions. For example, Ambition scores should be related to a person's status level in his or her occupation, but unrelated to his or her social security number. Seen in these terms, test validation is formally identical to the general process of theory construction in science *(cf. Hogan & Nicholson, 1988)*.

The process that we have just described is called construct validation *(Cronbach & Meehl, 1955; Loevinger, 1957)*. Many forms of evidence are required to build a case for the construct validity of a measure. This chapter presents three types of evidence regarding the construct validity of the primary scales of the HPI: correlations with the scales of other well-validated tests, correlations with peer ratings, and correlations with measures of organizational performance. This evidence reveals convergent and discriminant relations between construct measures.

3.1 Correlations With Other Tests

Tables 3.1 through 3.18 present correlations between the HPI scales and other well known psychological measures. These tables include four categories of tests: measures of cognitive ability, motives and interests, normal personality, and career derailers.

Cognitive Ability Tests. The cognitive ability tests include the Armed Services Vocational Aptitude Battery *(ASVAB; U. S. Department of Defense, 1984)*, selected PSI Basic Skills Tests for Business, Industry, and Government *(BST; Ruch, Weiner, McKillip, & Dye, 1985)*, the General Aptitude Test Battery *(GATB; U.S. Department of Labor, 1970; Segall & Monzon, 1995)*, the Watson-Glaser Critical Thinking Appraisal *(W-GCTA, 2002)*, the Bennett Mechanical Comprehension Test *(BMCT; Bennett, 1992)*, and the Hogan Business Reasoning Inventory *(HBRI; Hogan Assessment Systems, 2007)*.

The ASVAB is a 334-item group test of general knowledge and cognitive ability administered to all military recruits for selection and placement decisions in the armed forces. The ASVAB consists of 10 subtests from which occupational composites are computed. The samples who provided data for the ASVAB and the HPI were enlisted male and female personnel (N=359) assigned to Navy Basic Electricity and Electronic training and Army Missile Repair training. The BST consist of 20 tests of cognitive and perceptual abilities as well as typing performance. The tests are designed to assess skills and abilities important for clerical work; they are widely used because they are practical, short, and well-validated. Table 3.1 reports correlations between the HPI and ASVAB subtests.

A sample of female claims examiners (N=49) in a national health insurance company provided data for the HPI and four BSTs including Reading Comprehension (#2), Computation (#4), Following Written Directions (#8), and Coding (#12). These four tests are part of a larger battery of 20 cognitive and perceptual abilities tests, as well as typing skills designed to predict performance of clerical employees. The tests are intended for use in personnel selection, they are timed, and supported by meta-analytic validities. Table 3.2 reports correlations between the HPI and BSTs.

The GATB was developed in 1947 by the United States Employment Service in response to the need for a comprehensive assessment of basic aptitudes used in a wide variety of occupations. The GATB has been the subject of continuous revision and consists of 12 tests that yield measures of nine aptitudes. These measures reduce to three factors or general abilities identified as cognitive, perception, and psychomotor. To map the cognitive domain, we administered three power subtests of the GATB *(Form E; Segall & Monzon, 1995)* including Arithmetic Reasoning, Vocabulary, and Three-Dimensional Space. A research sample (N = 292) of male and female upper division university students completed the GATB and the HPI as part of a larger assessment project. Table 3.3 reports correlations between the HPI and GATB subtests.

Table 3.1
Correlations Between the ASVAB Composites and the HPI Scales

ASVAB	ADJ	AMB	SOC	INP	PRU	INQ	LRN
AFQTa	.11	.10	.06	.01	-.10	.20**	.31***
EL	.11	.08	-.04	-.00	.01	.28***	.19**
ST	.11	.07	-.02	-.02	-.03	.33***	.17**
MM	.06	.06	.03	.03	-.09	.24***	.09
CL	.10	.06	-.05	-.02	.01	.22**	.23**
GT	.09	.07	-.04	.02	.04	.21**	.23***
OF	.07	.07	.04	.02	-.09	.26***	.14*
GM	.00	.02	.00	.06	-.03	-.01	.05
SC	.09	.06	.01	.01	-.07	.27***	.13*
CO	.06	.06	.03	.03	-.08	.22**	.14*
FA	.08	.04	-.01	-.00	-.03**	.20	.18**
MKb	.08	.22**	.18*	.04	.00	.21**	.46***
EI	.12	.12	.00	-.15*	-.18*	.30***	.16*
MC	.14*	.20**	.13	-.03	-.23**	.30***	.27***
GS	.07	.10	.12	-.01	-.14*	.43***	.28***

Note. a N= 204; AFQT = Armed Forces Qualification Test, EL = Electronics, ST = Skilled Technical, MM = Mechanical Maintenance, CL = Clerical, GT = General Technical, OF = Operator and Food, GM = General Maintenance, SC = Surveillance and Communication, CO = Combat, FA = Field Artillery; b N = 155; MK = Mathematics Knowledge, EI = Electronics Information, MC = Mechanical Comprehension, GS = General Science; ADJ = Adjustment; AMB = Ambition; SOC = Sociability; INP = Interpersonal Sensitivity; PRU = Prudence; INQ = Inquisitive; LRN = Learning Approach; * p < .05 ** p < .01 *** p < .001, one-tailed.

Table 3.2
Correlations Between the PSI Basic Skills Tests and the HPI Scales

BST #	ADJ	AMB	SOC	INP	PRU	INQ	LRN
TEST 2a	-.12	-.07	.18	-.05	-.22	.24*	.44***
TEST 4	-.18	-.03	.18	-.17	-.32*	.13	.33**
TEST 8	-.06	.16	.25*	.01	-.32*	.27*	.32*
TEST 12	-.10	-.05	.34*	-.01	-.27*	.29*	.30*

Note. N = 49. ADJ = Adjustment; AMB = Ambition; SOC = Sociability; INP = Interpersonal Sensitivity; PRU = Prudence; INQ = Inquisitive; LRN = Learning Approach. a TEST 2 = Reading Comprehension; TEST 4 = Computation; TEST 8 = Following Written Directions; TEST 12 = Coding; * p < .05 ** p < .01 *** p < .001, one-tailed.

Table 3.3
Correlations Between GATB (Form E) and the HPI Scales

Scales	ADJ	AMB	SOC	INP	PRU	INQ	LRN
GATB – AR	.092	.100	-.008	.084	.059	.077	.363**
GATB – VO	.092	.139*	-.031	.023	.002	-.031	.225**
GATB – 3D	.043	.036	.052	.046	.002	.181**	.089
GATB Total Score	.101	.119*	.023	.079	.023	.151**	.297**

Note. N = 292. AR = Arithmetic Reasoning; VO = Vocabulary; 3D = Three-Dimensional Space; ADJ = Adjustment; AMB = Ambition; INQ = Inquisitive; INP = Interpersonal Sensitivity; PRU = Prudence; LRN = Learning Approach; SOC = Sociability. *p < .05 **p < .01, two-tailed, directional relationships not hypothesized a priori.

The WGCTA *(Watson & Glaser, 2002)* is a widely-used measure of critical thinking, composed of 20 items across five content areas. These include drawing inferences, recognizing assumptions, argument evaluation, deductive reasoning, and logical interpretation. For each area, verbal stimulus passages are presented as propositions and several conclusions follow. The respondent examines each conclusion and makes decision about its appropriateness or validity. Correct responses are summed for a total score. A sample of managerial job candidates (N = 375) completed the WGCTA and the HPI as part of an assessment battery for employment at one of the five largest transportation companies in the US. Table 3.4 reports correlations between the HPI and the WGCTA total score.

The BMCT *(Bennett, 1992)* assesses problem solving ability in applying physical laws and mechanical operations. This 68-item test is used for personnel selection in mechanical, technical, and manufacturing jobs. A sample of manufacturing job applicants (N = 62) completed the BMCT and the HPI as part of a selection validation project. Table 3.5 reports correlations between the HPI and the BMCT total score.

HBRI *(Hogan Assessment Systems, 2007)* assesses tactical and strategic reasoning through business-relevant problems. This 24-item inventory is used in career assessment and development for jobs within the managerial and professionals job families. Scores for tactical reasoning, strategic reasoning, and a total were calculated. The managerial sample (N = 2,340) who completed the WGCTA also completed the HBRI and the HPI online. Table 3.6 reports correlations between the HPI and the HBRI scales.

Table 3.4
Correlations Between WGCTA (Form B) and the HPI Scales

Scales	ADJ	AMB	SOC	INP	PRU	INQ	LRN
Inferences	.011	.138**	.083	.057	-.066	.078	.009
Recognition of Assumptions	.021	-.002	.079	.022	-.038	.011	.067
Deduction	.015	.064	.137**	-.002	-.091	.131*	.127*
Interpretation	.063	.039	.050	.073	-.055	.015	.085
Evaluation of Arguments	.090	.014	.109*	.005	-.003	.146*	.141**
Total Score	.055	.073	.136**	.043	-.076	.110*	.125*

Note. N = 375. ADJ = Adjustment; AMB = Ambition; SOC = Sociability; INP = Interpersonal Sensitivity; PRU = Prudence; INQ = Inquisitive; LRN = Learning Approach. * p < .05 ** p < .01, two-tailed, directional relationships not hypothesized a priori.

Table 3.5
Correlations Between BMCT and the HPI Scales

Scales	ADJ	AMB	SOC	INP	PRU	INQ	LRN
BMCT Total Score	.112	.240	.167	.196	-.130	.279*	.049

Note. N = 62. ADJ = Adjustment; AMB = Ambition; SOC = Sociability; INP = Interpersonal Sensitivity; PRU = Prudence; INQ = Inquisitive; LRN = Learning Approach. * p < .05 ** p < .01, two-tailed, directional relationships not hypothesized a priori.

Table 3.6
Correlations Between HBRI and the HPI Scales

Scales	ADJ	AMB	SOC	INP	PRU	INQ	LRN
Strategic Reasoning	.24*	.19**	.05*	.09**	.08**	.14**	.19**
Tactical Reasoning	.35**	.03**	-.01	.19**	.22**	.11**	.18**
HBRI Total Score	.33**	.28**	.03	.15**	.16**	.14**	.21**

Note. N = 2,340. ADJ = Adjustment; AMB = Ambition; SOC = Sociability; INP = Interpersonal Sensitivity; PRU = Prudence; INQ = Inquisitive; LRN = Learning Approach. * p < .05 ** p < .01, two-tailed, directional relationships not hypothesized a priori.

Researchers' attempts to integrate the cognitive and non-cognitive domains have been through correlating construct measures. An alternative strategy is to propose different abilities or constructs to account for individual differences in cognitive style. When the first approach is used, the test-test correlates that we report here corroborate the general findings in a research literature (Chamorro-Premuzic & Furnham, 2005) where the results are sparce. In their review of that literature, Chamorro-Premuzic and Furnham (2005, pp.42-67) point out that probably less than a dozen recent quantitative studies exist that integrate well-validated personality and intelligence measures. There are two consistent personality-cognitive performance findings. First, there appears to be a modest, but significant correlation (r = -.15) between FFM emotionally stability and psychometric intelligence that has been interpreted as producing test anxiety. This finding was reported by Ackerman and Heggestad (1997), which followed the earlier review of 273 studies that resulted in a mean correlation of r = -.18 between ability test performance and test anxiety (Hembree, 1988). We find a moderate relation between HPI Adjustment and measures of cognitive ability; however, we would be unable to support an interpretation of possible test anxiety for low scorers on Adjustment. A more likely interpretation is that low scorers are self doubting, and afraid of making mistakes.

Second, there are consistent relations between a range of cognitive ability tests and FFM Intellect/Openness to Experience measures, including HPI Inquisitive and/or Learning Approach. This is supported by all HPI results presented in Tables 3.1 to 3.6. Some researchers interpret this relation as a prediction of self-assessed ability (Cattell, Eber, & Tatsuoka, 1970), while others argue that a portion of true variance in the Intellect/Openness to Experience factor can be attributed to intelligence (Brand, 1994). We draw an interpersonal interpretation from the relation. People who are intellectually competent are seen by others as imaginative, curious, open-minded, interested in intellectual pursuits, and resourceful problem solvers. In our view, it is these interests, values, and behavioral styles that are shared by higher scorers on FFM Intellect/Openness to Experience and intelligence–based measures.

Motives and Interest Inventories. The motives and interest inventories include the Myers-Briggs Type Indicator (MBTI; Myers & McCaulley, 1985), the Self-Directed Search (SDS; Holland, 1985b), and the Motives, Values, Preferences Inventory (MVPI; J. Hogan & Hogan, 1996). The MBTI is the most widely used assessment device in modern America; it is designed to assess the 16 "types" defined by Jungian theory (Jung, 1923). Four theoretically independent dimensions of cognitive style are combined to create these 16 types. A sample (N = 53) of male and female psychology graduate students provided data for the HPI and the MBTI (see Table 3.7) The SDS is a self-administered vocational counseling measure used to assess the six occupational types proposed in Holland's (1985a) theory of careers. Each type is defined by a distinctive pattern of interests and abilities and, like Jungian theory, each is a personality type. The sample (N = 237) used to compute correlations between the SDS and the HPI included male and female undergraduate students, graduate students, and cases gathered during individualized assessment (see Table 3.8). Finally, the MVPI is designed to assess individual differences in the strength of 10 core values emphasized by motivational theorists from McDougall (1908) to McClelland (1985). The sample (N = 1,806) who provided data for the HPI and the MVPI were male and female job applicants and incumbents (see Table 3.9).

Table 3.7
Correlations Between the MBTI and the HPI Scales

Scales	ADJ	AMB	SOC	INP	PRU	INQ	LRN
EI	-.15	-.31*	-.55***	-.41***	-.03	-.34**	-.07
SN	-.08	.17	.52***	.18	-.32**	.20	-.18
TF	.01	-.01	-.19	-.23	-.26*	.03	-.25*
JP	.05	.07	.43***	.27*	-.26*	.03	-.15

Note. N= 53; Ela = Extraversion–Introversion; SN = Sensing-Intuition; TF = Thinking-Feeling; JP = Judging-Perceiving; ADJ = Adjustment; AMB = Ambition; SOC = Sociability; INP = Interpersonal Sensitivity; PRU = Prudence; INQ = Inquisitive; LRN = Learning Approach; *p < .05 **p < .01 ***p < .001, one-tailed.

Table 3.8
Correlations Between the SDS and the HPI Scales

Scales	ADJ	AMB	SOC	INP	PRU	INQ	LRN
Realistic	-.03	.04	.03	-.07	-.07	.35***	-.04
Investigative	.09	.11	-.01	-.07	.04	.36***	.34***
Artistic	-.01	.01	.21***	.09	-.13*	.49***	.01
Social	.06	.31***	.27***	.47***	-.00	.15*	-.09
Enterprising	.05	.43***	.36***	.22***	-.03	.19***	-.04
Conventional	.02	.14*	-.02	.05	.21***	-.03	.01

Note. N = 237. ADJ = Adjustment; AMB = Ambition; SOC = Sociability; INP = Interpersonal Sensitivity; PRU = Prudence; INQ = Inquisitive; LRN = Learning Approach. * p < .05 **p < .01 ***p <.001, one-tailed.

Table 3.9
Correlations Between the MVPI the HPI Scales

Scales	ADJ	AMB	SOC	INP	PRU	INQ	LRN
Aesthetic	-.19***	-.05**	.22***	-.02	-.14***	.388**	.16***
Affiliation	.32***	.37***	.42***	.43***	.16***	.24***	.14***
Altruism	.14***	.07***	.03	.30***	.25***	.16***	.05**
Commercial	.12***	.30***	.25***	.11***	.19***	.24***	.21***
Hedonism	-.28***	-.11***	.32***	-.02	-.32***	.05**	-.09***
Power	.07***	.42***	.37***	.05**	.03	.30***	.23***
Recognition	-.13***	.16***	.51***	.01	-.18***	.24***	.05**
Scientific	.09***	.14***	.18***	.02	.04*	.54***	.31***
Security	.06***	-.06***	-.24***	.05**	.36***	-.13***	-.04*
Tradition	.09***	.108**	-.06***	.11**	.24***	.06***	.08***

Note. N = 1,806. ADJ = Adjustment; AMB = Ambition; SOC = Sociability; INP = Interpersonal Sensitivity; PRU = Prudence; INQ = Inquisitive; LRN = Learning Approach. *p < .05 **p < .01 ***p < .001, one-tailed.

Normal Personality Inventories. The measures of normal personality include the Interpersonal Adjective Scales *(IAS; Wiggins, 1991)* and Big-Five factor markers *(Goldberg, 1992)*. The IAS assesses eight dimensions of interpersonal style defined by Wiggins *(1991)*, drawing on earlier work by Leary *(1957)* concerning the psychology of interpersonal relationships. The sample (N=331) consisted of male and female applicants for entry-level firefighter jobs (see Table 3.10). The Big-Five factor markers consist of 100 unipolar terms that load in a specific way on each of the FFM dimensions. These terms provide univocal measures of the five domains underlying most English-language personality terms. These markers can be considered criterion indicators of the FFM. The sample (N=168) consisted of college students who completed the HPI and the 100 unipolar markers (see Table 3.11).

In addition, the HPI was included as an instrument administered to the Eugene-Springfield Community Sample, recruited under direction of Lewis R. Goldberg from the Oregon Research Institute *(Goldberg, 2005)*. The HPI was administered in the winter of 1997 to 742 volunteers who ranged in age from 18 to 85 years. Of the original sample, 88% completed various assessments over a ten year period from 1993 to 2003. Matched data sets for the HPI and 27 other assessment instruments are available from Goldberg *(2005)*. For purposes of this manual, correlation matrices are reproduced for some of the most widely used personality measures available to business and industry. These include the 16 Personality Factor Questionnaire *(16PF; Conn & Rieke, 1994)*, California Psychological Inventory *(CPI; Gough, 1996)*, Jackson Personality Inventory-Revised *(JPI-R; Jackson, 1994)*, Multidimensional Personality Questionnaire *(MPQ; Tellegen, in press)* and NEO PI-R *(Costa & McCrae, 1992)*. The correlation matrices for the HPI scales and each of these inventories are presented in Tables 3.12 to 3.16, respectively.

Finally, we report correlations between the HPI and two FFM measures used in business and industry. The Personal Characteristics Inventory *(PCI: Mount & Barrick, 2001)* consists of 150 items with five primary scales. The sample that completed both inventories included undergraduate business students (N = 154) who were participating in a research study conducted by Ones, Schmidt, and Viswesvaran *(1995)*. The HPI and PCI scale correlations appear in Table 3.17.

Jesus Salgado developed the Inventario de Personalidad de Cinco Factores *(Salgado & Moscoso, 1999)*, as a Spanish FFM for personality assessment. Salgado gathered data from Spanish-speaking students (*N* = 200) on his inventory and the Spanish HPI translation. Table 3.18 shows the scale correlations between the two inventories.

The convergent and discriminant relations between personality scales are instructive and provide a source of accumulated evidence of construct validity for the HPI scales. To reflect construct validity for a measure, the correlations between similar construct measures should be significantly larger than the correlations between dissimilar constructs. As seen in tables 3.10 to 3.18, the correlations between the HPI scales and similar construct measures from other well-validated personality inventories converge. Conversely, correlations between scales purporting to measure dissimilar constructs are lower. As shown in

Figure 3. 1 for FFM measures alone, uncorrected correlations among similar construct measures with the HPI scales range as follows with medians displayed in the figure: Adjustment/EmotionalStability/Neuroticism (.66 to .72); Ambition/Extraversion/Surgency (.39 to .60); Sociability/Extraversion/Surgency (.44 to .64); Interpersonal Sensitivity/Agreeableness (.37 to .61); Prudence/Conscientiousness (.36 to .59); Inquisitive/Opennesss/Intellect (.to .69); and Learning Approach/Opennesss/Intellect (.24 to .35).

Table 3.10
Correlations Between the IAS and the HPI Scales

Scales	ADJ	AMB	SOC	INP	PRU	INQ	LRN
PA	.01	.49***	.39***	.02	-.07	.31***	.27***
BC	-.21***	.11*	.31***	-.26***	-.31***	.18***	.06
DE	-.22***	-.15***	-.12*	-.41***	-.22***	-.16**	-.12*
FG	-.29***	-.42***	-.28***	-.47***	-.27***	-.18***	-.14**
HI	-.16**	-.55***	-.34***	-.18***	-.03	-.30***	-.18***
JK	.12**	-.12**	-.27***	.19***	.22***	-.10*	-.04
LM	.15**	.08	.18***	.29***	.18***	.18***	.11*
NO	.19***	.34***	.35***	.40***	.27***	.27***	.17***

Note. N = 331. PA = Assured-Dominant; BC = Arrogant-Calculating; DE = Cold-Hearted; FG = Aloof-Introverted; HI = Unassured-Submissive; JK = Unassuming-Ingenuous; LM = Warm-Agreeable; NO = Gregarious-Extraverted; ADJ = Adjustment; AMB = Ambition; SOC = Sociability; INP = Interpersonal Sensitivity; PRU = Prudence; INQ = Inquisitive; LRN = Learning Approach; *p < .05 **p < .01 ***p < .001, one-tailed.

Table 3.11
Correlations Between Goldberg's Big-Five Markers and the HPI Scales

Scales	ADJ	AMB	SOC	INP	PRU	INQ	LRN
Factor I - Surgency	.04	.55**	.44***	.31***	-.24**	.29***	-.03
Factor II - Agreeableness	.13	-.11	.02	.56***	.23**	-.12	-.17*
Factor III - Conscientiousness	.10	.24**	-.26***	-.07	.36***	-.17*	-.08
Factor IV - Emotional Stability	.70***	.39***	-.04	.27***	.01	.28***	.11
Factor V - Intellect	.05	.22**	-.04	-.01	.03	.33***	.35***

Note. N = 168. ADJ = Adjustment; AMB = Ambition; SOC = Sociability; INP = Interpersonal Sensitivity; PRU = Prudence; INQ = Inquisitive; LRN = Learning Approach. *p < .05 **p < .01 ***p < .001, one-tailed.

Table 3.12
Correlations Between 16PF and the HPI Scales

Scales	ADJ	AMB	SOC	INP	PRU	INQ	LRN
Warmth	.090*	.207**	.174**	.504**	.133**	-.161**	-.016
Reasoning	.127**	.174**	.125**	-.090*	-.117**	.346**	.384**
Emotional Stability	.658**	.520**	.129**	.317**	.213**	.124**	.112**
Dominance	-.064	.502**	.424**	-.079*	-.252**	.325**	.131**
Liveliness	.002	.226**	.642**	.288**	-.214**	.159**	.008
Rule Consciousness	.098*	-.006	-.270**	.133**	.491**	-.193**	-.101
Social Boldness	.239**	.599**	.484**	.354**	-.011	.188**	.115**
Vigilance	-.376**	-.190**	-.093*	-.281**	-.222**	-.075	-.187**
Abstractedness	-.247**	-.040	.249**	-.067	-.523**	.283**	.047
Privateness	-.087*	-.181**	-.279**	-.310**	.014	-.019	-.002
Apprehension	-.516**	-.447**	-.158**	-.087*	.053	-.180**	-.096*
Q1 - Openness to Change	.033	.253**	.346**	.129**	-.333**	.452**	.198**
Q2 – Self-Reliance	-.120**	-.141**	-.273**	-.371**	-.105**	.030	.052
Q3 – Perfectionism	-.044	.062	-.143**	-.004	.395**	-.080*	.004
Q4 – Tension	-.417**	-.145**	.023	-.384**	-.240**	-.016	-.028

Note. N = 629. ADJ = Adjustment; AMB = Ambition; SOC = Sociability; INP = Interpersonal Sensitivity; PRU = Prudence; INQ = Inquisitive; LRN = Learning Approach. *p < .05 **p < .01, two-tailed, directional relationships not hypothesized a priori.

Table 3.13
Correlations Between CPI and the HPI Scales

Scales	ADJ	AMB	SOC	INP	PRU	INQ	LRN
Do (Dominance)	.249**	.782**	.498**	.200**	-.064	.370**	.293**
Cs (Capacity for Status)	.298**	.548**	.481**	.262**	-.110**	.419**	.270**
Sy (Sociability)	.294**	.640**	.599**	.381**	-.040	.355**	.238**
Sp (Social Presence)	.277**	.559**	.616**	.234**	-.252**	.396**	.217**
Sa (Self-acceptance)	.210**	.679**	.561**	.201**	-.194**	.418**	.273**
In (Independence)	.367**	.658**	.298**	.054	-.148**	.401**	.293**
Em (Empathy)	.324**	.497**	.508**	.339**	-.113**	.415**	.259**
Re (Responsibility)	.382**	.256**	-.055	.273**	.352**	.060	.245**
So (Socialization)	.522**	.195**	-.106**	.249**	.481**	-.160**	.092*
Sc (Self-control)	.497**	.015	-.454**	.211**	.562**	-.216	.048
Gi (Good Impression)	.557**	.222**	-.181**	.325**	.531**	-.063	.089*
Cm (Communality)	.135**	.217**	.130**	.187**	.047	.148**	.017
Wb (Well-being)	.627**	.424**	.061	.303**	.260**	.141**	.127**
To (Tolerance)	.374**	.175**	-.004	.275**	.197**	.043	.148**
Ac (Achievement via Conformance)	.421**	.486**	.037	.256**	.404**	.136**	.328**
Ai (Achievement via Independence)	.328**	.334**	.179**	.145**	-.049	.403**	.356**
Ie (Intellectual Efficiency)	.411**	.484**	.250**	.189**	-.007	.446**	.475**
Py (Psychological-mindedness)	.345**	.391**	.139**	.104**	-.001	.386**	.322**
Fx (Flexibility)	.085*	.052	.231**	.135**	-.302**	.216**	.118**
F/M (Femininity/ Masculinity)	-.234**	-.345**	-.229**	.159**	.172**	-.375**	.006
V.1 Externality/ Internality	-.064	-.659**	-.655	-.132**	.239**	-.401**	-.262**
V.2 Norm-doubting/ Norm-favoring	.337**	.211**	-.053	.181**	.487**	-.097*	.100
V.3 Ego-integration	.488**	.350**	.119**	.274**	.123**	.256**	.285**

Note. N = 648. ADJ = Adjustment; AMB = Ambition; SOC = Sociability; INP = Interpersonal Sensitivity; PRU = Prudence; INQ = Inquisitive; LRN = Learning Approach. *p < .05 ** p < .01, two-tailed, directional relationships not hypothesized a priori.

Table 3.14
Correlations Between JPI-R and the HPI Scales

Scales	ADJ	AMB	SOC	INP	PRU	INQ	LRN
Complexity	-.108**	.142**	.271**	.000	-.258**	.362**	.300**
Breadth of Interest	.123**	.302**	.352**	.188**	-.140**	.517**	.280**
Innovation	-.015	.380**	.429**	.089*	-.330**	.599**	.162**
Tolerance	.204**	.183**	.194**	.370**	-.060	.227**	.123**
Empathy	-.194**	-.059	.092*	.321**	.095*	-.040	.014
Anxiety	-.669**	-.393**	-.021	-.195**	-.098*	-.155**	-.110**
Cooperativeness	-.232**	-.240**	-.063	.028	.252**	-.239**	-.099*
Sociability	.053	.249**	.403**	.427**	.063	.040	-.040
Social Confidence	.214**	.711**	.589**	.301**	-.142**	.361**	.205**
Energy Level	.309**	.487**	.266**	.118**	.027	.334**	.191**
Social Astuteness	-.101*	.227**	.371**	.080*	-.215**	.200**	.111**
Risk Taking	-.036	.329**	.489**	-.118**	-.470**	.448**	.083*
Organization	.116**	.195**	-.064	.004	.339*	-.049	.130**
Traditional Values	.043	-.021	-.266**	.059	.406**	-.250**	-.144**
Responsibility	.217**	.080*	-.141**	.265**	.399**	-.083*	.073

Note. N = 643. ADJ = Adjustment; AMB = Ambition; SOC = Sociability; INP = Interpersonal Sensitivity; PRU = Prudence; INQ = Inquisitive; LRN = Learning Approach. *p < .05 ** p < .01, two-tailed, directional relationships not hypothesized a priori.

Table 3.15
Correlations Between MPQ the HPI Scales

Scales	ADJ	AMB	SOC	INP	PRU	INQ	LRN
WB (Wellbeing)	.431**	.423**	.262**	.386**	.095*	.218**	.166**
SP (Social Potency)	-.019	.608**	.605**	.110**	-.217**	.352**	.165**
AC (Achievement)	-.045	.314**	.177**	.050	.066	.303**	.149**
SC (Social Closeness)	.164**	.299**	.307**	.516**	.143**	-.002	.003
SR (Stress Reaction)	-.720**	-.461**	-.069	-.282**	-.139**	-.167**	-.148**
AL (Alienation)	-.349**	-.173**	.001	-.207**	-.165**	.004	-.110**
AG (Aggression)	-.348**	.007	.245**	-.355**	-.381**	.136**	-.047
CO (Control)	.161**	.026	-.311**	-.016	.488**	-.141**	.076*
HA (Harmavoidance)	.017	-.163**	-.315**	.041	.335**	-.394**	-.034
TR (Traditionalism)	-.009	-.060	-.222**	-.004	.369**	-.237**	-.217**
AB (Absorption)	-.144**	.026	.261**	.149**	-.232**	.342**	.064

Note. N = 662. ADJ = Adjustment; AMB = Ambition; SOC = Sociability; INP = Interpersonal Sensitivity; PRU = Prudence; INQ = Inquisitive; LRN = Learning Approach. *p < .05 ** p < .01, two-tailed, directional relationships not hypothesized a priori.

Table 3.16

Correlations Between the NEO-PI-R and the HPI Scales

Scale	ADJ	AMB	SOC	INP	PRU	INQ	LRN
Extraversion	.16**	.54**	.63**	.44**	-.06	.22**	.08*
Agreeableness	.31**	-.12**	-.24**	.47**	.46**	-.20**	-.08*
Conscientiousness	.24**	.37**	-.05	.08	.42**	.05	.16**
Neuroticism	-.72**	-.53**	-.08*	-.27**	-.22**	-.15**	-.17**
Openness	.01	.20**	.38**	.19**	-.31**	.52**	.24**

Note. N = 679. ADJ = Adjustment; AMB = Ambition; SOC = Sociability; INP = Interpersonal Sensitivity; PRU = Prudence; INQ = Inquisitive; LRN = Learning Approach. * p < .05 ** p < .01, two-tailed; directional relationships not hypothesized a priori.

Table 3.17

Correlations Between the PCI Primary Scales and the HPI Scales

Scale	ADJ	AMB	SOC	INP	PRU	INQ
Extraversion	.04	.39*	.64*	.26*	-.09	.18
Agreeableness	.50*	.25*	.09	.61	.21	-.03
Conscientiousness	.24*	.39*	-.06	.17	.59*	.08
Stability	.69*	.59*	-.02	.46*	.25*	.06
Openness	.12	.36*	.15	.17	-.05	.57*

Note. N = 154. ADJ = Adjustment; AMB = Ambition; SOC = Sociability; INP = Interpersonal Sensitivity; PRU = Prudence; INQ = Inquisitive. * p < .01.

Table 3.18

Correlations Between the Inventario de Personalidad de Cinco Factores and the HPI Scales

Scale	ADJ	AMB	SOC	INP	PRU	INQ
Extraversion	.24	.60	.62	.35	.04	.41
Agreeableness	.22	-.12	-.10	.37	.25	-.10
Conscientiousness	.22	.35	.08	.30	.49	.19
Stability	-.66	-.50	-.16	-.31	-.32	-.26
Openness	.11	.44	.51	.25	-.15	.69

Note. N = 200. Critical probability values were not provided in the study. ADJ = Adjustment; AMB = Ambition; SOC = Sociability; INP = Interpersonal Sensitivity; PRU = Prudence; INQ = Inquisitive.

Figure 3.1

Relations Between FFM Inventories and the HPI Scales

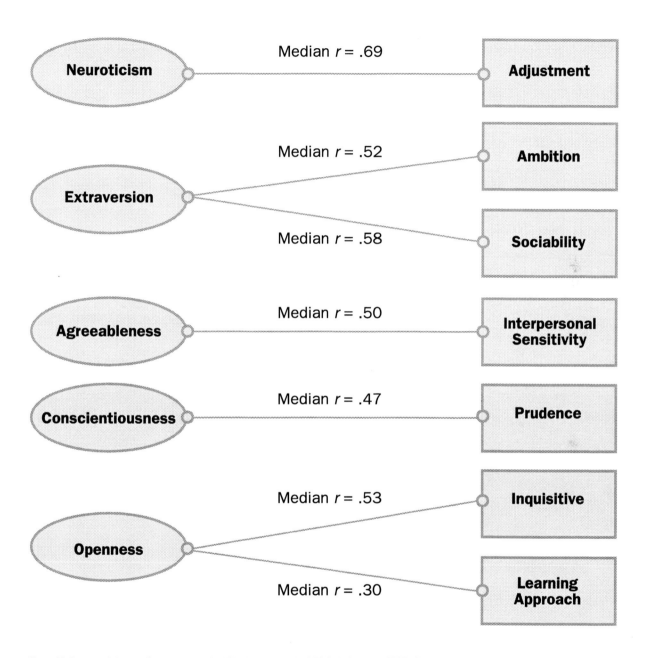

Note. Median correlation coefficients summarize HPI relations with the NEO PI-R (Goldberg, 2000), Goldberg's (1992) Big-Five Markers (R. Hogan & Hogan, 1995), Personal Characteristics Inventory (Mount & Barrick, 2001), and the Inventario de Personalidad de Cinco Factores (Salgado & Moscoso, 1999). The coefficient ranges are as follows: Adjustment/Emotional Stability/Neuroticism (.66 to .72); Ambition/Extraversion/Surgency (.39 to .60); Sociability/Extraversion/Surgency (.44 to .64); Interpersonal Sensitivity/Agreeableness (.37 to .61); Prudence/Conscientiousness (.36 to .59); Inquisitive/Openness/Intellect (.33 to .69); Learning Approach/Openness/Intellect (.24 to .35). Reprinted with permissions from the authors. All rights reserved.

Career Derailers. The Hogan Development Survey *(HDS; R. Hogan & Hogan, 1997)* is a measure of personality characteristics that can derail careers, relationships, and productive life activities. The 11 scales evaluate behavioral tendencies that can affect leadership styles, team effectiveness, performance competencies, and response tendencies under stress. These responses are not regarded as abnormal or clinical because virtually every person exhibits at least one of them when under pressure or when they let down their interpersonal guard. These characteristics might be best described as extensions of each end of the continuum of the FFM personality dimensions. For example, consider the case of FFM Conscientiousness, where at one extreme there is perfectionism and micromanaging and at the other there is risk-taking and limit-testing.

The structure of the HDS scales is defined by three factors. Factor I is a complex syndrome that can be labeled "negative affectivity" *(Tellegen, 1985)*. The scales that load on this factor are Excitable, Skeptical, Cautious, Reserved, and Leisurely. High scorers see the world as a dangerous place; as a result, they are alert for signs of criticism, rejection, betrayal, or hostile intent; they are easily upset and hard to sooth. When high scorers think they have detected a threat, they react vigorously in a variety of ways to remove the threat. Low scorers are mellow, calm, and placid.

HDS Factor II is a complex syndrome that can be labeled "positive affectivity" *(Tellegen, 1985)*. The scales that load on this factor are Bold, Mischievous, Colorful, and Imaginative. High scorers expect to be liked, admired, and respected; they are self-confident, self-centered, charming, attractive, and driven by their personal agendas. They expect to succeed at every undertaking, they resist acknowledging their mistakes and/or failures (which they blame on others), and they are often unable to learn from experience. Low scorers are typically modest, restrained, and humble.

HDS Factor III is a complex syndrome that can be labeled "restraint" *(Tellegen, 1985)*. The scales that compose this factor are Diligent and Dutiful. High scorers want to please figures of authority; as a result, they have high standards of performance for themselves and others, they work hard, pay attention to details, follow the rules, worry about making mistakes, are easy to supervise and popular with their bosses. Their respect for authority seems inversely related to their concern for the welfare of their subordinates. Low scorers are typically independent, skeptical of authority, and considerate of subordinates.

The sample (N=16,528) who provided data for the HDS and the HPI consisted of male and female job incumbents and applicants who were part of the norming sample for this version of the HPI manual. Although the HPI norming sample contains 156,614 cases, this sample contains individuals who completed both assessments between 2003-2004. Table 3.19 presents the HPI and HDS correlations.

Table 3.19
Correlations Between the HDS and the HPI Scales

Scales	ADJ	AMB	SOC	INP	PRU	INQ	LRN
Excitable	-.70	-.43	-.12	-.43	-.39	-.18	-.21
Skeptical	-.41	-.11	.05	-.30	-.33	.00	-.07
Cautious	-.50	-.66	-.33	-.31	-.15	-.27	-.26
Reserved	-.31	-.35	-.33	-.54	-.26	-.14	-.13
Leisurely	-.29	-.23	-.03	-.17	-.19	-.04	-.05
Bold	-.02	.29	.32	.03	-.04	.24	.21
Mischievous	-.09	.20	.45	-.03	-.40	.33	.07
Colorful	.04	.45	.62	.19	-.16	.28	.19
Imaginative	-.22	.09	.38	-.04	-.36	.30	.08
Diligent	-.01	.04	-.03	.08	.31	.09	.07
Dutiful	-.03	-.18	-.03	.22	.21	-.01	-.07

Note. N = 16,528, ADJ = Adjustment; AMB = Ambition; SOC = Sociability; INP = Interpersonal Sensitivity; PRU = Prudence; INQ = Inquisitive; LRN = Learning Approach. Critical value r = .02, p < .05; r = .03, p < .01, two-tailed, directional relationships not hypothesized a priori.

3.2 Interpretive Summaries of the HPI Scale Correlations with Other Tests

We organize our summary of these four sources of correlational data in terms of each HPI scale. The source data for this discussion appear in Tables 3.1 to 3.19 presented previously.

Adjustment. Tables 3.1 through 3.6 contain correlations between HPI Adjustment and both cognitive ability and skill tests. Although the research literature suggests an overlap between these types of measures that reflects test anxiety, we expected and found virtually no relations between intellectual measures and emotional stability as reflected by Adjustment scores. Only modest correlations appeared with the HBRI, which should be interpreted conservatively due to the large sample size. Again, we suggest low scorers may be fearful of making mistakes and, subsequently, being criticized.

Table 3.7 concerns the relation between the HPI and the MBTI. The MBTI types are composed of combinations of four dimensions: (a) Extraversion-Introversion (EI) is defined by what one pays attention to, people or ideas and concepts; (b) Sensation-Intuition (SN) is defined by how one processes information, empirically or intuitively; (c) Thinking-Feeling (TF) is defined by how one reaches conclusions, logically or emotionally; and (d) Judging-Perceiving (JP) is an odd dimension that concerns structure and planning at the Judging end and flexibility and spontaneity at the Perceiving end. We would expect Adjustment to be moderately correlated with Extraversion because the two constructs (Extraversion and Adjustment) share the underlying construct of social self-confidence; this expectation is confirmed in Table 3.3 (high scores on Adjustment are correlated with low scores on EI). Table 3.8 contains correlations between the HPI and the SDS. Because Artistic types tend to be disaffected and critical of their culture, we expected a negative correlation between Adjustment and the SDS Artist scale; this expectation is not confirmed, i.e., the correlation is not significant. Table 3.9 concerns relations between the HPI and the MVPI. We expected a negative correlation between Adjustment and the Aesthetic scale for the same reason that we expected a negative correlation with the SDS Artistic scale. We expected a positive correlation with the MVPI Affiliation scale because Adjustment and Affiliation share the underlying construct of social self-confidence. The correlation with the Hedonism measure of pleasure seeking and self-indulgence was unexpected. It suggests that hedonistic people may be self-derogatory and inclined to take criticism personally.

Table 3.10 contains correlations between the HPI and the IAS. We expected Adjustment to be correlated negatively with the dimensions of BC (Arrogant-Calculating), DE (Cold Hearted), and FG (Aloof-Introverted) because they share the underlying construct of empathy. Low scores on Adjustment and high scores on BC, DE, and FG reflect a lack of interpersonal sensitivity and responsiveness. Table 3.11 presents correlations between the HPI and the Big Five factor markers. Because the HPI was designed to parallel the five factors, we would predict that Adjustment would have its single highest correlation with Factor IV Emotional Stability and, in fact, the resulting .70 correlation is the highest in the matrix. Similarly, we examined the five matrices from Goldberg's *(2005)* Community Sample for convergent validity (see Tables 3.12 through 3.16). In all cases, the highest correlations for Adjustment were achieved with other personality scales of emotional stability. These ranged from -.72 for the MPQ (Stress Reaction) and the NEO-PI-R (Neuroticism) to .63 for the CPI (Well-being). Discriminant validity is indicated by relatively low (or nonsignificant) correlations between Adjustment and other FFM construct measures. The median correlation shown in Figure 3.1 suggests that the Adjustment scale can be a proxy for the FFM Emotional Stability dimension in validity generalization applications.

Table 3.19 contains correlations between the HPI and the HDS. We predicted that Adjustment would be negatively correlated with every HDS scale and that the largest correlations would be with scales loading on the first factor of the HDS, because these scales concern flawed interpersonal tendencies associated with anxiety. As Table 3.19 shows, we were partially correct. Adjustment is indeed negatively correlated with every scale except HDS Colorful, and the correlation with HDS Excitable is the largest in the table. However, we did not expect the near zero relations with the scales on the second and third HDS factors.

Ambition. There is no reason to expect Ambition to be strongly correlated with measures of cognitive ability, and the results in Tables 3.1 through 3.6, in general, confirm this expectation.

On the other hand, Ambition is fulfilled by means of social interaction, and the relatively large correlation with the EI scale of the MBTI shown in Table 3.7 was predicted. For Holland's SDS, we predicted the largest correlations for Ambition would be with Enterprising, followed by Social, and then Conventional interests. The correlations in Table 3.8 nicely confirm this prediction. We predicted that persons with high scores on Ambition are primarily motivated by MVPI Power, Commercial, and Affiliation motives. Table 3.9 correlations support this prediction.

As noted above, Ambition has a large component of social competence; we predicted, therefore, that Ambition should have positive correlations with the IAS Assured-Dominant and Gregarious-Extraverted scales, and negative correlations with Aloof-Introverted and Unassured-Submissive. These predictions are verified in Table 3.10. For the FFM, we proposed that Ambition and Sociability would be related to Factor I, Surgency. Table 3.11 shows that Ambition has its highest correlation with Factor I of the Big-Five markers, which ties it to such lexical themes as "energetic," "bold," "assertive," and "daring" (Goldberg, 1992). Next, we examined the five matrices from Goldberg's (2005) Community Sample for convergent validity (see Tables 3.12 through 3.16). In all cases, the highest correlations for Ambition were achieved with other personality scales of social potency. These ranged from .78 for the CPI (Dominance) and .71 for the JPI-R (Social Confidence) to .54 for the NEO-PI-R (Extraversion). Discriminant validity is indicated by relatively low (or non-significant) correlations between Ambition and other FFM construct measures. The median correlation shown in Figure 3.1 suggests that the Ambition scale can be a proxy for the FFM Extraversion dimension in validity generalization applications.

Table 3.19 contains correlations between Ambition and the HDS. We predicted that Ambition would be negatively correlated with scales defining the first factor of the HDS, positively correlated with the second factor, and uncorrelated with the third factor. Generally, these predictions were supported. All scale correlations between Ambition and scales defining the HDS Factor I were negative and significant indicating that low ambition scores are associated with negative affectivity. The positive correlations between Ambition and HDS Factor II indicate that high ambition scores are associated with positive affectivity. The negative correlation between Ambition and HDS Factor III Dutiful scale suggest that high ambition scores are associated with independence.

Sociability. Because Sociability combines a need for social interaction with a need for stimulation, there is no reason to expect the scale to be associated with measures of cognitive ability. Tables 3.1 through 3.6 show that, in general, there is little relation between Sociability and cognitive measures. The small number of significant correlations that do appear is positive and low, with no obvious interpretive pattern.

The same construct underlies the HPI Sociability and the MBTI Extraversion-Introversion scale. Consequently, Sociability should have the highest correlation of all the HPI scales with EI. Table 3.7 shows that this is indeed the case. In fact, the Sociability scale is the best single HPI predictor of MBTI scales. In Holland's (1985a) theory of vocational interests, the Social and Enterprising types are the most extraverted. Consequently, Sociability should have its largest correlations with the SDS scales for Social and Enterprising; Table 3.8 indicates that this is so. The correlation with Artistic interests is unexpected. Because persons with high scores on Sociability need to interact and want to be noticed, Sociability should have its highest correlations with the Affiliation and Recognition scales of the MVPI. Table 3.9 verifies this prediction. The correlation with Hedonism adds an impulsive and fun-loving component to the meaning of Sociability.

Because Sociability is at the core of interpersonal behavior, we expected the scale to be correlated with all of Wiggins' IAS dimensions, but to have its largest positive correlations with the Gregarious-Extraverted and Assured-Dominant scales. We expected the largest negative correlations to be with the Aloof-Introverted and Unassured-Submissive scales. As Table 3.10 shows, these expectations were correct. Similarly, we predicted that Sociability would have its highest correlation with Factor I (Surgency) of the Big-Five factor markers and results in Table 3.11 support this expectation. The impulsive and fun-loving theme is reflected in the negative correlation between Sociability and Factor III, Conscientiousness. The adjectival markers for this factor suggest that high Sociability scorers are "disorganized," "careless," "inconsistent," and "sloppy" *(Goldberg, 1992)*. Next, we examined the five matrices from Goldberg's *(2005)* Community Sample for convergent validity (see Tables 3.12 through 3.16). In all cases, the highest correlations for Sociability were achieved with other personality scales of broad bandwidth extraversion. These ranged from .64 for the 16PF (Liveliness) and .63 for the NEO-PI-R (Extraversion) to .40 for the JPI-R (Sociability). Discriminant validity is indicated by relatively low (or non-significant) correlations between Sociability and other FFM construct measures. The median correlation shown in Figure 3.1 suggests that the Sociability scale can be a proxy for the FFM Extraversion dimension in validity generalization applications.

Table 3.19 contains correlations between Sociability and the HDS. We predicted that Sociability would be negatively correlated with Cautious and Reserved scales on the first factor of the HDS, positively correlated with the second factor, and uncorrelated with the third factor. Generally, these predictions were supported. Scale correlations between Sociability and scales reflecting social withdrawal on the HDS Factor I were negative and significant. The positive correlations between Sociability and HDS Factor II indicate that high Sociability scores are associated with positive affectivity, social presence, and attention seeking. The near zero correlations between Sociability and HDS Factor III Diligent and Dutiful scales suggest that Sociability is unrelated to restraint, self-reliance, and independence.

Interpersonal Sensitivity. The Interpersonal Sensitivity construct concerns charm, tact, and interpersonal skill. Consequently, it should be relatively independent of cognitive ability. Tables 3.1 though 3.6 verify this expectation.

It is not clear that Interpersonal Sensitivity is an important part of any of the Jungian dimensions unless enjoying social interaction is part of the MBTI EI construct at the Extraverted end. Table 3.7 suggests that this is the case. The Interpersonal Sensitivity scale and the SDS Social type share the underlying construct of sympathy, tolerance, and warmth. As Table 3.8 shows, Interpersonal Sensitivity has its largest correlation with the SDS Social scale. As for the motivational base of Interpersonal Sensitivity, we predicted that persons with high scores on this scale should enjoy social interaction and should like to help others. Table 3.9 shows that Interpersonal Sensitivity is significantly correlated with Affiliation and Altruism motives.

Because Interpersonal Sensitivity is a fundamental evaluative aspect of social interaction, we predicted that the scale would be significantly correlated with every IAS scale. Table 3.10 shows significant correlations with seven of the eight scales. The highest correlations are with Aloof-Introverted and Cold Hearted in the negative direction and with Gregarious-Extraverted in the positive direction. The correlation with Warm-Agreeable (.29), although significant, is somewhat lower than we expected. The Interpersonal Sensitivity scale was intended to be a proxy for the agreeableness dimension in the FFM; Table 3.11 indicates that Factor II Agreeableness is substantially correlated with Interpersonal Sensitivity scale scores. Next, we examined the five matrices from Goldberg's (2005) Community Sample for convergent validity (see Tables 3.12 through 3.16). In all cases, the highest correlations for Interpersonal Sensitivity were achieved with other personality scales of agreeableness. These ranged from .52 for the MPQ (Social Closeness) and .50 for the 16PF (Warmth) to .32 for the CPI (Good Impression). Discriminant validity is indicated by modest (or non-significant) correlations between Interpersonal Sensitivity and other FFM construct measures. The median correlation shown in Figure 3.1 suggests that the Interpersonal Sensitivity scale can be a proxy for the FFM Agreeableness dimension in validity generalization applications.

Table 3.19 contains correlations between Interpersonal Sensitivity and the HDS. We predicted that Interpersonal Sensitivity would be negatively correlated with HDS Factor I scales, uncorrelated with the second factor, and positively correlated with the third factor. Generally, these predictions were supported. Scale correlations between Interpersonal Sensitivity and scales reflecting social withdrawal on the HDS Factor I were negative and significant. The only meaningful positive correlation between Interpersonal Sensitivity and the HDS Factor II Colorful indicate that high Interpersonal Sensitivity scores are associated with social skill, self-expression, and attention seeking behavior. The positive correlations between Interpersonal Sensitivity and HDS Factor III Diligent and Dutiful scales suggest that Interpersonal Sensitivity is associated with conformity and being eager to please others—getting along.

Prudence. The Prudence construct concerns cautiousness, attention to detail, and most of all, self-control. This dimension is typically related to academic performance, but it is not expected to be related to cognitive ability, per se. Table 3.1 shows that it is unrelated to scores on the ASVAB composites, but is negatively related to the electronics, mechanics, and science primary scales. Table 3.2 shows a persistent pattern of negative correlations with the BST, suggesting that persons with low scores on Prudence will do better on these measures. We can only speculate as to the meaning of these negative correlations; perhaps guessing is rewarded in the scoring keys, and persons with low Prudence scores are more likely to guess than persons with high scores. Tables 3.4 through 3.6 show no relations between business-oriented cognitive tests and conscientiousness, defined by the Prudence scale.

On the MBTI (see Table 3.7), the Sensation-Intuition dimension is a measure of creative tendencies. Because low Prudence is also associated with creativity *(cf. Barron, 1965)*, we expected a negative correlation between these two measures. The Thinking-Feeling and Judging-Perceiving scales also concern being flexible and open-minded at the low ends; again, we predicted negative correlations between Prudence and these scales. As Table 3.7 shows, these expectations were confirmed. On the SDS, the Conventional type should have the highest scores for Prudence, and the Artistic type should have the lowest scores. Although the correlations are quite modest, Table 3.8 confirms these predictions. In terms of the motivational basis of Prudence, persons with high scores should need Security and Tradition, and should deny Hedonism needs. Table 3.9 supports these predictions. The positive correlation with Altruism motives is a surprise and somewhat softens the interpretation of high Prudence scores.

In terms of the IAS, the psychopathic tone of the Arrogant-Calculating scale suggests it should be negatively correlated with Prudence. Table 3.10 shows that the largest correlation for Prudence (-.31) is with this scale. The other correlations are less theoretically meaningful and have less bearing on the construct validity of the Prudence scale. In Table 3.11, Prudence has its highest correlation with Factor III Conscientiousness of the Big-Five factor markers. Adjectival markers for this factor are organized, systematic, thorough, and neat *(Goldberg, 1992)*. Next, we examined the five matrices from Goldberg's *(2005)* Community Sample for convergent validity (see Tables 3.12 through 3.16). In all cases, the highest correlations for Prudence were achieved with other personality scales of broad bandwidth conscientiousness. These ranged from .56 for the CPI (Self-control) and .49 for the 16PF (Rule Consciousness) to .42 for the NEO-PI-R (Conscientiousness). Discriminant validity is indicated by modest (or non-significant) correlations between Prudence and other FFM construct measures. The median correlation shown in Figure 3.1 suggests that the Prudence scale can be a proxy for the FFM Conscientiousness dimension in validity generalization applications.

Table 3.19 contains correlations between Prudence and the HDS. We predicted that Sociability would be negatively correlated with HDS Factor I and Factor II scales, but positively correlated with HDS Factor III. Generally, these predictions were supported. Scale correlations between Prudence and scales reflecting social withdrawal on the HDS Factor I were negative and significant. The negative correlations between Prudence and HDS Factor II indicate that low Prudence scores are associated with impulsive, risk-taking, and limit-testing tendencies. The positive correlations between Prudence and HDS Factor III Diligent and Dutiful scales suggest that Prudence is related to overly-conscientious and deferential behavior.

Inquisitive. The Inquisitive scale contains a component of intellectual talent in the sense that persons with high scores seem bright. Consequently, we would expect modest positive correlations between Inquisitive and measures of cognitive ability. Tables 3.1 and 3.2 support this expectation. We also expected modest, non-zero correlations between Inquisitive scores and scale scores for the business-oriented cognitive tests in Tables 3.3 through 3.6. Although some correlations emerged, these were neither as high nor as uniform as the correlations for the more general ability tests.

On the MBTI, Introversion (I) concerns interest in ideas, and Intuition (N) concerns creativity. Consequently, we expected Inquisitive to be correlated negatively with EI, and positively with SN. Table 3.7 shows that this is the case. In terms of Holland's *(1985a)* theory, the Investigative and Artistic types are the most creative of the six types. We predicted the largest positive correlations would occur between Inquisitive and the Investigative and Artistic scales of the SDS. Table 3.8 supports this prediction. The correlation with Realistic interests suggests that Realistic types are more imaginative than we thought. We expected persons with high scores on Inquisitive to be motivated primarily by Aesthetic and Scientific interests. Table 3.9 shows that Inquisitive indeed has its highest correlations with these two MVPI scales.

Inquisitive is not necessarily or primarily a dimension of interpersonal performance. As a result, we made no predictions concerning correlations between Inquisitive and the personality scales of the IAS. As Table 3.10 shows, persons with high scores on Inquisitive tend to be described as Assured-Dominant and as Gregarious-Extraverted. This probably reflects the underlying link between Inquisitive and Ambition. On the other hand, we expected both the Inquisitive scale and the Learning Approach scale from the HPI to correlate with Factor V Intellect of the Big-Five factor markers and results in Table 3.11 show this is the case. Adjectival descriptors associated with high scores on Factor V include "intellectual," "creative," "complex," and "imaginative" *(Goldberg, 1992)*. Next, we examined the five matrices from Goldberg's *(2005)* Community Sample for convergent validity (see Tables 3.12 through 3.16). In all cases, the highest correlations for Inquisitive were achieved with other personality scales of Intellect/Openness to Experience. These ranged from .52 for the JPI-R (Breadth of Interest) and .45 for the CPI (Intellectual Efficiency) to .30 for the MPQ (Achievement). Discriminant validity is indicated by relatively low (or non-significant) correlations between Inquisitive and other FFM construct measures. The median correlation shown in Figure 3.1 suggests that the Inquisitive scale can be a proxy for the FFM Intellect/Openness to Experience dimension in validity generalization applications.

Table 3.19 contains correlations between Inquisitive and the HDS. We predicted that Inquisitive would be negatively correlated with HDS Factor I Cautious and positively correlated with HDS Factor II Mischievous and Imaginative. We predicted that Inquisitive would be unrelated to HDS Factor III. The relations between Inquisitive and the specific scale predictions were supported and we interpret these high scores on Inquisitive to reflect openness to innovation, willingness to accept challenges and risks, and a willingness to express unconventional and original ideas. The positive correlations between Inquisitive and HDS Factor II scales indicate that high Inquisitive scores generally are associated with positive affectivity, social presence, and attention seeking. The near zero correlations between Inquisitive and HDS Factor III Diligent and Dutiful scales suggest that Inquisitive is unrelated to restraint and self-reliance.

Learning Approach. Learning Approach concerns interest in and aptitude for learning and training. Intelligence and diligence are the major requirements for academic performance and we expected Learning Approach to be correlated with indices of these two constructs. Tables 3.1 and 3.2 show that Learning Approach is steadily and moderately correlated with measures of cognitive ability. Similar to the pattern of correlations with Inquisitive, we also expected modest, non-zero correlations between Learning Approach scores and scale scores for the business-oriented cognitive tests in Tables 3.3 through 3.6. Again, although some correlations emerged, these were neither as high nor as uniform as the correlations for the more general ability tests.

In terms of the scales of the MBTI in Table 3.7, Learning Approach is modestly correlated with the planful and inflexible end of the MBTI scales. On the SDS, the Investigative type is concerned with academic performance. The only significant correlation in Table 3.8 is between Learning Approach and the Investigative scale of the SDS. We thought that the motivational basis for Learning Approach would be a need for achievement and, perhaps, intellectual curiosity. These two needs are reflected in the MVPI scales for Power and Science. Table 3.9 shows that Learning Approach has its largest correlations with these two motive measures.

The Learning Approach construct has only minimal interpersonal implications. Table 3.10 shows that, other than a .27 correlation with the IAS Assured-Dominant scale, School Success is unrelated to Wiggins' *(1991)* dimensions of interpersonal style. Similarly, Table 3.11 shows that Learning Approach is related to Factor V (Intellect) of the Big-Five factor markers. Next, we examined the five matrices from Goldberg's *(2005)* Community Sample for convergent validity (see Tables 3.12 through 3.16). In all cases, the highest correlations for Inquisitive were achieved with other personality scales of intellect/openness to experience. These ranged from .47 for the CPI (Intellectual Efficiency) to .15 for the MPQ (Achievement). Discriminant validity is indicated by relatively low (or non-significant) correlations between Learning Approach and other FFM construct measures. The median correlation shown in Figure 3.1 suggests that the Inquisitive scale is a rough proxy for the FFM Intellect/Openness to Experience dimension in validity generalization applications.

Table 3.19 contains correlations between Learning Approach and the HDS. We predicted that Learning Approach would have a pattern of correlations with the HDS scales that is similar to those for Inquisitive reported in Table 3.19. As such, we predicted that Learning Approach would be negatively correlated with HDS Factor I Cautious and positively correlated with HDS Factor II Mischievous and Imaginative. We predicted that Inquisitive would be unrelated to HDS Factor III. The relations between Inquisitive and the specific scale correlations were in the predicted directions; however, the correlations with HDS Bold and Colorful were higher than expected. The overall pattern of relations suggests that high scores on Inquisitive are open to innovation, competitive, and like being recognized for their accomplishments. The near low correlations between Learning Approach and HDS Factor III Diligent and Dutiful scales suggest that Sociability is unrelated to restraint.

3.2 Correlations Between the HPI and Others' Descriptions

A primary goal of HPI is to predict how a respondent will be described by others who know him or her, i.e., to predict his or her reputation (see Chapter 1). If certain descriptive terms are reliably associated with HPI scale scores, then this helps us understand the meaning of the scores. In addition, we can use those scores to predict how peers will describe others with comparable scores and to predict how they will behave in non-testing situations because a person's characteristic social behavior generates his or her reputation, and reputation is reflected in peer descriptions.

According to socioanalytic theory, the same process underlies social interaction and responding to the HPI or any other assessment procedure. In theory, this is the reason certain scale scores are linked to certain peer descriptions *(Mills & Hogan, 1976)*. Thus, finding correlations between peer descriptions and HPI scores allows us to evaluate the validity of the HPI and to evaluate the theory of personality on which the HPI rests.

Undergraduate and graduate student volunteers (N=128) completed the HPI; they also gave personality rating forms to two persons who had known them for at least two years. The peer rating form was organized in three sections. The first section contained items that paralleled the content of the 43 HICs on the HPI. For example, the Ambition scale has a HIC entitled Leadership. We developed a rating item for the Leadership HIC that reads, "This person is a leader, not a follower." Respondents rated the target person on the 43 items (corresponding to the 43 HICs) using a 5-point Likert scale, where "1" indicated "strongly disagree" and "5" indicated "strongly agree."

The second section of the rating form contained 21 California Q-Set *(Block, 1961)* items that correlated above .5 with markers for the FFM in research conducted by John *(1990)*; these Q-Set items are proxies for the dimensions of the FFM. Respondents described the target person by checking "yes" or "no" to each Q-Set item (e.g., arouses liking in others). The third section contained 112 adjectives from Gough and Heilbrun's *(1983)* Adjective Check List (ACL); John *(1990)* identified these adjectives as prototypical markers of the dimensions of the FFM. The response format was the same as that used in the previous section. We assigned the subjects scores for the primary HPI scales. We combined the ratings of the two respondents on the rating forms and computed scores for the rating dimensions in each section of the form.

The 7 HPI-based peer rating scales in the first section were labeled Rated Adjustment (RTADJ), Rated Ambition (RTAMB), Rated Sociability (RTSOC), Rated Interpersonal Sensitivity (RTINP), Rated Prudence (RTPRU), Rated Inquisitive (RTINQ), and Rated Learning Approach (RTLRN). In the second section of the peer rating form, we formed the following scale scores: Q-Set Adjustment (QSADJ); Q-Set Ambition (QSAMB); Q-Set Sociability (QSSOC); Q-Set Interpersonal Sensitivity (QSINP); Q-Set Prudence (QSPRU); and Q-Set Inquisitive (QSINQ). The ACL scales in the third section were labeled Emotional Stability

(EMOTS), Extraversion (EXTRA), Agreeableness (AGREE), Conscientiousness (CONSC), and Intellectual Openness (INTOP).

Table 3.20 presents means, standard deviations, coefficient alphas *(Cronbach, 1951)*, and interrater reliabilities for each peer description variable. Note that the ACL-based scales yielded the highest alphas and the Q-Set scales had the lowest alphas. Note also that the Adjustment descriptors consistently had the lowest reliabilities, whereas the Conscientiousness (Prudence) ratings consistently had the highest. This means that it is relatively easier to rate Prudence than Adjustment.

Table 3.20
Characteristics of Rated Personality Description Scales

Peer Rating Scales	Mean	Standard Deviation	Number of Items	Alpha	Interrater Reliability
HPI Ratings					
RTADJ	37.3	6.0	5	72	.25
RTAMB	46.1	6.8	6	.65	.45
RTSOC	24.5	6.0	4	.71	.55
RTINP	44.8	5.2	6	.61	.42
RTPRU	36.2	5.9	5	.61	.59
RTINQ	38.7	4.7	5	.57	.38
RTLRN	37.7	6.2	5	.60	.56
Q-Set Ratings					
QSADJ	4.5	1.5	3	.46	.08
QSAMB	3.4	1.0	2	.38	.26
QSSOC	6.5	1.6	4	.53	.32
QSINP	6.8	1.3	4	.41	.15
QSPRU	4.5	1.4	3	.47	.39
QSINQ	5.5	2.1	5	.41	.34
ACL Ratings					
EMOTS	25.8	5.6	18	.78	.24
EXTRA	29.4	6.9	21	.86	.53
AGREE	50.7	6.7	28	.90	.33
CONSC	33.4	6.9	20	.89	.68
INTOP	41.7	6.6	25	.82	.40

Table 3.21
Scale Correlates of Rated Personality Descriptions

Rated Personality[a]							
HPI-based	**ADJ**	**AMB**	**SOC**	**INP**	**PRU**	**INQ**	**LRN**
RTADJ	.74	.37	.17	.43	.33	.45	.12
RTAMB	.46	.67	.45	.10	.19	.53	.18
RTSOC	.06	-.18	.74	.12	-.64	-.06	-.09
RTINP	.41	.04	.16	.73	.20	-.08	.12
RTPRU	.08	-.07	-.42	.21	.79	-.06	.01
RTINQ	.31	.40	.43	.36	.11	.77	.32
RTLRN	.04	.09	-.26	.05	.59	.46	.68
Q-SET-based	**ADJ**	**AMB**	**SOC**	**INP**	**PRU**	**INQ**	**LRN**
QSADJ	.55	.57	.34	.69	.41	.66	.46
QSAMB	-.06	.37	.18	-.12	-.19	.41	.34
QSSOC	.26	.40	.82	.72	-.29	.19	-.06
QSINP	.51	-.22	.11	.94	-.30	.13	-.22
QSPRU	.06	-.44	-.44	.00	.45	.09	-.14
QSINQ	.22	.43	.17	.24	.18	.42	.45
ACL-based[b]	**ADJ**	**AMB**	**SOC**	**INP**	**PRU**	**INQ**	**LRN**
EMOTS	.69c	.33	.33	.52	.40	.34	-.01
EXTRA	.11	.44	.62	.27	-.45	.19	-.03
AGREE	.34	-.03	.04	.81	.32	.02	-.15
CONSC	-.13	.07	-.21	.05	.54	.09	.06
INTOP	.15	.39	.07	.44	.42	.66	.43

Note. Critical value r= .23, p=.01, one-tailed test (N =100); [a]Sample sizes: HPI-based (N =108); Q-SET-based (N =105); ACL-based (N =100); ADJ = Adjustment; AMB = Ambition; SOC = Sociability; INP = Interpersonal Sensitivity; PRU = Prudence; INQ = Inquisitive; LRN = Learning Approach. [b]EMOTS (Emotional Stability); EXTRA (Extraversion); AGREE (Agreeableness); CONSC (Conscientiousness); INTOP (Intellectual Openness); cCorrelation is uncorrected; correction yielded a coefficient in excess of 1.00.

We computed correlations between HPI scale scores and all the peer rating scale scores. Correlations were corrected for the unreliability of the peer ratings using methods discussed by Spearman *(cf. Ghiselli, Campbell, & Zedeck, 1981, p. 290)*, and these results appear in Table 3.21. The correlations between test-non-test measures of the same construct should be positive, significant, and larger than the other possible correlations. As Table 3.21 indicates, this pattern occurs in 19 of 21 cases, and this pattern supports the construct validity of the HPI scales.

Then, we computed correlations between individual ACL items and the HPI scales. Table 3.22 lists the ten adjectives most highly correlated with each scale. These adjectival correlates are a major source of information regarding the meaning of the HPI scales.

Table 3.22

Adjectival Correlates of the HPI Scales

Adjustment		Ambition		Sociability	
Tense	-.53	Outgoing	.32	Quiet	-.45
Worrying	-.49	Shy	-.31	Talkative	.48
Moody	-.46	Retiring	-.30	Shy	-.42
Unstable	-.43	Assertive	.28	Outgoing	.37
Self Pitying	-.39	Spunky	.28	Silent	-.37
Temperamental	-.39	Polished	.28	Reserved	-.35
Nervous	-.37	Silent	-.27	Show-off	.33
Fearful	-.37	Active	.26	Spunky	.32
Self Punishing	-.36	Sociable	.26	Outspoken	.32
High Strung	-.35	Forceful	.24	Withdrawn	-.32
Interpersonal Sensitivity		**Prudence**		**Inquisitive**	
Sympathetic	.44	Noisy	-.43	Narrow Interests	-.42
Praising	.44	Through	.38	Ingenious	.34
Outgoing	.43	Wise	.37	Artistic	.31
Soft-hearted	.37	Precise	.37	Imaginative	.30
Enthusiastic	.37	Irresponsible	-.36	Inventive	.30
Sociable	.37	Stable	.30	Sharp-witted	.30
Friendly	.36	Show-Off	-.34	Active	.29
Polished	.33	Cautious	.30	Energetic	.26
Sensitive	.33	Efficient	.31	Witty	.26
Pleasant	.31	Practical	.31	Original	.25
Learning Approach					
Narrow Interests	-.26				
Insightful	.24				
Ingenious	.23				
Foresighted	.22				
Clever	.21				
Good Natured	-.22				
Thorough	.19				
Precise	.18				
Touchy	-.17				
Painstaking	.16				

3.3 HPI Correlates of Organizational Behavior

This section examines the relationship between HPI scale scores and various aspects of organizational behavior. We are concerned with how the HPI scale scores are related to non-test behaviors, where the construct of interest is hypothesized to underlie both the HPI scale and the criterion assessed. Earlier research concerning the relationship between personality and occupational performance often failed to distinguish correctly between the various components of personality, e.g., because Adjustment and Prudence are both measures of personality, they were thought to be somehow interchangeable.

The earlier research also failed on many occasions to use measures that were appropriate for the non-test criteria in terms of the underlying construct (e.g., measures of adjustment might be used to predict training performance). Results presented by Hough et al. *(1990)* illustrate the point. When any personality scale is used to predict any criteria, virtually no relationships emerge *(see also Pearlman, 1985)*. Using measures of single constructs to predict any criteria leads to modest results. However, when measures of single constructs are used to predict relevant criteria, the correlations improve substantially. The results described by Hough et al. *(1990)* provide empirical support for Campbell's *(1990)* point that meaningful test-non-test correlations can only be found when the latent structure underlying both the predictor and the criterion constructs is similar.

Figure 3.2 describes the performance implications of the socioanalytic themes of "getting along" and "getting ahead" as well as the construct measures of the HPI. In the figure, example performance criteria for each dimension are specified. For example, the HPI Inquisitive and Learning Approach scales measure the FFM culture factor. These scales should be related to training and academic performance because persons with high scores on measures of culture are curious, have wide interests, and enjoy education for its own sake; conversely, persons with low scores are practical, concrete-minded, and have narrow interests. We used this method to specify the performance domain for each of the other factors. Each of the proposed relations in Figure 3.2 is testable. J. Hogan and Holland *(2003; the text that follows is reproduced with permission)* describe research that resulted in the classification of criteria listed in Figure 3.2 and the personality correlates of these performance dimensions.

Figure 3.2
Example Criteria Representing Getting Along, Getting Ahead, and HPI Personality Scales

Theme/Construct	Sample Criteria[1]
Getting Along	Demonstrates Interpersonal skill
	Works with Others
	Shows Positive Attitude
	Shares Credit
Getting Ahead	Works with Energy
	Exhibits Effort
	Values Productivity
	Shows Concern for Quality
Adjustment	Remains Even Tempered
	Manages People, Crisis, & Stress
	Shows Resiliency
	Demonstrates Patience
Ambition	Exhibits Leadership
	Demonstrates Effectiveness
	Takes Initiative
	Generates New Monthly Accounts
Interpersonal Sensitivity	Shows Interpersonal Skill
	Exhibits Capacity to Compromise
	Demonstrates Tactfulness & Sensitivity
	Shares Credit
Prudence	Stays Organized
	Works With Integrity
	Abides by Rules
	Follows Safety Procedures
Inquisitive	Achieves Quality with Information
	Analyzes Finances/Operations
	Seems Market Savvy
	Displays Good Judgment
Learning Approach	Capitalizes on Training
	Exhibits Technical Skill
	Makes Progress in Training
	Possesses Job Knowledge

[1] All example criteria are ratings except for "Generates New Monthly Accounts"

We now describe HPI-based meta-analyses that evaluate the links between personality and job performance. This research provides further evidence for the construct validity of the primary HPI scales.

Methods Used for Meta-Analysis. We identified 43 independent samples (total N = 5,242) from published articles, chapters, technical reports, and dissertations between 1980 and 2000 that were catalogued in the Hogan Assessment Systems' archive. The studies met the following criteria: (a) they used job analysis to estimate personality-based job requirements; (b) they used a concurrent (k = 41) or predictive (k = 2) validation strategy with working adults; (c) the criteria were content explicit, not just overall job performance, and these were classified reliably by subject matter experts using the constructs listed in Figure 3.2; and (d) the predictor variables were scales of the HPI. We excluded studies using: (a) clinical patients and therapists; (b) undergraduate or graduate students; (c) self-reported performance criteria; (d) performance criteria other than ratings and objective productivity/personnel measures; (e) only an overall performance criterion; (f) laboratory or assessment center studies; and (g) studies unrelated to work contexts.

Table 3.23 lists the distribution of studies (k = 43) by job title and Holland *(1985)* occupational type. Most job titles correspond to the Holland Realistic, Social, Enterprising, and Conventional types; no studies involved Investigative and Artistic occupations. Ideally, every Holland type would be present in the analysis, but our sample composition reflects the base rate of occupations in the U.S. economy. Gottfredson and Holland *(1989; 1996)* report that the majority of occupations are Realistic (66.7%), Conventional (13.4%), and Enterprising (11.1%); Social (4.6%), Investigative (3.0%), and Artistic (1.2%) occupations are less common. The jobs in the table represent the most frequent types in the U. S. economy.

Table 3.23
Distribution of Studies Based on Holland Code and Job Title

Holland Codes		DOT Code	DOT Job Title	# Studies
Conventional 10 Studies	CES	239.367-010	Customer Service Representative	5
	CSE	211.362-010	Cashier	1
	CSE	209.362-010	Clerk, General	3
	CSE	243.367-014	Post Office Clerk	1
Enterprising 16 Studies	ECS	369.467-010	Manager, Branch Store	2
	ERS	250.357-022	Sales Representative	3
	ERS	239.167-014	Telephone/Telegraph Dispatcher	1
	ESA	189.167-022	Manager, Department	6
	ESC	299.357-014	Telephone Solicitor	1
	ESR	187.117-010	Administrator, Hospital	1
	ESR	189.117-022	Manager, Industrial Organization	1
	ESR	184.167-114	Manager, Warehouse	1
Realistic 10 Studies	RCS	905.663-014	Truck Driver, Heavy	3
	REI	891.684-010	Dock Hand	1
	REI	590.382-010	Operator, Automated Process	2
	RES	913.463-010	Bus Driver	1
	RES	910.363-014	Locomotive Engineer	1
	RIE	019.061-022	Ordnance Engineer	1
	RSE	962.362-010	Communications Technician	1
Social 7 Studies	SEC	193.262-014	Dispatcher, Governmental Services	1
	SER	372.667-018	Corrections Officer	1
	SER	377.677-018	Deputy Sheriff, Civil Division	1
	SER	355.674-014	Nurse Aide	1
	SER	375.263-014	Police Officer	2
	SIE	168.267-014	Claims Examiner, Insurance	1

Note. Classifications based on work by Gottfredson and Holland (1989; 1996).

All studies included one or more types of job analyses during the initial stages of the research. Approximately 30% of the studies (k = 13) used the critical incidents method *(Flanagan, 1954)* to define exceptional behavior *(for example, see Hogan & Lesser, 1996)*. Over half of the studies used worker-oriented methods to determine the knowledge, skills, and abilities required for successful job performance. These job analyses generally followed the Goldstein, Zedeck, and Schneider (1993) method for content validation research (cf. R. Hogan & Hogan, 1995, p. 75). The remaining studies (k = 18) used the Performance Improvement Characteristics (PIC) job analysis approach (Hogan & Rybicki, 1998). This personality-based job analysis uses a 48-item PIC checklist to profile jobs in terms of the FFM dimensions. Raymark, Schmit, and Guion (1997) describe a similar method for evaluating personality-based job requirements. Although job analysis results often are used to justify predictor measures, these results were used to develop criterion dimensions.

Meta-Analysis Procedures. We used the meta-analytic procedures specified by Hunter and Schmidt (1990) to cumulate results across studies and to assess effect sizes. All studies used zero-order product-moment correlations, which eliminated the need to convert alternative statistics to values of r. Corrections were made for sampling error, unreliability in the measures, and range restriction. Reliability of the personality measures was estimated using within-study coefficient alpha [M = .78; range = .71 (Prudence) to .84 (Adjustment)], rather than relying exclusively on the values reported in the HPI manual. Although some researchers (e.g., Murphy & De Shon, 2000) argue against the use of rater-based reliability estimates, we followed procedures outlined by Barrick and Mount (1991) and Tett et al. (1991), and used the .508 reliability coefficient proposed by Rothstein (1990) as the estimate of the reliability of supervisory ratings of job performance. For objective criterion data, we (conservatively) assumed perfect reliability, following Salgado's (1997) method. Note that Hunter, Schmidt, and Judiesch (1990) recommend a reliability estimate of .55 for objective criteria. The frequency-weighted mean of the job performance reliability distribution was .59, which is comparable to the value of .56 reported by Barrick and Mount (1991), and the mean square root reliability of .76 corresponds to the value of .778 reported by Tett et al. (1991). We also computed a range restriction index for HPI scales. Following procedures described by Hunter and Schmidt (1990), we divided each HPI scale's within-study standard deviation by the standard deviation reported by Hogan and Hogan (1995). This procedure produced an index of range restriction for each HPI scale [M = .87; range = .81 (Ambition) to .94 (Learning Approach)] within each study, and we used this value to correct each predictor scale for range restriction.

Hunter and Schmidt (1990) point out that meta-analytic results can be biased unless each sample contributes about the same number of correlations to the total. To eliminate such bias, we averaged correlations within studies so that each sample contributed only one point estimate per predictor scale. For example, if more than one criterion from any study was classified as getting along, the correlations between each predictor scale and those criteria were averaged to derive a single point estimate of the predictor-criterion relationship. Note that this procedure uses both negative and positive correlations rather than mean absolute values for averaging correlations. This is the major computational difference between the current analyses and those presented by Tett et al. (1991, p. 712). We did not correct correlation coefficients to estimate validity at the construct level. Although some (e.g., Mount & Barrick, 1995a; Ones, Schmidt, & Viswesvaran, 1994) argue this is a relevant artifact that can be corrected, we believe it is premature to estimate the validity of the perfect construct when there is no firm agreement on the definition of the perfect construct.

Results. Table 3.24 presents the results for the HPI scales when the criterion themes of getting along and getting ahead are combined as global measures of job performance. As seen in the table, the sample weighted and estimated true validities for HPI Adjustment, Ambition, and Prudence are .19 (.32), .13 (.22), and .14 (.24), respectively. The estimated validity of the Adjustment scale exceeds previously reported values for the Emotional Stability construct, which are .15 *(Neuroticism; Tett et al., 1991)* and .09 *(Emotional Stability; Hurtz & Donovan, 2000; Salgado, 1997)*. The FFM Extraversion factor is represented by HPI Ambition and Sociability scales. Similar to results reported by Vinchur et al. *(1998)*, Ambition, not Sociability (r = .01) predicts the criteria. In previous meta-analyses, the estimated true validity of Extraversion for predicting global performance ranged from .13 *(Barrick & Mount, 1991)* to .16 *(Tett, et al., 1991)*, but these analyses combine facets of Ambition with Sociability. The estimated true validity of HPI Learning Approach is less than Tett et al's. finding for Openness (r = .27), but larger than the reported estimates from other omnibus meta-analyses. Moreover, the results for Sociability, Interpersonal Sensitivity, and Inquisitive do not generalize based on the 90% credibility values, which is consistent with results reported by Hurtz and Donovan *(2000)* and Tett et al. *(1991)*. Table 3.24 validities represent the most global level of analysis.

Table 3.25 presents 14 meta-analyses using HPI scales to predict getting along or getting ahead criteria considered separately. As seen, between 22 (N = 2,553) and 42 (N = 5,017) studies were used in these analyses. Getting along criteria are best predicted by HPI Adjustment, Prudence, and Interpersonal Sensitivity, with estimated true validities of .34, .31, and .23, respectively. HPI Sociability and Inquisitive scales are unrelated to criteria for getting along. Getting ahead criteria are best predicted by the HPI Ambition (r = .26), Adjustment (r = .22), and Prudence (r = .20) scales. Again note that Ambition, not Sociability, predicts getting ahead. Validities and the credibility intervals for the HPI Sociability and Interpersonal Sensitivity scales indicate that they are not practically useful for predicting getting ahead criteria. Although the pattern of variances differ, the results in Table 3.25 suggest that the Adjustment, Prudence, and Ambition scales generally are valid for predicting criteria reflecting getting along and getting ahead at work.

Table 3.26 presents validity results for HPI scales aligned by construct-classified criteria. Forty-two meta-analyses were computed; there were too few studies with criteria categorized as Sociability-related to compute meta-analyses for the HPI Sociability scale. However, there were sufficient studies to compute meaningful analyses for the other scales. The sample weighted mean correlations and the estimated true validities across scales are consistently larger than validities associated with the more global criteria of getting along and getting ahead. The estimated true validities range from .25 (HPI Learning Approach) to .43 (HPI Adjustment). These findings support Campbell's *(1990)* strategy of organizing the predictor and criterion domains based on their latent structure. In fact, aligning predictors and criteria increases the sample-weighted validities over the aggregate performance index [M = 43%; range = 24% (Adjustment) to 75% (Inquisitive)], Getting Along criteria [M = 47%; range = 24% (Adjustment) to 90% (Inquisitive)], and Getting Ahead criteria [M = 47%; range = 25% (Ambition) to 65% (Inquisitive)]. The lower bound credibility intervals are all greater than .20, except for Learning Approach, which suggests that scale validity generalizes across samples when criteria are classified by construct. In every case, the credibility intervals support the targeted validity coefficients.

Table 3.26 also shows the convergent and discriminant validity of the HPI scales. For each dimension except HPI Learning Approach, the correlations are highest between personality scales and the aligned, construct-specific criterion variables, indicating convergence. The estimated true validity for HPI Adjustment (.43) is the largest in the table. Similarly, validity coefficients are smallest for the personality scales that are not aligned with specific constructs. For example, HPI Inquisitive is unrelated to Adjustment, Interpersonal Sensitivity, and Prudence criteria; HPI Sociability predicts none of the construct-based criteria. This pattern of lower correlations for the off-diagonal scales supports discriminant validity. Another index of discriminant validity comes from the overlap of the credibility values among scales. Except for HPI Learning Approach, no lower-bound credibility values for construct-aligned measures overlap any other scale, which suggests independence. This pattern of findings further supports the discriminant validity of the predictor scales.

The off-diagonal correlations in Table 3.26 show the magnitude of relations between Adjustment, Prudence and, to a lesser extent, Ambition with non-aligned performance criteria. Adjustment's estimated true validity meets or exceeds .20 across 80% of the criterion dimensions with the exception of the Inquisitive-based criteria. Although the magnitude of the relations between Adjustment and non-aligned criteria exceed previous estimates for the Emotional Stability construct, the generally consistent pattern corresponds to some previous results *(cf. Hurtz & Donovan, 2001)*. The HPI Prudence scale is related to Adjustment (.32) and Interpersonal Sensitivity (.21) criteria. Prudence, Adjustment, and Interpersonal Sensitivity concern interpersonal aspects of work *(Hurtz & Donovan, 2000)*, which may account for the circular predictive pattern among these scales. Finally, the Ambition scale predicts criteria classified into the Inquisitive (.23) and Learning Approach (.27) categories; this is sensible because the Inquisitive criteria reflect intellectual striving and the Learning Approach criteria reflect academic achievement.

Table 3.24
Meta-Analysis Results Across Getting Along and Getting Ahead Criteria Combined

HPI Scales	1	2	3	4	5	6	7	8	9	10
	k	N	avg N	r obs	SD r	rv	r	SD r	%VE	90% CV
Adjustment	43	5,242	122	.19	.147	.28	.32	.191	35	.08
Ambition	43	5,242	122	.13	.129	.20	.22	.153	48	.02
Sociability	43	5,242	122	.00	.122	.00	.01	.134	55	-.16
Interpersonal Sensitivity	43	5,242	122	.09	.128	.13	.17	.156	50	-.03
Prudence	43	5,242	122	.14	.132	.20	.24	.168	45	.03
Inquisitive	43	5,242	122	.05	.101	.08	.08	.070	80	-.01
Learning Approach	33	4,222	128	.09	.095	.12	.14	.061	85	.06

Note. k = number of studies; N = total number of participants across k studies; average N = average number of participants within each study; r obs = mean observed validity; SD r = SD of observed correlations; rv = operational validity; r = true validity at scale level; SD r = SD of true validity; %VE = percentage of variance explained; 90% CV = credibility value.

Table 3.25
Meta-Analysis Results for Getting Along and Getting Ahead Criteria Separated

	1	2	3	4	5	6	7	8	9	10
Getting Along	k	N	avg N	r obs	SD r	rv	r	SD r	%VE	90% CV
Adjustment	26	2,949	113	.19	.093	.31	.34	.034	92	.30
Ambition	26	2,949	113	.10	.101	.15	.17	.060	89	.09
Sociability	26	2,949	113	.01	.099	.01	.01	.047	93	-.05
Interpersonal Sensitivity	26	2,949	113	.12	.088	.19	.23	.000	115	.23
Prudence	26	2,949	113	.14	.105	.21	.31	.106	72	.18
Inquisitive	26	2,949	113	.02	.098	.03	.03	.038	95	-.02
Learning Approach	22	2,553	116	.08	.096	.12	.12	.024	98	.09
Getting Ahead										
Adjustment	42	5,017	129	.14	.138	.20	.22	.167	42	.01
Ambition	42	5,017	129	.15	.130	.23	.26	.155	47	.06
Sociability	42	5,017	129	.02	.123	.04	.04	.132	56	-.13
Interpersonal Sensitivity	42	5,017	129	.07	.127	.09	.11	.000	52	.11
Prudence	42	5,017	129	.12	.138	.17	.20	.177	43	-.03
Inquisitive	42	5,017	129	.07	.105	.11	.12	.081	75	.02
Learning Approach	32	4,211	132	.09	.095	.13	.15	.060	83	.07

Note. k = number of studies; N = total number of participants across k studies; average N = average number of participants within each study; r obs = mean observed validity; SD r = SD of observed correlations; rv = operational validity; r = true validity at scale level; SD r = SD of true validity; %VE = percentage of variance explained; 90% CV = credibility value.

Table 3.26
Meta-Analysis Results for Criteria Aligned by Personality Construct

Scales	k	N	avg N	r obs	SD r	rv	r	SD r	%VE	90% CV
Adjustment										
Adjustment	**24**	**2,573**	**107**	**.25**	**.114**	**.37**	**.43**	**.117**	**62**	**.28**
Ambition	24	2,573	107	.08	.153	.13	.16	.201	39	-.10
Sociability	24	2,573	107	-.06	.131	-.08	-.10	.151	53	-.29
Interpersonal Sensitivity	24	2,573	107	.09	.081	.13	.16	.000	136	.16
Prudence	24	2,573	107	.18	.114	.27	.32	.109	69	.18
Inquisitive	24	2,573	107	-.00	.132	-.00	-.00	.150	51	-.19
Learning Approach	21	2,311	110	.08	.091	.13	.14	.000	108	.14
Ambition										
Adjustment	28	3,698	132	.11	.115	.18	.20	.130	53	.03
Ambition	**28**	**3,698**	**132**	**.20**	**.077**	**.31**	**.35**	**.000**	**119**	**.35**
Sociability	28	3,698	132	.04	.106	.07	.08	.096	71	-.04
Interpersonal Sensitivity	28	3,698	132	.06	.069	.09	.10	.000	170	.10
Prudence	28	3,698	132	.10	.105	.15	.17	.112	63	.03
Inquisitive	28	3,698	132	.07	.076	.11	.12	.000	121	.12
Learning Approach	25	3,448	138	.09	.080	.14	.15	.000	109	.15
Interpersonal Sensitivity										
Adjustment	17	2,500	147	.16	.101	.23	.28	.114	59	.14
Ambition	17	2,500	147	.07	.095	.09	.11	.086	77	-.00
Sociability	17	2,500	147	.05	.081	.06	.08	.000	108	.08
Interpersonal Sensitivity	**17**	**2,500**	**147**	**.18**	**.094**	**.25**	**.34**	**.100**	**68**	**.21**
Prudence	17	2,500	147	.12	.087	.17	.21	.040	93	.16
Inquisitive	17	2,500	147	-.00	.067	-.00	-.00	.000	156	-.00
Learning Approach	15	2,399	150	.06	.237	.08	.10	.390	11	-.40
Prudence										
Adjustment	26	3,379	130	.18	.130	.24	.28	.158	41	.08
Ambition	26	3,379	130	.07	.133	.08	.10	.159	45	-.10
Sociability	26	3,379	130	-.04	.098	-.07	-.07	.062	84	-.15
Interpersonal Sensitivity	26	3,379	130	.09	.141	.12	.17	.184	40	-.07
Prudence	**26**	**3,379**	**130**	**.22**	**.113**	**.313**	**.36**	**.125**	**55**	**.20**
Inquisitive	26	3,379	130	-.01	.120	-.03	-.02	.125	56	-.18
Learning Approach	20	2,603	130	.07	.108	.09	.10	.096	69	-.02
Inquisitive										
Adjustment	7	1,190	170	.05	.116	.07	.08	.150	44	-.11
Ambition	7	1,190	170	.13	.082	.20	.23	.046	90	.17
Sociability	7	1,190	170	.06	.132	.09	.11	.191	34	-.14
Interpersonal Sensitivity	7	1,190	170	-.02	.073	-.03	-.03	.000	113	-.03
Prudence	7	1,190	170	-.03	.078	-.04	-.05	.000	100	-.05
Inquisitive	**7**	**1,190**	**170**	**.20**	**.037**	**.29**	**.34**	**.000**	**357**	**.34**
Learning Approach	3	643	214	.10	.017	.14	.17	.000	1667	.17
Learning Approach										
Adjustment	9	1,366	152	.11	.103	.17	.20	.119	57	.05
Ambition	9	1,366	152	.14	.098	.22	.27	.110	63	.13
Sociability	9	1,366	152	.02	.102	.03	.03	.103	67	-.10
Interpersonal Sensitivity	9	1,366	152	.04	.076	.07	.07	.000	121	.07
Prudence	9	1,366	152	.09	.096	.14	.17	.107	65	.03
Inquisitive	9	1,366	152	.03	.083	.05	.05	.000	101	.05
Learning Approach	**9**	**1,366**	**152**	**.15**	**.132**	**.22**	**.25**	**.184**	**34**	**.01**

Note. k = number of studies; N = total number of participants across k studies; average N = average number of participants within each study; r obs = mean observed validity; SD r = SD of observed correlations; rv = operational validity; r = true validity at scale level; SD r = SD of true validity; %VE = percentage of variance explained; 90% CV = credibility value.

3.4 HPI Validity for Personnel Selection in Seven Job Families

This section reviews the validity of the HPI for personnel selection in seven job families: Managers & Executives, Professionals, Technicians & Specialists, Sales & Customer Support, Administrative & Clerical, Operations & Trades, and Service & Support. Validity generalization procedures are used to evaluate the validity of the HPI for predicting job performance within each family and these include meta-analysis, transportability, and synthetic/job component validity.

Specifically, validity generalization methods are used to identify scales from the HPI that are significantly correlated with performance across and within seven job families.

According to the *Uniform Guidelines on Employee Selection Procedures*, when jobs are similar and the selection procedures are valid and fair, test validity from one job can be used for decision-making in similar jobs. For each of the seven job families, transportability of validity evidence is based on data from multiple jobs in the Hogan Archive; job similarity was determined using job descriptions, previous job analysis information, and US Department of Labor and Occupational Information Network job codes. The original validation studies provided the predictor-criterion relations necessary to transport the HPI scales for future selection. Results from archival studies revealed that cutoff scores for the HPI can be used to predict performance for each job family and will yield no adverse impact.

Synthetic/job component validity involves: (a) defining critical job components or competencies for each job family through a review of job analysis information; (b) identifying valid predictors of those job components within archival studies; and (c) applying the results to the same components in each of the seven job families. Synthetic/job component validity evidence is an additional justification for using designated HPI scales as a selection battery to predict job components required in each job family.

We began research to identify valid scales for the HPI's use with job families in April 2004. We finalized job family descriptions in June 2004 and completed the validity generalization procedures in March 2006. All validation research contained in the Hogan Archives that is used for these analyses was conducted in the United States between 1982 and 2005. We evaluated the validity of the HPI for performance prediction in each job family based on evidence that personality measures predict critical competencies for these jobs (Hogan & Holland, 2003). The research setting was the Hogan technical validation archives and the HPI data warehouse. Prior to 2001, all HPI data in the archive were machine scored using computerized scoring software. In May 2001, HPI data began being collected from the Web-based Assessment Management (WAM) system, which produces a scored database from internet administration of the HPI. We launched a replacement to WAM. The most recent Hogan platform, HALO, offers significant system enhancements such as greater search capability, a more intuitive interface, a configurable start page, and advanced security features.

The scope of the research is defined by the job families. No assessment distinctions are made for the variety of jobs included in a job family. This is a limitation of the research because subtle differences between jobs within a family are not reflected in this classification scheme.

Job families are groups of occupations classified as similar based on work performed, skills, education, training, and credentials required for competence. The seven job families used for this analysis were derived from nine "job classifications" used by the Equal Employment Opportunity Commission (EEO) for employers in the United States. These nine EEO job classifications are used to capture information about an organization's ethnic make-up. We used this scheme for two reasons: (a) a large percentage of employers within the United States are familiar with the EEO job classifications; and (b) the job classifications are conceptually clear and easy to use for reporting purposes.

Based on prior experience with competencies, we determined that the same competency models could be used for the original EEO job classifications of Craft Worker, Operative, and Laborer. Each of these job classifications are combined into the Operations and Trades job family. We made additional modifications to job family names for the purpose of creating a less bureaucratic, more functional scheme of titles.

Table 3.27 presents the seven job families along with the Hogan descriptions of those families, the US Department of Labor (DoL) classifications *(US DoL, 2001)*, and the corresponding Occupational Information Network *(O*NET OnLine, 2005)* job categories. The DoL Standard Occupational Classification (SOC) System was developed by the US Department of Labor in response to a growing need for a universal occupational classification system *(US DoL, 1991)*. The SOC System contains 22 occupational categories that are used to classify all jobs within the US workforce. O*NET is the product of a large-scale effort to transfer SOC information to a searchable, web-based platform *(Dye & Silver, 1999)*.

Table 3.27
US Department of Labor Job Categories and SOC Codes Categorized by Job Family

Job Families	Definitions	O*NET & SOC Job Categories
Managers & Executives	Employees assigned to positions of administrative or managerial authority over the human, physical, and financial resources of the organization.	Management
Professionals	Employees with little legitimate authority, but high status within the organization because of the knowledge and/or skills they possess. These employees are usually experts with a broad educational background and rely primarily on their knowledge and intellect to perform their duties.	Architecture and Engineering Art, Design, Entertainment, Sports, and Media Business and Financial Operations Community and Social Service Education, Training, and Library Health Practitioner and Technical Legal Life, Physical, and Social Science
Techncians & Specialists	Employees who rely on the application of highly specific knowledge in skilled manipulation (e.g., operation, repair, cleaning, and/or preparation) of specialized technology, tools, and/or machinery.	Computer and Mathematical Science Installation, Maintenance, and Repair
Operations & Trades	Craft workers (skilled), operatives (semi-skilled), and laborers (unskilled) whose job knowledge and skills are primarily gained through on-the-job training and experience; little prerequisite knowledge or skill is needed.	Building and Grounds Cleaning and Maintenance Construction and Extraction Farming, Fishing, and Forestry Military Specific Production Transportation and Material Moving
Sales & Customer Support	Employees who use appropriate interpersonal style and communication techniques to establish relationships, sell products or services that fulfill customers' needs, and provide courteous and helpful service to customers after the sale.	Sales and Related
Administrative & Clerical	Employees who plan, direct, or coordinate supportive services of an organization. The main function of these employees is to facilitate the function of professionals by completing jobs that require little formal education or skill to complete (e.g., professional assistants, secretaries, and clerks).	Healthcare Support Office and Administrative Support
Service & Support	Employees that perform protective services for individuals and communities (e.g., police, fire fighters, guards) and non-protective services for individuals that require little to no formal training but a high degree of interaction with people (e.g., food service, recreation and amusement).	Food Preparation and Serving Related Personal Care and Service Protective Service

Validity generalization (VG) evidence, when available, may be used in place of local validation studies to support the use of a selection procedure *(Gatewood & Feild, 1994; Society for Industrial and Organizational Psychology, 2003)*. As indicated by the *Principles*:

> At times, sufficient accumulated validity evidence is available for a selection procedure to justify its use in a new situation without conducting a local validation research study. In these instances, use of the selection procedure may be based on demonstration of the generalized validity inferences from that selection procedure, coupled with a compelling argument for its applicability to the current situation. Although neither mutually exclusive nor exhaustive, several strategies for generalizing validity evidence have been delineated: (a) transportability, (b) synthetic validity/job component validity, and (c) meta-analytic validity generalization (p. 27).

The *Principles* recognize meta-analysis as a method "that can be used to determine the degree to which predictor-criterion relationships are specific to the situations in which the validity data have been gathered or are generalizable to other situations, as well as to determine the sources of cross-situation variability *(Aguinis & Pierce, 1998)*" *(p. 28)*. Pearson *(1904; as cited in Rosenthal & DiMatteo, 2001)* reported meta-analytic results evaluating the efficacy of vaccinations over 100 years ago. However, the method was only used to evaluate selection test validity in the late 1970s, and it was not the first method to be used *(cf. Lawshe, 1952)*. Of the three VG methods, meta-analysis provides the most generalizable results, but it relies exclusively on criterion-related validity studies. Transportability and synthetic/job component validity research is less generalizable, but can use either content or criterion-related research as source data.

According to the *Principles*, "reliance on meta-analysis results is more straightforward when they are organized around a construct or set of constructs" *(p. 30)*. Schmidt and Hunter *(1977)* used a construct orientation in their well-known meta-analysis of cognitive ability measures. Hogan and Holland *(2003)* did the same in a meta-analysis of the validity of personality predictors. A construct-driven approach has two advantages. First, theory drives professional judgment, which is unavoidable when compiling data from multiple studies. Second, a theory-driven approach provides a framework for interpreting the results. Generalization of Validity Evidence. Both the *Uniform Guidelines* and the *Principles* recommend transporting validity evidence to a new situation based on validation research conducted elsewhere. A key consideration for generalizing validity is showing that jobs are comparable in terms of content or requirements. The rationale for generalizing test validity across jobs can be summarized in three points:

- Hogan has conducted over 200 criterion-related validity studies assessing the relationship between scores on the HPI and job performance. Results of these studies are available in the Hogan Archive.

- Criterion-related validation results are available for the following seven job families: Managers & Executives, Professionals, Technicians & Specialists, Sales & Customer Support, Administrative & Clerical, Operations & Trades, and Service & Support.

- Results from these studies can be used to determine the validity of the HPI for predicting job performance for each of seven job families.

Because the Hogan Archive contains multiple studies of performance in seven job families and they are generalizable in terms of job requirements, validity evidence for these jobs can be meta-analyzed. We used the meta-analytic procedures specified by Hunter and Schmidt *(1990)* to cumulate results across studies and to assess effect sizes. All studies used zero-order product-moment correlations. Corrections were made for sampling error, unreliability in the measures, and range restriction. Reliability of the personality measures was estimated using within-study coefficient alpha [$M = .78$; range = .71 (Prudence) to .84 (Adjustment)], rather than relying exclusively on the values reported in the 1995 HPI manual. We followed procedures outlined by Barrick and Mount *(1991)* and Tett et al. *(1991)*, and used the .508 reliability coefficient proposed by Rothstein *(1990)* as the estimate of the reliability of supervisory ratings of job performance. We also computed a range restriction index for HPI scales. Following procedures described by Hunter and Schmidt *(1990)*, we divided each HPI scale's within-study standard deviation by the standard deviation reported by R. Hogan and Hogan *(1995)*. This procedure produced an index of range restriction for each HPI scale for each study. Mean replacement within job family was used to estimate range restriction correction factors for each scale when within study standard deviation was unavailable.

Hunter and Schmidt *(1990)* point out that meta-analysis results can be biased unless each sample contributes about the same number of correlations to the total. To eliminate such bias, we averaged correlations within studies so that each sample contributed only one point estimate per predictor scale. For example, if more than one criterion was available for any study, the correlations between each predictor scale and those criteria were averaged to derive a single point estimate of the predictor-criterion relationship. Note that this procedure uses both negative and positive correlations rather than mean absolute values for averaging correlations. This is the major computational difference between the current analyses and those presented by Tett et al. *(1991, p. 712)*. These results, which are derived from the meta-analytic procedures outlined above, represent true relationships between observed scores on each HPI scale and job performance within each specific job family.

Synthetic Validity/Job Component Validity. The *Uniform Guidelines* is vague about technical requirements and documentation for synthetic/job component validity as a method for establishing the validity of a selection procedure. However, the *Principles* explicitly includes this strategy as a way to establish the generalized validity of inferences based on test scores. The concept of synthetic validity was introduced by Lawshe *(1952)* over 50 years ago; however, it was largely ignored during the time when people believed that test validity is specific to situations. An exception was an interpretive review and demonstration by Mossholder and Arvey *(1984)*. Drawing on Mossholder and Arvey, the term synthetic validity "describes the logical process of inferring test-battery validity from predetermined validities of the tests for basic work components" *(p. 323)*. If the important components of a job are known, researchers can review previous criterion-related studies that contain those jobs' components and their significant predictors. The valid predictors of job components can be "synthesized" into a valid test battery for the job being considered *(Lawshe, 1952)*. Balma *(1959)* summarized Lawshe's definition stating that synthesis "...is the combination of separate elements into a whole" *(p. 395)*. Operational definitions of the synthetic validity process are available from Primoff *(1959)*, Guion *(1965)*, and McCormick, DeNisi, and Shaw *(1979)*. Hoffman, Holden, and Gale *(2000)*, Jeanneret and Strong *(2003)*, Johnson, Carter, Davison, and Oliver *(2001)*, and McCloy *(1994, 2001)* have published synthetic validity research, and Scherbaum *(2005)* reviews of the field. Brannick and Levine *(2002)* point out that synthetic validity approaches allow us to build up validity evidence from small samples with common job components. The process of synthetic validation proceeds by estimating validity for a current job criterion from previously established predictor-criterion relations. Using synthetic validation to devise a selection battery, evidence can be accumulated at the level of criterion similarity as opposed to job similarity, as in the case of transporting validity.

Synthetic validation is a logical procedure that relies heavily on archival research. The process of establishing synthetic validity proceeds by: (a) identifying the important performance criteria of a job; (b) reviewing previous criterion-related validation research that examines the prediction of each criterion; and (c) aggregating predictor-criterion correlations across multiple studies for the various criteria (components) that compose the job to form a test battery using component validities *(Scherbaum, 2005)*. Mossholder and Arvey *(1984)* corroborate these requirements and summarize their final requirement as follows:

> *When test battery validity is inferred from evidence showing that tests measure broad characteristics necessary for job performance, the process resembles a construct validation strategy. When scores are correlated with component performance measures, the process involves criterion-related validation. The nature of the tests used in the process (e.g., work sample vs. aptitude) may determine in part the appropriate validational strategy. (p. 323)*

Subsequent sections of this report describe the job performance criteria (job components) and the validity of the HPI scales for predicting performance criteria across job families. For purposes of this discussion and because the concept of synthetic validity has evolved over 50 years, we use interchangeably the terms criteria, performance dimensions, job components, work components, competencies, and domains of work.

3.41 Managers & Executives Job Family

Overview of Job Family. The Managers & Executives job family consists of jobs that have administrative or managerial authority over the human, physical, and financial resources of an organization. These jobs involve establishing broad policies, planning, forecasting, prioritizing, allocating, and directing work to achieve efficient use of resources at each level of the organization. Personnel who advance into these jobs typically are scientific, professional, or administrative specialists. We distinguish the following three levels of Managers & Executives:

1. Executive Management – Senior-most business and business unit heads (e.g., Corporate-Levels, Executive Vice Presidents, Senior Vice Presidents, Vice Presidents, General Managers, Directors).

2. Middle Management – Positions with second-level management direct reports and higher (e.g., department heads, business unit heads).

3. Supervisors & Entry-level Management – First-level supervisors and the positions to whom they report (e.g., general supervisor, first-level manager, unit head).

Meta-Analysis Results. The Hogan Archive was searched for HPI validation studies that included Managers & Executives. Thirty-five studies were identified in the review, and these are listed in Table 3.28. Each study reported correlations between the personality scales and job performance criteria. The correlations for each scale are aggregated across studies, using meta-analysis to estimate the relationship between the predictor variables and job performance.

Table 3.28
Managers & Executives Jobs with Criterion-Related Data for Meta-Analysis

Study #	Job Title
10, 14, 61, 114, 158, 182, 192, 193, 219, 319	Managers
157	Volume Business Managers
157	Specialist Business Managers
83, 103, 175	Store Managers
10	Terminal Managers
67	Managers & Assistants Managers
73	Account Manager at Sales Rep
73	Account Executive at Sales Rep
256	Telemarketing Supervisors
274	Executive Directors
10	Coordinators
118	Facility Administrators
320	Assistant Project Managers
219	Field Sales Managers
278	Restaurant Managers
151, 155	Supervisors
99	Assistant Managers
122	Expatriate Managers in Turkey
309, 324	Management-level Employees
200	Terminal Managers
267	Supervisory Officers
301	Branch Managers

Note. Study # reference citations appear in Appendix C with (Tech. Rep. No.) designations.

The HPI meta-analytic correlations are presented in Table 3.29.

Table 3.29

Meta-Analytic Correlations Between HPI Scales and Performance Criteria for Managers & Executives Jobs

	HPI Scales								
	N	**K**	**ADJ**	**AMB**	**SOC**	**INP**	**PRU**	**INQ**	**LRN**
Validation Samples	3,751	35	**.20**	**.29**	.07	**.13**	**.11**	.07	.09

Note. N = number of participants across K studies; K = number of studies; ADJ = Adjustment; AMB = Ambition; SOC = Sociability; INP = Interpersonal Sensitivity; PRU = Prudence; INQ = Inquisitive; LRN = Learning Approach.

These results support those found in the published meta-analysis literature. HPI Adjustment and Ambition are the best predictors of job performance. Interpersonal Sensitivity and Prudence also predict job performance. Finally, although Sociability, Inquisitive, and Learning Approach had lower correlations with job performance, the relationships were still positive, suggesting that they might be important for some jobs within the Managers & Executives job family. These data suggest that being calm and self-confident (HPI Adjustment), energetic and leaderlike (HPI Ambition), popular and tactful (HPI Interpersonal Sensitivity), and dependable and organized (HPI Prudence) are characteristics important to successful performance for Managers and Executives. We combined the validities across personality predictors into a single coefficient representing the link between the predictor battery and total job performance. There are several methods for doing this and they are reviewed by Scherbaum *(2005)*. Peterson, Wise, Arabian, & Hoffman *(2001)* specifically discuss various weighting options for predictor batteries. Although these authors find little difference in the outcomes of the various methods, there are differences in data requirements (e.g., need for job analysis data). The data in the Hogan Archive (i.e., competency ratings) dictated that we use the weighting procedure recommended by Johnson, Carter, and Tippins *(2001)*. To assess the predictive validity of this test battery, Nunnally's *(1978)* correlation of linear sums was used to estimate the overall correlation between the composite of selected HPI scales (i.e., Adjustment, Ambition, Interpersonal Sensitivity, and Prudence) and Managers and Executives' performance:

$$r_{y_c x_c} = \frac{\overline{r_{y_i x_i}}}{\sqrt{r_{yy}} \sqrt{r_{xx}}}$$

Based on the Hogan Archive of validity results, the overall estimated validity of the test battery is $r = .31$.

Synthetic Validity/Job Component Validity. Synthetic validity/job component validity procedures permit inferences based on previous studies using the HPI. The process requires: (1) identifying the relevant performance criteria for a job family; (2) reviewing previous criterion-related validation research; and (3) aggregating predictor-criterion correlations across multiple studies for the various criteria that compose the job family.

The Managers & Executives competency model we developed was used to identify the relevant performance criteria for these positions. For each job component, studies from the Hogan Archive using similar performance criteria were identified, and the correlations from those studies were aggregated using meta-analysis. These correlations, which represent validities for the HPI scales across performance criteria, are presented in Table 3.30.

The results indicate that Adjustment, Ambition, Interpersonal Sensitivity, and Prudence scales predict performance in the Managers & Executives job family. Note that the HPI scales best predict dimensions with a similar conceptual foundation (e.g., Adjustment and Maintaining Optimism, Ambition and Persuading Others, Prudence and Acting with Integrity). The convergence of HPI scales and dimensions illustrates the complimentary nature of HPI scales. A combination of HPI scales creates a data-based profile of effectiveness, which can be used for personnel decision making.

This evidence supports the use of the HPI Adjustment, Ambition, Interpersonal Sensitivity, and Prudence scales to predict performance. Synthetic validity evidence suggests that being calm and self-confident (HPI Adjustment); energetic and leaderlike (HPI Ambition); perceptive and tactful (HPI Interpersonal Sensitivity); and dependable and organized (HPI Prudence) are characteristics important to successful performance for Managers and Executives. To assess the predictive validity of the synthetic test battery, Nunnally's *(1978)* correlation of linear sums *(cf. Johnson, et al., 2001)* was used to estimate the overall synthetic correlation between the composite of the selected HPI scales (i.e., Adjustment, Ambition, Interpersonal Sensitivity, and Prudence) and Managers and Executives' performance. Based upon synthetic validity results, the overall estimated validity of the test battery is $r = .25$.

Table 3.30
HPI Synthetic Validity/Job Component Validity for Managers & Executives Job Family Competencies

Criterion	K	N	ADJ	AMB	SOC	INP	PRU	INQ	LRN
Category 1 – Leading Organizational Action									
Setting Strategic Vision	1	50	.04	.06	.02	-.08	**.29**	**-.14**	–
Showing Entrepreneurial Acumen	1	89	**.46**	**.51**	**.10**	**.30**	**.17**	**.25**	-.06
Sponsoring Change	1	44	.07	**.19**	**-.24**	**.14**	**.33**	**-.37**	-.07
Growing Organizational Capability	48	4,496	.09	**.20**	.00	.03	.07	.02	.04
Category 2 – Exercising Business Skills									
Implementing Business Strategies	26	3,947	**.17**	.06	.09	.08	**.13**	**.14**	**.13**
Planning and Organizing	22	2,166	**.11**	**.51**	.01	.06	**.14**	-.01	.04
Allocating and Leveraging Resources	3	381	**-.16**	**.19**	**.33**	.00	-.06	**.25**	-.03
Demonstrating Technical Capabilities	29	2,546	.06	**.20**	-.04	-.04	.05	.04	.06
Communicating Business Concepts	51	5,225	**.11**	**.13**	.03	**.10**	.07	.04	.05
Category 3 – Solving Problems and Making Decisions									
Using Industry and Org. Knowledge	11	1,179	**.15**	**.14**	-.01	.05	.00	.08	.04
Using Creative Problem Solving	51	5,940	**.13**	**.12**	-.04	.02	.08	.04	.07
Dealing with Complexity	22	3,126	**.17**	**.21**	.09	**.10**	.06	.08	.09
Making Decisions	8	1,105	**.12**	**.20**	**.11**	.06	-.01	**.20**	**.15**
Category 4 – Building and Maintaining Relationships									
Focusing on the Customer	39	3,840	**.17**	**.11**	.02	**.14**	**.15**	-.03	.00
Persuading Others	6	1,063	**.25**	**.38**	**.21**	**.25**	**.18**	.05	.02
Negotiating	6	1,063	**.25**	**.38**	**.21**	**.25**	**.18**	.05	.02
Teaming with Others	36	4,417	**.19**	.05	-.04	**.13**	**.20**	-.03	.05
Building Alliances	7	435	**.17**	**.15**	.02	**.10**	.08	.06	.09
Category 5 – Managing & Developing People									
Delegating and Monitoring Assignments	1	290	**.35**	**.17**	**-.16**	**.12**	.04	.02	.09
Building and Coaching Teams	4	342	**.31**	**.24**	-.02	**.24**	**.23**	.06	-.02
Developing and Supporting People	10	1,414	.06	**.29**	**.16**	**.14**	.09	**.10**	.03
Category 6 – Showing Drive and Motivation									
Exhibiting Motivation and Commitment	49	5,064	.09	.07	.00	.06	**.14**	.03	.00
Maintaining Optimism	15	1,820	**.36**	**.15**	**-.11**	**.12**	**.22**	-.03	**.13**
Driving for Results	48	4,496	.09	**.20**	.00	.03	.07	.02	.04
Category 7 – Demonstrating Integrity and Professionalism									
Showing Emotional Maturity	52	5,676	**.30**	**.10**	-.04	**.16**	**.19**	.00	.05
Pursuing Self-Development	20	2,282	.01	**.16**	.00	-.03	.01	**.11**	.05
Acting with Integrity	36	3,660	**.17**	.02	-.05	**.13**	**.24**	-.03	.03

Note. K = Number of Studies; N = Total Sample Size; ADJ = Adjustment, AMB = Ambition, SOC = Sociability, INP = Interpersonal Sensitivity, PRU = Prudence, INQ = Inquisitive, LRN = Learning Approach.

Overview of Job Family. The Professionals job family consists of occupations concerned with theoretical and applied aspects of such fields as art, science, engineering, education, medicine, law, computer science, business relations, and other technical specializations. Professional employees may have little supervisory or managerial responsibility; however, these positions generally require substantial educational preparation for professional practice. Personnel who advance in these jobs are experts in their field and usually have a high level of training and experience. We distinguish the following three levels of Professionals:

1. Senior Professionals – Senior-most, non-management contributors with advanced post-graduate degrees, specialized expertise, related credentialing, and substantial work experience (e.g., senior scientists, physicians, researchers, R&D consultants, attorneys, consultant advisors).

2. Mid-Level Professionals – Positions that require a college degree, along with special training, credentialing, and prior job experience; a post-graduate degree might be required. These positions are generally equivalent in compensation to mid-level managers, but focus on a specific professional discipline (e.g., engineering, law, medicine, accounting, finance, marketing, human resources, IT, education).

3. Entry-Level Professionals - Positions that require a college degree, special training, or credentialing requirements; little prior work experience required.

Meta-Analysis Results. The Hogan Archive was searched for HPI validation studies involving Professionals. Twelve studies were identified in the review and these are listed in Table 3.31. Two studies overlapped with managerial level jobs that were included in the validity analysis computed for the Managers & Executives job family. Because job analysis results for both jobs indicated a significant portion of the responsibilities included professional activities, the studies were included in the validity analyses computed for Professionals. Table 3.32 reports correlations between scales and job performance criteria with the correlations for each scale aggregated across studies, using meta-analysis.

Table 3.31
Professionals Jobs with Criterion-Related Data for Meta-Analysis

Study #	Job Title
172	Auditors
84	Trading Assistants
71	Licensed Practical Nurses
168	Recreation Leaders
174	Trading Assistants
77	Marketing Personnel
78	Insurance Personnel
182	Manager
301	Loan Officers
320	Assistant Project Managers
101	Small Business Bankers
326	Financial Specialists

Note. Study # reference citations appear in Appendix C with (Tech. Rep. No.) designations.

The HPI meta-analytic correlations are presented in Table 3.32.

Table 3.32
Meta-Analytic Correlations Between HPI Scales and Performance Criteria for Professionals Jobs

					HPI Scales				
	N	*K*	ADJ	AMB	SOC	INP	PRU	INQ	LRN
Validation Samples	1,149	12	.14	.12	-.04	.09	.08	.00	.01

Note. N = number of participants across K studies; K = number of studies; ADJ = Adjustment; AMB = Ambition; SOC = Sociability; INP = Interpersonal Sensitivity; PRU = Prudence; INQ = Inquisitive; LRN = Learning Approach.

These results are consistent with those reported in the published meta-analysis literature. HPI Adjustment and Ambition are the most significant predictors of job performance. Interpersonal Sensitivity and Prudence have small positive relationships with job performance for Professionals. It is likely that these characteristics will be more important for positions that involve interactions and procedures than positions where professionals are working alone with little job structure. These data suggest that being calm and self-confident (HPI Adjustment) and energetic and leader-like (HPI Ambition) are characteristics important to successful performance for Professionals. To assess the predictive validity of this test battery, Nunnally's *(1978)* correlation of linear sums *(cf. Johnson, et al., 2001)* was used to estimate the overall correlation among the composite of the selected HPI scales (i.e., Adjustment and Ambition) and Professionals' performance. Based on the Hogan Archive validity results, the overall estimated validity of the test battery is $r = .19$.

Synthetic Validity/Job Component Validity. The Professionals competency model we developed was used to identify the relevant performance criteria for these jobs. For each job component, studies from the Hogan Archive using similar performance criteria were identified, and the correlations from those studies were aggregated using meta-analysis. These correlations, which represent validities for the HPI scales across performance criteria, are presented in Table 3.33.

Table 3.33
HPI Scale Synthetic Validity/Job Component Validity for Professionals Job Family Competencies

Criterion	K	N	ADJ	AMB	SOC	INP	PRU	INQ	LRN
Category 1 – Delivering Professional Expertise									
Demonstrating Technical Capabilities	29	2,546	.06	**.14**	-.04	-.04	.05	.04	.06
Building Credibility	44	4,907	**.17**	.06	-.06	.06	**.14**	-.03	.02
Translating Skills into Action	29	2,546	.06	**.14**	-.04	-.04	.05	.04	.06
Growing Organizational Capability	48	4,496	.09	**.20**	.00	.03	.07	.02	.04
Category 2 – Exercising Business Skills									
Planning and Organizing	22	2,166	**.11**	**.14**	.01	.06	**.14**	-.01	.04
Allocating and Leveraging Resources	3	381	**-.16**	**.32**	.33	.00	-.06	**.25**	-.03
Exercising Business Acumen	1	89	**.46**	**.51**	.10	**.30**	**.17**	**.25**	-.06
Presenting Ideas Clearly	51	5,225	**.11**	**.13**	.03	.10	**.07**	.04	.05
Category 3 – Solving Problems and Making Decisions									
Seeking Out Information	26	3,947	**.17**	**.32**	.09	.08	**.13**	**.14**	**.13**
Analyzing Information Creatively	51	5,940	**.13**	**.12**	-.04	.02	.08	.04	.07
Dealing with Complexity	22	3,126	**.17**	**.21**	.09	**.10**	.06	.08	.09
Making Decisions	8	1,105	**.12**	**.20**	**.11**	.06	-.01	**.20**	**.15**
Category 4 – Building and Maintaining Relationships									
Focusing on the Customer	39	3,840	**.17**	**.11**	.02	**.14**	**.15**	-.03	.00
Impacting and Influencing Others	6	1,063	**.25**	**.38**	**.21**	**.25**	**.18**	.05	.02
Teaming and Collaborating	36	4,417	**.19**	.05	-.04	**.13**	**.20**	-.03	.05
Demonstrating Organizational Savvy	3	439	**.27**	**.15**	.02	**.21**	**.16**	-.09	.05
Category 5 – Showing Drive and Motivation									
Exhibiting Motivation and Commitment	49	5,064	.09	.07	.00	.06	**.14**	.03	.00
Maintaining Optimism	15	1,820	**.36**	**.15**	-.11	**.12**	**.22**	-.03	**.13**
Driving for Results	48	4,496	.09	**.20**	.00	.03	.07	.02	.04
Category 6 – Integrity and Professionalism									
Showing Emotional Maturity	52	5,676	**.30**	**.10**	-.04	**.16**	**.19**	.00	.05
Pursuing Self-Development	20	2,282	.01	**.16**	.00	-.03	.01	**.11**	.05
Acting with Integrity	36	3,660	**.17**	.02	-.05	**.13**	**.24**	-.03	.03

Note. K = Number of Studies; N = Total Sample Size; ADJ = Adjustment, AMB = Ambition, SOC = Sociability, INP = Interpersonal Sensitivity, PRU = Prudence, INQ = Inquisitive, LRN = Learning Approach.

The results indicate that Adjustment, Ambition, Interpersonal Sensitivity, and Prudence predict performance in Professional jobs. Note that the HPI scales best predict dimensions with a similar conceptual foundation (e.g., Adjustment and Maintaining Optimism, Ambition and Impacting and Influencing Others, Prudence and Acting with Integrity). The convergence of HPI scales and dimensions illustrates the complimentary nature of HPI scales. By combining HPI scales to create a data-based profile of effectiveness, the likelihood of making accurate human resource decisions is maximized. Synthetic validity evidence suggests that being calm and self-confident (HPI Adjustment); energetic and leaderlike (HPI Ambition); perceptive and tactful (HPI Interpersonal Sensitivity); and dependable and organized (HPI Prudence) are characteristics important to successful performance for Professionals. To assess the predictive validity of the synthetic test battery, Nunnally's *(1978)* correlation of linear sums *(cf. Johnson, et al., 2001)* was used to estimate the overall synthetic correlation among the composite of the selected HPI scales (i.e., Adjustment, Ambition, Interpersonal Sensitivity, and Prudence) and Professionals' performance. Based upon synthetic validity results, the overall estimated validity of the test battery is $r = .24$.

3.43 Technicians & Specialists Job Family

Overview of Job Family. The Technicians & Specialists job family consists of jobs in which employees work to solve practical problems encountered in fields of specialization (e.g., engineering, machine trades, processing, etc.). These jobs require specialized knowledge and skills to perform activities directed by a professional. Personnel who work in these occupations usually complete two years of college, technical school, or thorough on-the-job training certification. We distinguish between technicians and specialists:

1. Technicians – Positions that typically do not require a college degree, but may involve associates-level, trade, vocational, or other school training (e.g., service and repair, installation and set-up, information collection, data basing jobs, specialized equipment operators).

2. Specialists - Positions that typically require a college degree in a specific area of study. (e.g., bookkeeping, IT specialties, drafting, engineering, healthcare specialists, paralegal, public safety).

Meta-Analysis Results. The Hogan Archive was searched for HPI validation studies involving Technicians & Specialists jobs. Thirteen studies were identified in the review and these are listed in Table 3.34. Each study reported correlations between scales and job performance criteria with the correlations for each scale aggregated across studies, using meta-analysis.

Table 3.34
Technicians & Specialists Jobs with Criterion-Related Data for Meta-Analysis

Study #	Job Title
8, 117, 124, 169, 241	Mechanics
69	Installers/Assemblers
126	Offshore Anchor Handlers (Riggers)
185	Engineer Trainees, Field Training
199	Information Technical Employees
185	Engineer Trainees, Classroom Training
247	Field Service Technicians
288	Field Service Representatives
107	Field Representatives

Note. Study # reference citations appear in Appendix C with (Tech. Rep. No.) designations.

The HPI meta-analytic correlations are presented in Table 3.35.

Table 3.35
Meta-Analytic Correlations Between HPI Scales and Performance Criteria for Technicians & Specialists Jobs

	HPI Scales							
	N	*K*	**ADJ**	**AMB**	**SOC**	**INP**	**PRU**	**INQ**	**LRN**
Validation Samples	2,207	13	**.22**	**.18**	-.07	**.11**	**.19**	.04	.05

Note. N = number of participants across K studies; K = number of studies; ADJ = Adjustment; AMB = Ambition; SOC = Sociability; INP = Interpersonal Sensitivity; PRU = Prudence; INQ = Inquisitive; LRN = Learning Approach.

These results support those found in the published meta-analysis literature. HPI Adjustment, Ambition, Interpersonal Sensitivity and Prudence scales predict job performance. The negative correlations associated with Sociability also suggest that this scale could be used to predict job performance for some Technician & Specialist positions, although lower scores on this scale are associated with higher levels of job performance. Generalized validity evidence suggests that being calm and self-confident (HPI Adjustment), energetic and leaderlike (HPI Ambition), perceptive and tactful (HPI Interpersonal Sensitivity), and dependable and organized (HPI Prudence) are characteristics important to successful performance for Technicians and Specialists. To assess the predictive validity of this test battery, Nunnally's (1978) correlation of linear sums (cf. Johnson, et al., 2001) was used to estimate the overall transportability correlation among the composite of the selected HPI scales (i.e., Adjustment, Ambition, Interpersonal Sensitivity, and Prudence) and Technicians and Specialists' performance. Based upon meta-analysis results, the overall estimated validity of the test battery is $r = .30$.

Synthetic Validity/Job Component Validity. The Technicians & Specialists competency model developed by Hogan was used to identify the relevant performance criteria for these jobs. For each job component, studies from the Hogan Archive using similar performance criteria were identified, and the correlations from those studies were aggregated using meta-analysis. These correlations, which represent validities for each personality scale across critical performance criteria, are presented in Table 3.36.

Table 3.36
HPI Scale Synthetic Validity/Job Component Validity for Technicians & Specialists Job Family Competencies

Criterion	K	N	ADJ	AMB	SOC	INP	PRU	INQ	LRN
Category 1 - Demonstrating Technical Skills									
Delivering Technical Expertise	29	2,546	.06	**.14**	-.04	-.04	.05	.04	.06
Translating Skills into Action	29	2,546	.06	**.14**	-.04	-.04	.05	.04	.06
Presenting Ideas Clearly	51	5,225	**.11**	**.13**	.03	**.10**	.07	.04	.05
Showing Personal Productivity	48	4,496	.09	**.20**	.00	.03	.07	.02	.04
Building Organizational Awareness	51	5,225	**.11**	**.13**	.03	**.10**	.07	.04	.05
Category 2 - Solving Problems and Making Decisions									
Seeking Out Information	26	3,947	**.17**	**.32**	.09	.08	**.13**	**.14**	**.13**
Analyzing Information Creatively	51	5,940	**.13**	**.12**	-.04	.02	.08	.04	.07
Dealing with Concepts	29	2,546	.06	**.14**	-.04	-.04	.05	.04	.06
Making Decisions	8	1,105	**.12**	**.20**	**.11**	.06	-.01	**.20**	**.15**
Category 3 - Building and Maintaining Relationships									
Focusing on the Customer	39	3,840	**.17**	**.11**	.02	**.14**	**.15**	-.03	.00
Showing Interpersonal Understanding	5	822	**.36**	**.13**	-.08	**.23**	**.23**	.05	.02
Impacting and Influencing Others	6	1,063	**.25**	**.38**	**.21**	**.25**	**.18**	.05	.02
Teaming and Collaborating	36	4,417	**.19**	.05	-.04	**.13**	**.20**	-.03	.05
Category 4 - Showing Drive and Motivation									
Exhibiting Motivation and Commitment	49	5,064	.09	.07	.00	.06	**.14**	.03	.00
Showing Flexibility	22	3,126	**.17**	**.21**	.09	**.10**	.06	.08	.09
Driving for Results	48	4,496	.09	**.20**	.00	.03	.07	.02	.04
Category 5 - Demonstrating Integrity and Professionalism									
Showing Emotional Maturity	52	5,676	**.30**	**.10**	-.04	**.16**	**.19**	.00	.05
Pursuing Self-Development	10	1,414	.06	**.29**	**.16**	**.14**	.09	**.10**	.03
Acting with Integrity	36	3,660	**.17**	.02	-.05	**.13**	**.24**	-.03	.03

Note. K = Number of Studies; N = Total Sample Size; ADJ = Adjustment, AMB = Ambition, SOC = sociability, INP = Interpersonal Sensitivity, PRU = Prudence, INQ = Inquisitive, LRN = Learning Approach.

The results indicate that Adjustment, Ambition, Interpersonal Sensitivity, and Prudence predict performance in the Technician & Specialist job family. Note that the HPI scales best predict dimensions with a similar conceptual foundation (e.g., Adjustment and Showing Emotional Maturity, Ambition and Impacting and Influencing Others, Prudence and Acting with Integrity). The convergence of HPI scales and dimensions illustrates the complimentary nature of HPI scales. By combining HPI scales to create a data-based profile of effectiveness, the likelihood of making accurate human resource decisions is maximized. Synthetic validity evidence suggests that being calm and self-confident (HPI Adjustment), energetic and leader-like (HPI Ambition), perceptive and tactful (HPI Interpersonal Sensitivity), and dependable and organized (HPI Prudence) are characteristics important to successful performance for Technicians and Specialists. To assess the predictive validity of the synthetic test battery, Nunnally's *(1978)* correlation of linear sums *(cf. Johnson, et al., 2001)* was used to estimate the overall synthetic correlation among the composite of the selected HPI scales (i.e., Adjustment, Ambition, Interpersonal Sensitivity, and Prudence) and Technicians and Specialists' performance. Based upon synthetic validity results, the overall estimated validity of the test battery is $r = .23$.

3.44 Operations & Trades Job Family

Overview of Job Family. The Operations & Trades job family consists of occupations that include craft workers (skilled), operatives (semi-skilled), and laborers (unskilled) whose job knowledge and skills are primarily gained through on-the-job training and experience; little prerequisite knowledge or skill is needed to enter these jobs.

Meta-Analysis Results. Meta-analyses for the Operations & Trades job family are similar to those for Technicians & Specialists. The consistencies are because: (a) most previous work in this area focuses on both skilled and semi-skilled employees as one group, which encompasses positions in both Operations & Trades and Technicians & Specialists job families; and (b) although the level of expertise and training required for positions within each family may differ, there is considerable overlap in the personality-based requirements and primary duties performed in both job families. Consequently, meta-analysis results presented for Technicians & Specialists are also applied to Operations & Trades jobs.

The Hogan Archive was searched for HPI validation studies involving Operations & Trades. Forty-four studies were identified in the review and these are listed in Table 3.37. Each study reported correlations between scales and job performance criteria with the correlations for each scale aggregated across studies, using meta-analysis.

Table 3.37
Operations & Trade Jobs with Criterion-Related Data for Meta-Analysis

Study #	Job Title
56, 58, 60, 62, 64, 76, 90, 91, 94, 96, 104, 110, 111, 116, 129, 134, 140, 148, 181, 209, 242	Drivers
60	Warehousers
65	Mechanic Operators
60	Loaders
270	Owner Operators
124	Road Drivers
124	City Drivers
112	Freight Handlers
330	Entry Level Factory Workers
280	Regional Drivers
11	Line Haul Drivers
130	Dock Workers
214	Crewmen
311, 323	Truck Drivers
244	Surfacing & Coating Employees
162	Utility & Service Personnel
124	Jockey
136	Pipe Manufacturing Workers
247, 288	Delivery Service Representatives
79	Machine Operators
102	Drivers & Delivery/Installation Service
203	Bus Operators

Note. Study # reference citations appear in Appendix C with (Tech. Rep. No.) designations.

The HPI meta-analytic correlations are presented in Table 3.38.

Table 3.38
Meta-Analytic Correlations Between HPI Scales and Performance Criteria for Operations & Trades Jobs

	HPI Scales							
	N	*K*	**ADJ**	**AMB**	**SOC**	**INP**	**PRU**	**INQ**	**LRN**
Validation Studies	3,021	44	**.27**	**.14**	.00	**.11**	**.18**	.03	.05

Note. N = number of participants across K studies; K = number of studies. ADJ = Adjustment; AMB = Ambition; SOC = Sociability; INP = Interpersonal Sensitivity; PRU = Prudence; INQ = Inquisitive; LRN = Learning Approach.

These results support those found in the published meta-analysis literature. HPI Adjustment and Prudence are the best predictors of job performance. Ambition and Interpersonal Sensitivity also have positive relations with job performance in Operations & Trades jobs. Generalized validity evidence suggests that being calm and self-confident (HPI Adjustment), energetic and leader-like (HPI Ambition), perceptive and tactful (HPI Interpersonal Sensitivity), and dependable and organized (HPI Prudence) are characteristics important to successful performance for Operations and Trades. To assess the predictive validity of this test battery, Nunnally's *(1978)* correlation of linear sums *(cf. Johnson, et al., 2001)* was used to estimate the overall transportability correlation among the composite of the selected HPI scales (i.e., Adjustment, Ambition, Interpersonal Sensitivity, and Prudence) and Operations and Trades' performance. Based upon meta-analysis results, the overall estimated validity of the test battery is $r = .30$.

Synthetic Validity/Job Component Validity. The Operations & Trades competency model developed by Hogan was used to identify relevant performance criteria for these jobs. For each job component, studies from the Hogan Archive using similar performance criteria were identified, and the correlations from those studies were aggregated using a meta-analysis. These correlations, which represent validities for each personality scale across performance criteria, are presented in Table 3.39.

Table 3.39
HPI Synthetic Validity/Job Component Validity for Operations & Trades Job Family Competencies

Criterion	K	N	ADJ	AMB	SOC	INP	PRU	INQ	LRN
Category 1 – Demonstrating Technical Skills									
Applying Job Skills	29	2,546	.06	**.14**	-.04	-.04	.05	.04	.06
Showing Personal Productivity	48	4,496	.09	**.20**	.00	.03	.07	.02	.04
Focusing on Safety	6	471	**.21**	**.27**	.01	**.12**	**.21**	.08	.01
Category 2 – Solving Problems and Making Decisions									
Analyzing Information Effectively	51	5,940	**.13**	**.12**	-.04	.02	.08	.04	.07
Troubleshooting and Solving Problems	51	5,940	**.13**	**.12**	-.04	.02	.08	.04	.07
Making Decisions	8	1,105	**.12**	**.20**	**.11**	.06	-.01	**.20**	**.15**
Learning from Experience	20	2,282	.01	**.16**	.00	-.03	.01	**.11**	.05
Category 3 – Building and Maintaining Relationships									
Focusing on the Customer	39	3,840	**.17**	**.11**	.02	**.14**	**.15**	-.03	.00
Showing Interpersonal Understanding	5	822	**.36**	**.13**	-.08	**.23**	**.23**	.05	.02
Communicating Effectively	51	5,225	**.11**	**.13**	.03	**.10**	.07	.04	.05
Teaming and Collaborating	36	4,417	**.19**	.05	-.04	**.13**	**.20**	-.03	.05
Category 4 – Showing Drive and Motivation									
Exhibiting Motivation and Commitment	49	5,064	.09	.07	.00	.06	**.14**	.03	.00
Showing Concern for Quality	6	991	**.24**	**.12**	-.02	**.11**	**.24**	**.10**	**.15**
Category 5 – Demonstrating Integrity and Professionalism									
Showing Emotional Maturity	52	5,676	**.30**	**.10**	-.04	**.16**	**.19**	.00	.05
Adapting to Change	22	3,126	**.17**	**.21**	.09	**.10**	.06	.08	.09
Acting with Integrity	36	3,660	**.17**	.02	-.05	**.13**	**.24**	-.03	.03

Note. K = Number of Studies; N = Total Sample Size; ADJ = Adjustment, AMB = Ambition, SOC = Sociability, INP = Interpersonal Sensitivity, PRU = Prudence, INQ = Inquisitive, LRN = Learning Approach.

The results indicate that Adjustment, Ambition, Interpersonal Sensitivity, and Prudence predict performance in Operations & Trades jobs. Note that the HPI scales best predict dimensions with a similar conceptual foundation (e.g., Adjustment and Showing Emotional Maturity, Ambition and Showing Personal Productivity, Prudence and Acting with Integrity). The convergence of HPI scales and dimensions illustrates the complimentary nature of HPI scales. Synthetic validity evidence suggests that being calm and self-confident (HPI Adjustment), energetic and leaderlike (HPI Ambition), and dependable and organized (HPI Prudence) are characteristics important to successful performance for Operations and Trades personnel. To assess the predictive validity of the synthetic test battery, Nunnally's *(1978)* correlation of linear sums *(cf. Johnson, et al., 2001)* was used to estimate the overall synthetic correlation among the composite of the selected HPI scales (i.e., Adjustment, Ambition, and Prudence) and Operations and Trades' performance. Based upon the synthetic validity results, the overall estimated validity of the test battery is $r = .23$.

3.45 Sales & Customer Support Job Family

Overview of Job Family. The Sales & Customer Support job family consists of jobs in which employees are responsible for selling and/or supporting products and services through interaction with prospects and clients using knowledge of the industry product. These employees rely on their interpersonal skills and communication techniques to sell products or services that meet customers' needs. They provide courteous and helpful service to customers after the sale. Hogan distinguishes the following three levels of Sales & Customer Support:

1. Senior Sales Executives – Positions that involve the handling of clients of major size and sensitivity, managing national or key accounts, or contributing to sales strategy. The positions may involve sales management responsibilities, but the primary focus is on managing large-scale relationships, ensuring continued sales with major customers, and finding additional, new major sales opportunities. College education, substantial experience, and substantial sales training are typically required.

2. Sales Professionals – Positions that involve all features of the sales process, from prospecting, to lead qualification, making sales presentations, follow through on opportunities, and closing sales. These positions typically involve face-to-face customer contact, but may include some higher-level telephone prospecting as well. This level may, or may not, require college education, but typically involves substantial company-specific sales training.

3. Telemarketers & Customer Support – Positions that handle either inbound or outbound customer contact for purposes of making sales, taking orders, handling service problems, or answering questions. Also included are positions in the service and retail trades, where the employee provides limited advice, sales support, service, and transaction processing face-to-face.

Meta-Analysis Results. The Hogan Archive was searched for HPI validation studies involving Sales & Customer Support jobs. Forty-eight studies were identified in the review and these are listed in Table 3.40. Each study reported correlations between scales and job performance criteria with the correlations for each scale aggregated across studies, using meta-analysis.

Table 3.40
Sales & Customer Support Jobs with Criterion-Related Data for Meta-Analysis

Study #	Job Title
60	Merchandisers
256, 263	Telephone Sales Representatives
19, 20, 88, 135	Telemarketers
190	Customer Service Operator
125	International Relocation Consultants
20, 91, 99, 102, 109, 131, 138, 149, 162, 165, 171	CSRs
216	Sales
83	Part Time Sales
60	Parts Specialists
70	Service Operations Coordinators
276	Customer Operations
179	Sales Associates
152	Sales Persons
7, 75, 196, 265, 319, 325	Sales Representatives
86	Customer Operations Representatives
123	Service Operation Coordinators
19	Account Executives
103	Financial Sales
66	Financial Consultants
297	NBA Sales
310	Account Managers
297	Consumer Sales
138	Customer and Policy Service
297	Care Employees
173	Termite Inspectors
121	Sales/Service Technicians
95	Sales and Service Technician
20, 219	Field Sales

Note. Study # reference citations appear in Appendix C with (Tech. Rep. No.) designations.

The HPI meta-analytic correlations are presented in Table 3.41.

Table 3.41

Meta-Analytic Correlations Between HPI Scales and Performance Criteria for Sales & Customer Support Jobs

			HPI Scales						
	N	*K*	ADJ	AMB	SOC	INP	PRU	INQ	LRN
Validation Studies	3,740	48	**.10**	**.17**	.07	.08	.06	.06	.06

Note. N = number of participants across K studies; K = number of studies; ADJ = Adjustment; AMB = Ambition; SOC = Sociability; INP = Interpersonal Sensitivity; PRU = Prudence; INQ = Inquisitive; LRN = Learning Approach.

These results support those found in the published meta-analysis literature. HPI Adjustment and Ambition predict job performance. Sociability, Interpersonal Sensitivity, Prudence, Inquisitive, and Learning Approach have positive relationships with job performance, although their particular predictive contribution may be moderated by the type of sales or customer service position an organization seeks to fill. Generalized validity evidence suggests that being calm and self-confident (HPI Adjustment) and energetic and leader-like (HPI Ambition) are characteristics important to successful performance for Sales and Customer Support jobs. To assess the predictive validity of this test battery, Nunnally's *(1978)* correlation of linear sums *(cf. Johnson, et al., 2001)* was used to estimate the overall correlation among the composite of the selected HPI scales (i.e., Adjustment and Ambition) and Sales and Customer Service performance. Based upon meta-analysis, the overall estimated validity of the test battery is $r = .20$.

Synthetic Validity/Job Component Validity. The Sales & Customer Support competency model developed by Hogan was used to identify the relevant performance criteria for these positions. For each job component, studies from the Hogan Archive using similar performance criteria were identified, and the correlations from those studies were aggregated using meta-analysis. These correlations, which represent validities for the HPI scales across performance criteria, are presented in Table 3.42.

Table 3.42
HPI Synthetic Validity/Job Component Validity for Sales & Customer Support Job Family Competencies

Criterion	K	N	ADJ	AMB	SOC	INP	PRU	INQ	LRN
Category 1 – Creating Sales Results									
Prospecting with Insight	24	2,981	.16	.24	.05	.14	.06	.06	.10
Demonstrating Product and Service Knowledge	11	1,179	.15	.14	-.01	.05	.00	.08	.04
Building Credibility	36	3,660	.17	.02	-.05	.13	.24	-.03	.03
Showing Personal Productivity	48	4,496	.09	.20	.00	.03	.07	.02	.04
Category 2 – Exercising Business Skills									
Implementing Sales Strategies	24	2,981	.16	.24	.05	.14	.06	.06	.10
Leveraging Resources	3	381	-.16	.32	.33	.00	-.06	.25	-.03
Demonstrating Business Acumen	1	89	.46	.51	.10	.30	.17	.25	-.06
Presenting Ideas Clearly	51	5,225	.11	.13	.03	.10	.07	.04	.05
Category 3 – Solving Problems and Making Decisions									
Using Industry and Organizational Knowledge	11	1,179	.15	.14	-.01	.05	.00	.08	.04
Analyzing Information Creatively	51	5,940	.13	.12	-.04	.02	.08	.04	.07
Dealing with Complexity	22	3,126	.17	.21	.09	.10	.06	.08	.09
Making Decisions	8	1,105	.12	.20	.11	.06	-.01	.20	.15
Category 4 – Building and Maintaining Relationships									
Focusing on the Customer	39	3,840	.17	.11	.02	.14	.15	-.03	.00
Impacting and Influencing Others	6	1,063	.25	.38	.21	.25	.18	.05	.02
Teaming and Collaborating	36	4,417	.19	.05	-.04	.13	.20	-.03	.05
Demonstrating Organizational Savvy	3	439	.27	.15	.02	.21	.16	-.09	.05
Category 5 – Showing Drive and Motivation									
Exhibiting Motivation and Commitment	49	5,064	.09	.07	.00	.06	.14	.03	.00
Demonstrating Resilience and Persistence	52	5,676	.30	.10	-.04	.16	.19	.00	.05
Driving for Results	48	4,496	.09	.20	.00	.03	.07	.02	.04
Category 6 – Demonstrating Integrity and Professionalism									
Showing Emotional Maturity	52	5,676	.30	.10	-.04	.16	.19	.00	.05
Pursuing Self-Development	20	2,282	.01	.16	.00	-.03	.01	.11	.05
Acting with Integrity	36	3,660	.17	.02	-.05	.13	.24	-.03	.03

Note. K = Number of Studies; N = Total Sample Size; ADJ = Adjustment, AMB = Ambition, SOC = Sociability, INP = Interpersonal Sensitivity, PRU = Prudence, INQ = Inquisitive, LRN = Learning Approach.

The results indicate that HPI Adjustment, Ambition, Interpersonal Sensitivity, and Prudence predict performance in the Sales & Customer Support job family. Note that the HPI scales best predict dimensions with a similar conceptual foundation (e.g., Adjustment and Maintaining Optimism, Ambition and Persuading Others, Prudence and Acting with Integrity). The convergence of HPI scales and dimensions illustrates the complimentary nature of HPI scales. Synthetic validity evidence suggests that being calm and self-confident (HPI Adjustment), energetic and leaderlike (HPI Ambition), perceptive and tactful (HPI Interpersonal Sensitivity), and dependable and organized (HPI Prudence) are characteristics important to successful performance for Sales and Customer Support jobs. To assess the predictive validity of the synthetic test battery, Nunnally's *(1978)* correlation of linear sums *(cf. Johnson, et al., 2001)* was used to estimate the overall synthetic correlation among the composite of the selected HPI scales (i.e., Adjustment, Ambition, Interpersonal Sensitivity, and Prudence) and Sales and Customer Support performance. Based upon synthetic validity results, the overall estimated validity of the test battery is $r = .23$.

3.46 Administrative & Clerical Job Family

Overview of Job Family. The Administrative & Clerical job family consists of jobs in which employees plan, direct, or coordinate supportive services as well as prepare/compile documents, compute accounts, and maintain records/files of an organization. These employees engage in variety of non-manual activities that can include maintaining records, distributing mail, handling information requests, operating telephone equipment, preparing correspondence, arranging conference calls, scheduling meetings, and providing other office support services.

Meta-Analysis Results. The Hogan Archive was searched for HPI validation studies involving Administrative & Clerical jobs. Fifteen studies were identified in the review and these are listed in Table 3.43. Each study reported correlations between scales and job performance criteria with the correlations for each scale aggregated across studies, using meta-analysis.

Table 3.43
Administrative & Clerical Jobs with Criterion-Related Data for Meta-Analysis

Study #	Job Title
63, 127	Certified Nursing Assistants
125	International Relocation Assistants
114	Administrative Personnel
114	Clerical Employees
2	Nursing Aides
138	Document Processor
138	Data Entry & Mailroom Positions
167	Clerical Workers
138	Data Entry Operator
142	Office Clerks
33	Claims Examiners
37	Clerical Workers
164	Auditor and Claims Examiner
137	Entry Level Administrative

Note. Study # reference citations appear in Appendix C with (Tech. Rep. No.) designations.

The HPI meta-analytic correlations are presented in Table 3.44.

Table 3 44
Meta-Analytic Correlations Between HPI Scales and Performance Criteria for Administrative & Clerical Jobs

			HPI Scales						
	N	*K*	ADJ	AMB	SOC	INP	PRU	INQ	LRN
Validation Studies	920	15	**.18**	.03	-.04	.03	**.15**	.00	.07

Note. N = number of participants across K studies; K = number of studies; ADJ = Adjustment; AMB = Ambition; SOC = Sociability; INP = Interpersonal Sensitivity; PRU = Prudence; INQ = Inquisitive; LRN = Learning Approach.

These results support those found in the published meta-analysis literature. HPI Adjustment and Prudence scales predicted job performance for positions in the Administrative & Clerical job family. Generalized validity evidence suggests that being calm and self-confident (HPI Adjustment) and dependable and organized (HPI Prudence) are characteristics important to successful performance in Administrative and Clerical jobs. To assess the predictive validity of this test battery, Nunnally's *(1978)* correlation of linear sums *(cf. Johnson, et al., 2001)* was used to estimate the overall transportability correlation among the composite of the selected HPI scales (i.e., Adjustment and Prudence) and Administrative and Clerical performance. Based upon meta-analysis, the overall estimated validity of the test battery is $r = .23$.

Synthetic Validity/Job Component Validity. The Administrative & Clerical competency model developed by Hogan was used to identify important performance criteria for these positions. For each job component, studies from the Hogan Archive using similar performance criteria were identified, and the correlations from those studies were aggregated using meta-analysis. These correlations, which represent validities for each personality scale across critical supervisory performance criteria, are presented in Table 3.45.

Table 3.45
HPI Synthetic Validity/Job Component Validity for Administrative & Clerical Job Family Competencies

Criterion	K	N	ADJ	AMB	SOC	INP	PRU	INQ	LRN
Category 1 – Exercising Job Skills									
Applying Job Skills	29	2,546	.06	**.14**	-.04	-.04	.05	.04	.06
Showing Personal Productivity	48	4,496	.09	**.20**	.00	.03	.07	.02	.04
Using Knowledge of the Organization	11	1,179	**.15**	**.14**	-.01	.05	.00	.08	.04
Category 2 – Solving Problems and Making Decisions									
Analyzing Information Effectively	51	5,940	**.13**	**.12**	-.04	.02	.08	.04	.07
Making Decisions	8	1,105	**.12**	**.20**	**.11**	.06	-.01	**.20**	**.15**
Learning from Experience	20	2,282	.01	**.16**	.00	-.03	.01	**.11**	.05
Category 3 – Building and Maintaining Relationships									
Focusing on the Customer	39	3,840	**.17**	**.11**	.02	**.14**	**.15**	-.03	.00
Showing Interpersonal Understanding	5	822	**.36**	**.13**	-.08	**.23**	**.23**	.05	.02
Communicating Effectively	51	5,225	**.11**	**.13**	.03	**.10**	.07	.04	.05
Teaming and Collaborating	36	4,417	**.19**	.05	-.04	**.13**	**.20**	-.03	.05
Category 4 – Showing Drive & Motivation									
Exhibiting Motivation and Commitment	49	5,064	.09	.07	.00	.06	**.14**	.03	.00
Showing Concern for Quality	6	991	**.24**	**.12**	-.02	**.11**	**.24**	**.10**	**.15**
Showing Flexibility	22	3,126	**.17**	**.21**	.09	**.10**	.06	.08	.09
Category 5 – Demonstrating Integrity and Professionalism									
Showing Emotional Maturity	52	5,676	**.30**	**.10**	-.04	**.16**	**.19**	.00	.05
Acting with Integrity	36	3,660	**.17**	.02	-.05	**.13**	**.24**	-.03	.03

Note. K = Number of Studies; N = Total Sample Size ADJ = Adjustment, AMB = Ambition, SOC = Sociability, INP = Interpersonal Sensitivity, PRU = Prudence, INQ = Inquisitive, LRN = Learning Approach.

The results indicate that HPI Adjustment, Ambition, Interpersonal Sensitivity, and Prudence predict performance in Administrative & Clerical jobs. Note that the HPI scales best predict dimensions with a similar conceptual foundation (e.g., Adjustment and Showing Emotional Maturity, Ambition and Showing Personal Productivity, Prudence and Acting with Integrity). The convergence of HPI scales and dimensions is important because it illustrates the complimentary nature of HPI scales. Synthetic validity evidence suggests that being calm and self-confident (HPI Adjustment), energetic and leaderlike (HPI Ambition), and dependable and organized (HPI Prudence) are characteristics important to successful performance for Administrative and Clerical jobs. To assess the predictive validity of the synthetic test battery, Nunnally's (1978) correlation of linear sums (cf. Johnson, et al., 2001) was used to estimate the overall synthetic correlation among the composite of the selected HPI scales (i.e., Adjustment, Ambition, and Prudence) and Administrative and Clerical performance. Based upon synthetic validity results, the overall estimated validity of the test battery is $r = .21$.

3.47 Service & Support Job Family

Overview of Job Family. The Service & Support job family consists of jobs in which employees perform protective (e.g., police, fire fighters, guards) and non-protective (e.g., food service, recreation and amusement, professional and personal service) services for others.

Meta-Analysis Results. The Hogan Archive was searched for HPI validation studies that included Service & Support jobs. Twenty-three studies were identified in the review and these are listed in Table 3.45. Each study reported correlations between scales and job performance criteria with correlations for each scale aggregated across studies, using meta-analysis.

Table 3.46
Service & Support Jobs with Criterion-Related Data for Transportability of Validity

Study #	Job Title
92	Cabin Supervisors & Managers
115	Conservation Officers
32	Basic Electronics School Students
20	Office Manager
20	Service Operation Dispatchers
85, 103, 287	Cashiers
170	Emergency Communication Officers
106	Reservation Sales Representative
72	Police Communication Operators
221	Navy Personnel
291	Dispatchers & Supervisors
80	Bank Tellers
166	Sheriff Deputies
220, 349	Fire Fighters and Officers
119, 284	Correctional Officers
120	Deputy Sheriffs
267	Non-Supervisory Officers
81	Police Officers
87	ROTC Students
194	Police Officers
213	Bank Tellers

Note. Study # reference citations appear in Appendix C with (Tech. Rep. No.) designations.

The HPI meta-analytic correlations are presented in Table 3.47.

Table 3.47

Meta-Analytic Correlations Between HPI Scales and Performance Criteria for Service & Support Jobs

			HPI Scales						
	N	*K*	ADJ	AMB	SOC	INP	PRU	INQ	LRN
Validation Studies	2,372	25	**.15**	.09	.02	**.10**	**.18**	.02	.03

Note. N = number of participants across K studies; K = number of studies; ADJ = Adjustment; AMB = Ambition; SOC = Sociability; INP = Interpersonal Sensitivity; PRU = Prudence; INQ = Inquisitive; LRN = Learning Approach.

These results supported those found in the published meta-analysis literature. HPI Adjustment, Interpersonal Sensitivity, and Prudence predict job performance. Ambition has a significant positive relationship with job performance, indicating that it may be relevant as a predictor in some Service & Support positions, depending on the specific requirements of those positions. Generalized validity evidence suggests that being calm and self-confident (HPI Adjustment), perceptive and tactful (HPI Interpersonal Sensitivity), and dependable and organized (HPI Prudence) are characteristics important to successful performance for Service and Support jobs. To assess the predictive validity of this test battery, Nunnally's *(1978)* correlation of linear sums *(cf. Johnson, et al., 2001)* was used to estimate the overall transportability correlation among the composite of the selected HPI scales (i.e., Adjustment, Interpersonal Sensitivity, and Prudence) and Service and Support performance. Based upon meta-analysis, the overall estimated validity of the test battery is $r = .22$.

Synthetic Validity/Job Component Validity. The Service & Support competency model developed by Hogan was used to aggregate the relevant criteria for these jobs. For each job component, studies from the Hogan Archive using similar performance criteria were identified, and the correlations from those studies were aggregated using meta-analysis. These correlations, which represent validities for each personality scale across critical supervisory performance criteria, are presented in Table 3.47.

Table 3.48
HPI Synthetic Validity/Job Component Validity for Service & Support Job Family Competencies

Criterion	K	N	ADJ	AMB	SOC	INP	PRU	INQ	LRN
Category 1 – Demonstrating Technical Skills									
Applying Job Skills	11	1,179	.15	.14	-.01	.05	.00	.08	.04
Showing Personal Productivity	48	4,496	.09	.20	.00	.03	.07	.02	.04
Focusing on Safety	6	471	.21	.27	.01	.12	.21	.08	.01
Category 2 – Solving Problems and Making Decisions									
Analyzing Information Effectively	51	5,940	.13	.12	-.04	.02	.08	.04	.07
Troubleshooting and Solving Problems	51	5,940	.13	.12	-.04	.02	.08	.04	.07
Making Decisions	8	1,105	.12	.20	.11	.06	-.01	.20	.15
Learning from Experience	20	2,282	.01	.16	.00	-.03	.01	.11	.05
Category 3 – Building and Maintaining Relationships									
Focusing on the Customer	39	3,840	.17	.11	.02	.14	.15	-.03	.00
Showing Interpersonal Understanding	5	822	.36	.13	-.08	.23	.23	.05	.02
Communicating Effectively	51	5,225	.11	.13	.03	.10	.07	.04	.05
Teaming and Collaborating	36	4,417	.19	.05	-.04	.13	.20	-.03	.05
Category 4 – Showing Drive and Motivation									
Exhibiting Motivation and Commitment	49	5,064	.09	.07	.00	.06	.14	.03	.00
Showing Concern for Quality	6	991	.24	.12	-.02	.11	.24	.10	.15
Category 5 – Demonstrating Integrity and Professionalism									
Showing Emotional Maturity	52	5,676	.30	.10	-.04	.16	.19	.00	.05
Adapting to Change	22	3,126	.17	.21	.09	.10	.06	.08	.09
Acting with Integrity	36	3,660	.17	.02	-.05	.13	.24	-.03	.03

7. K = Number of Studies; N = Total Sample Size; ADJ = Adjustment, AMB = Ambition, SOC = Sociability, INP = Interpersonal Sensitivity, PRU = Prudence, INQ = Inquisitive, LRN = Learning Approach.

The results indicate that Adjustment, Ambition, Interpersonal Sensitivity, and Prudence predict performance in the Service & Support job family. Note that the HPI scales best predict dimensions with a similar conceptual foundation (e.g., Adjustment and Showing Emotional Maturity, Ambition and Showing Personal Productivity, Prudence and Acting with Integrity). The convergence of HPI scales and dimensions illustrates the complimentary nature of HPI scales. Synthetic validity evidence suggests that being calm and self-confident (HPI Adjustment), energetic and leader-like (HPI Ambition), and dependable and organized (HPI Prudence) are characteristics important to successful performance in Service and Support jobs. To assess the predictive validity of the synthetic test battery, Nunnally's *(1978)* correlation of linear sums *(cf. Johnson, et al., 2001)* was used to estimate the overall synthetic correlation among the composite of the selected HPI scales (i.e., Adjustment, Ambition, and Prudence) and Service and Support performance. Based upon synthetic validity results, the overall estimated validity of the test battery is $r = .23$.

4. Interpretation

The HPI is designed primarily for use in personnel selection, individualized assessment, development, and career-related decision making. It provides information regarding what we call the "bright side" of personality–characteristics that appear in social interaction and that facilitate or inhibit a person's ability to get along with others and to achieve his or her goals.

- The HPI, based on the Five-Factor Model of personality, assesses normal personality and interpersonal characteristics, and predicts occupational success.

- The HPI provides information on how a person is perceived by others instead of how the person sees him- or herself. This perspective is possible because the HPI was validated using observers' descriptions of behavior and job performance (e.g., 360º ratings, supervisor ratings, etc.).

- The 206 items comprise seven primary scales, one validity scale, and 41 subscales. The subscales also are also called Homogeneous Item Composites (HICs), and present more specific information concerning a person's primary scale scores than the primary scales alone. The data are presented in terms of percentiles.

- Scores at the 65th percentile and above are considered High.

- Scores between the 36th and 64th percentiles are considered Average.

- Scores at the 35th percentile and below are considered Low.

- There are strengths and shortcomings associated with High, Average, and Low scores.

- The Validity Scale detects careless or erratic responding. When the Validity Scale score is less than 10, the HPI is invalid and cannot be interpreted. Ninety-eight percent of the people who take the HPI have a score of 10 or greater.

- The interpretive statements for each scale are empirically based.

A detailed interpretation of the HPI scales, configurations, and profiles along with uses and applications appears in R. Hogan, Hogan, and Warrenfeltz *(2007)*. In addition, Hogan certification training is available to qualified professionals under the American Psychological Association's sponsor approval system.

4.1 Adjustment

The Adjustment scale measures the degree to which a person appears calm and self-accepting or conversely, self-critical and tense.

Performance Implications of High Scores (65% - 100%)

- ***Positive Performance Implications***. High-scoring individuals adjust to fast paced environments and/or heavy workloads, stay calm under pressure, avoid overreacting, and do not react negatively to stress. They are even-tempered, confident in their abilities, and others will value their resiliency in urgent, stressful times. These individuals are trusting of others and tend to see the glass as half full rather than half empty.

- ***Negative Performance Implications***. Because high-scoring individuals are so calm, they may not realize when others are stressed, may continue to pile work onto others, and may not be empathic. They tend to view positive feedback as a means of "patting themselves on the back" and, because of their high level of self-confidence, they tend to discount, or even ignore, negative feedback. High-scoring individuals also tend to ignore their mistakes and overestimate their workplace contributions.

Performance Implications of Average Scores (36% - 64%)

- ***Positive Performance Implications***. Average-scoring individuals are seen as balanced, stable, and remain calm under stress and pressure. They will also listen to others' suggestions and apply feedback from others.

- ***Negative Performance Implications***. Average-scoring individuals may tend to appear nonchalant in their approach to work tasks and priority assignments. Others may perceive them as not being truly aware of their circumstances.

Performance Implications of Low Scores (0% - 35%)

- ***Positive Performance Implications***. Low-scoring individuals will be introspective, vigilant, concerned about their work products, and will use feedback as a means to improve performance. These individuals should be responsive to coaching and feedback.

- ***Negative Performance Implications***. Low-scoring individuals are overly self-critical, tend to be their own worst enemy, and are inclined to take criticism personally. They are perceived as remorseful, unhappy, intense, edgy, stress prone, tense under pressure, anxious, and self-derogatory. Setbacks and inconveniences will annoy them and cause stress.

4.2. Ambition

The Ambition scale measures the degree to which a person appears socially self-confident, leader-like, competitive, and energetic.

Performance Implications of High Scores (65% - 100%)

- *Positive Performance Implications*. High-scoring individuals tend to be leader-like, energetic, driven, competitive, and focused on achieving results and success. They also will take initiative, be persistent when completing a task, and are eager to advance in the organization. These individuals are self-confident and comfortable when presenting their ideas in front of groups, and they will lead others to focus on major business goals and initiatives.

- *Negative Performance Implications*. High-scoring individuals may tend to compete with their peers or subordinates to facilitate their own advancement. They may assume they have all the answers, and may not seek others' input when generating ideas. These individuals will become restless in jobs that lack career progression and move on to other opportunities if they see no room for advancement.

Performance Implications of Average Scores (36% - 64%)

- *Positive Performance Implications*. Average-scoring individuals are seen as relatively ambitious, reasonably hardworking, and good team players. Although they are not driven by status concerns, they normally do not mind moving into positions of authority, and they support team efforts to complete projects.

- *Negative Performance Implications*. Average-scoring individuals may be seen as indifferent and not very strategic in their decision making; consequently, others may have difficulty maintaining confidence in these individuals' leadership potential. Because of their tendency to not seek out challenges, they may be seen as lacking both the skill and desire to achieve high-impact results.

Performance Implications of Low Scores (0% - 35%)

- *Positive Performance Implications*. Low-scoring individuals will prefer to have tasks assigned to them and will be more comfortable following others than leading. They tend not to engage in "political behavior" and will work well in team and subordinate roles.

- *Negative Performance Implications*. Low-scoring individuals will be perceived as unassertive, indecisive, uninterested in advancement, satisfied with the status quo, and lacking focus or a clear vision. They tend to not take initiative unless asked, and may reject offers of leadership or advancement.

4.3 Sociability

The Sociability scale measures the degree to which a person seems to need and/or enjoy interacting with others.

Performance Implications of High Scores (65% - 100%)

- ***Positive Performance Implications***. High-scoring individuals tend to be described as approachable, gregarious, outgoing, talkative, entertaining, and dynamic. They will make a positive first impression and be comfortable in high profile positions–especially if they can be the center of attention. These individuals meet strangers well, enjoy interacting with others, and are seen as being socially skilled by both peers and customers.

- ***Negative Performance Implications***. High-scoring individuals may have difficulty engaging in active listening and may frequently interrupt others. They tend to compete for center stage instead of understanding their role in the bigger picture. Over time, more reserved coworkers may see these individuals as loud and overbearing, which will reduce their effectiveness. They also may also be impulsive and not think through the consequences of their actions, which puts them at risk of making hasty and poor decisions (check for low Prudence).

Performance Implications of Average Scores (36% - 64%)

- ***Positive Performance Implications***. Average-scoring individuals are neither extroverted nor socially retiring. They will be seen by others as friendly and congenial, but not overly attention seeking. Customers and coworkers will see them as approachable, accessible, and willing to listen to their needs before offering suggestions.

- ***Negative Performance Implications***. Average-scoring individuals tend not to seek recognition for their performance; consequently, they may be viewed as lacking involvement or dedication. They tend to not voice their ideas and opinions to avoid drawing too much attention to themselves.

Performance Implications of Low Scores (0% - 35%)

- ***Positive Performance Implications***. Low-scoring individuals tend not to engage in small talk, and consequently will be more business focused and task oriented. They will enjoy and excel at solitary tasks, will be good listeners, and will not need continuous social interaction to keep them interested and satisfied with their job.

- *Negative Performance Implications*. Low-scoring individuals tend to be described as being reserved, quiet, and somewhat shy. They may also be described as cold and socially aloof, and may use their shyness as a manipulation technique. As managers, they may hold back during discussions, not give enough feedback to their staff, and seem unapproachable.

4.4 Interpersonal Sensitivity

The Interpersonal Sensitivity scale measures the degree to which a person is seen as perceptive, tactful, and socially sensitive.

Performance Implications of High Scores (65% - 100%)

- *Positive Performance Implications*. High-scoring individuals will be seen as diplomatic, trustworthy, friendly, warm, considerate, and nurturing in relationships. They tend to be perceptive, thoughtful, and cooperative team members who try to build and maintain coalitions with others. They encourage cooperation and teamwork, and foster trust and respect from their peers and staff.

- *Negative Performance Implications*. High-scoring individuals have a propensity to avoid confrontation. They tend to be focused on getting along with others; consequently, they may not address poor performance issues in a timely manner, which can create perceptions of favoritism. Others may take advantage of this person.

Performance Implications of Average Scores (36% - 64%)

- *Positive Performance Implications*. Average-scoring individuals are seen as cooperative and friendly, but are still able to voice their opinions. These individuals will be comfortable confronting conflict and tend to do so in a tactful way.

- *Negative Performance Implications*. Average-scoring individuals may become impatient with others' shortcomings and avoid interacting with them at a professional level.

Performance Implications of Low Scores (0% - 35%)

- *Positive Performance Implications*. Low-scoring individuals will confront nonperformance issues promptly, using a frank and direct manner. They will not be swayed easily by others' emotions or personal concerns, and will be comfortable enforcing tough rules and procedures.

- *Negative Performance Implications*. Low-scoring individuals will be seen as direct, blunt, tough, and possibly insensitive. They may be harsh, unconcerned with staff morale, and indifferent to others' feelings; consequently, others will not turn to them in a time of need. These individuals tend to be socially imperceptive and say things without realizing the consequences of their words and actions (e.g., they may give orders instead of making suggestions). They may also be seen as becoming easily impatient with others' shortcomings (check for low Adjustment).

4.5 Prudence

The Prudence scale measures the degree to which a person seems conscientious, conforming, and dependable.

Performance Implications of High Scores (65% - 100%)

- **Positive Performance Implications**. High-scoring individuals are seen as orderly, dependable, planful, organized, reliable, and responsible. They will hold high standards for their own and others' performance, and will be described as procedurally driven and attentive to details. These individuals tend to be good organizational citizens who are attentive to the rules and procedures of the organization. They will gather all information necessary to make an informed decision.

- **Negative Performance Implications**. High-scoring individuals may be overly controlling and have difficulty managing change. They will be described by others as micro-managing the details of projects, and being somewhat unable to delegate tasks to others. These individuals tend to not be visionary or "big picture" oriented (check for low Inquisitive), which may reduce their overall effectiveness. Individuals with very high scores (90th percentile and above) tend to be seen as rigid and inflexible.

Performance Implications of Average Scores (36% - 64%)

- **Positive Performance Implications**. Average-scoring individuals will be seen as responsible employees who are planful, mindful of details, and able to tolerate close supervision. They are open to new experiences, ideas, and initiatives, and will look beyond standard procedures to solve problems.

- **Negative Performance Implications**. Average-scoring individuals may have difficulty prioritizing work, being flexible in uncertain situations, and knowing when they have enough information to make a decision.

Performance Implications of Low Scores (0% - 35%)

- **Positive Performance Implications**. Low-scoring individuals will be quick to act and make things happen within the organization. They will be flexible, open, and comfortable with change, innovation, and new initiatives.

- *Negative Performance Implications*. Low-scoring individuals tend to be impulsive and careless with respect to rules, policies, and procedures. They tend to be inattentive to details, resist supervision, ignore small process steps, not plan ahead, and rarely think through the consequences of their actions.

4.6 Inquisitive

The Inquisitive scale measures the degree to which a person is perceived as bright, creative, and interested in intellectual matters.

Performance Implications of High Scores (65% - 100%)

- *Positive Performance Implications*. High-scoring individuals tend to be imaginative, have a lot of ideas, and are resourceful problem solvers. They often are creative (check for low Prudence), adventurous, inquisitive, curious, open-minded, and focused on the bigger picture. These individuals usually are strategic "outside-the-box" thinkers who can bring a variety of ideas and solutions to the table.

- *Negative Performance Implications*. High-scoring individuals may become easily bored without new and stimulating activities. They may have difficulty diagnosing the practicality of ideas and concepts, downplay operational or process matters, and prefer conceptualizing over implementation. Individuals with very high scores (above 90%) often are often perceived as easily distractible (especially when performing tedious tasks), unpredictable, and overly passionate about topics of personal interest.

Performance Implications of Average Scores (36% - 64%)

- *Positive Performance Implications*. Average-scoring individuals will be seen as being somewhat imaginative and having varying degrees of interest in creativity or conceptual thinking. While they will contribute to the strategic planning of the organization, they will tend to stay in the background and evaluate ideas rather than generating their own. These individuals often enjoy taking visionary ideas and translating them into workable solutions.

- *Negative Performance Implications*. Average-scoring individuals may lose sight of the big picture and not be enthusiastic about strategic planning. Others may see them as lacking ideas and being indifferent to change and advancement in technology or operating procedures.

Performance Implications of Low Scores (0% - 35%)

- *Positive Performance Implications*. Low-scoring individuals will be seen as practical, level headed, process focused, and tolerant of repetitive tasks. They tend to have a practical, hands-on approach to problem solving, and are good with applications.

- *Negative Performance Implications*. Low-scoring individuals will be cautious in their acceptance of new ideas and experiences, making them uncomfortable in ambiguous situations. They tend to focus on details and operational matters and ignore the big picture. These individuals prefer to use familiar, instead of creative ways to solve problems, and may ignore the constructive advice of peers or superiors on new ways to perform familiar tasks.

4.7 Learning Approach

The Learning Approach scale measures the degree to which a person seems to enjoy academic activities and to value educational achievement.

Performance Implications of High Scores (65% - 100%)

- *Positive Performance Implications*. High-scoring individuals value education and view learning as an end unto itself. They tend to be up-to-date with current trends in their profession, and will push for learning and training opportunities for themselves and their staff. These individuals are achievement oriented, goal-focused, enjoy applying their knowledge to current situations, and will work to improve their skills.

- *Negative Performance Implications*. High-scoring individuals may tend to focus more on learning rather than doing "non-interesting," yet required, tasks. They may tend to jump on the newest technology without verifying its usefulness and may overwhelm others with their zeal for training opportunities. These individuals may be perceived as dogmatic about the value of knowledge; consequently, they may be seen as a "know-it-all" by others, causing them to lose credibility over time.

Performance Implications of Average Scores (36% - 64%)

- *Positive Performance Implications*. Average-scoring individuals will seek learning opportunities, but not with great urgency. They will encourage others to stay up to date on current trends, but will not make it mandatory. Although the prevailing perception is that these individuals are informed of the latest procedures, they may be caught off guard by those who dig deeper into new advancements.

- *Negative Performance Implications*. Average-scoring individuals may delay their learning of new information, which can be a detriment to the organization. Because they show little urgency, others may perceive them as uncommitted to the tasks at hand. Further, they may tend to talk about employee development and staying current on trends, but rarely provide their staff with the opportunities to do so.

Performance Implications of Low Scores (0% - 35%)

- *Positive Performance Implications*. Low-scoring individuals look to hands-on, nontraditional venues of training and learning, versus traditional educational media. They usually prefer to apply skills rather than learning new methods and concepts.

- *Negative Performance Implications*. Low-scoring individuals tend to view traditional venues of education as something to be endured rather than enjoyed. Consequently, they often seem unconcerned with staff development, and may ignore opportunities for continuing education for both themselves and their staff. They may not set clear goals and objectives for themselves or others, and/or equip their staff with the necessary skills to carry out their assignments.

4.8 Adjectival Correlates of HPI Scale Scores

A primary goal of the HPI is to predict how a respondent will be described by others who know him or her, i.e., to predict his or her reputation (see Chapter 1). If certain descriptive terms are reliably associated with HPI scale scores, then this helps to understand the meaning of the scores. In addition, those scores can be used to predict how peers will describe others with comparable scores and to predict behavior in non-testing situations.

According to socioanalytic theory, the same process underlies social interaction and responding to the HPI or any other assessment procedure. In theory, this is the reason why certain scale scores are linked to certain peer descriptions *(Mills & Hogan, 1978)*. Thus, finding correlations between peer (and other) descriptions and HPI scores allows us to evaluate the validity of the HPI and to evaluate the theory of personality on which the HPI rests.

Data were collected from 86 graduate and undergraduate students. Participants varied in age (M = 26, SD = 7,the 13% not reporting), gender (58% male, 33% female, 9% not reporting), and ethnicity (63% White, 7% Black, 6% Hispanic, 5% Asian American, 6% American Indian/Alaskan Native, 2% other, 12% not reporting).

Participants completed the HPI and gave adjectival rating forms to two persons who knew them well (e.g., family members, friends, roommates, etc.) These rating forms were organized into two sections. The first section included all 100 items from the California Q-Set *(CQS; Block, 1961)*. Respondents were asked to check items from the Q-Set (e.g., arouses liking in others) that described the study participant. Each checked item was assigned a dummy code of 1, and each unchecked item was assigned a dummy code of 0. The second section included all 300 items of the Adjective Check List (ACL; Gough & Heilbrun, 1983). The response format and item coding were the same as that used for the Q-Set. Average scores for each item from both raters were computed and used in subsequent analyses. Results for each item and phrase were then correlated with each HPI scale. Selected results are presented for each HPI scale in Tables 4.1 through 4.7. Complete scale by item matrices are presented in Appendix D.

Table 4.1
Adjustment Correlations with CQS and ACL Items

CQS Statements		ACL Adjective	
Has a clear-cut, internally consistent personality.	0.34	Self-confident	0.37
Is calm, relaxed in manner.	0.30	Active	0.34
Is subjective unaware of self-concern; feels satisfied with self.	0.28	Easy-going	0.32
Judges self and others in conventional terms like "popularity," "the correct thing to do," social pressures, etc.	0.26	Humorous	0.31
Is a genuinely dependable and responsible person.	0.26	Cooperative	0.31
Is comfortable with uncertainty and complexity.	0.26	Energetic	0.30
Has fluctuating moods.	-0.37	Practical	0.28
Is thin-skinned; sensitive to anything that can be construed as criticism or an interpersonal slight.	-0.34	Relaxed	0.27
Extrapunitive; tends to transfer or project blame.	-0.32	Realistic	0.26
Is self-defeating.	-0.31	Confident	0.26
Is sensitive to anything that can be construed as a demand.	-0.31	Patient	0.25
Is basically anxious.	-0.30	Adaptable	0.22
Feels cheated and victimized by life; self-pitying.	-0.29	Moody	-0.31
Over-reactive to minor frustrations; irritable.	-0.28	Quarrelsome	-0.30
Reluctant to commit self to any definite course of action; tends to delay or avoid action.	-0.24	Pessimistic	-0.29
		Temperamental	-0.29
		Bitter	-0.27
		Distrustful	-0.26
		Cynical	-0.23
		Nagging	-0.23

Table 4.2
Ambition Correlations with CQS and ACL Items

CQS Statements		ACL Adjective	
Regards self as physically attractive.	0.41	Self-confident	0.39
Has a clear-cut, internally consistent personality.	0.35	Masculine	0.37
Values own independence and autonomy.	0.28	Handsome	0.36
Appears straightforward, forthright, and candid in dealing with others.	0.27	Outspoken	0.29
Appears to have a high degree of intellectual capacity.	0.25	Active	0.27
Is power oriented; values power in self or others.	0.25	Energetic	0.26
Is comfortable with uncertainty and complexity.	0.22	Confident	0.25
Has a brittle ego-defense system; has a small reserve of integration; would be disorganized and maladaptive when under stress or trauma.	-0.30	Lazy	-0.30
Is vulnerable to real or fancied threat, generally fearful.	-0.26	Moderate	-0.29
		Quiet	-0.28
		Mild	-0.26
		Changeable	-0.25
		Affected	-0.24
		Silent	-0.24
		Unexcitable	-0.22

Table 4.3
Sociability Correlations with CQS and ACL Items

CQS Statements		ACL Adjective	
Emphasizes being with others; gregarious.	0.45	Flirtatious	0.52
Is a talkative individual.	0.39	Outgoing	0.43
Initiates humor.	0.32	Sociable	0.41
Interested in establishing relationships.	0.32	Talkative	0.38
Is facially and/or gesturally expressive.	0.31	Outspoken	0.37
Tends to arouse liking and acceptance in people.	0.29	Adventurous	0.37
Is cheerful.	0.28	Humorous	0.31
Has a rapid personal tempo; behaves and acts quickly.	0.27	Excitable	0.29
Is skilled in social techniques of imaginative play, pretending and humor.	0.26	Jolly	0.29
Is socially perceptive of a wide range of interpersonal cues.	0.22	Loud	0.29
Keeps people at a distance; avoids close interpersonal relationships.	-0.23	Mischievous	0.23
Does not vary roles; relates to everyone in the same way.	-0.22	Reckless	0.23
		Quiet	-0.39
		Silent	-0.30
		Unaffected	-0.30
		Industrious	-0.29
		Discreet	-0.28
		Cautious	-0.24
		Moderate	-0.23
		Rigid	-0.22

Table 4.4
Interpersonal Sensitivity Correlations with CQS and ACL Items

CQS Statements		ACL Adjective	
Emphasizes being with others; gregarious.	0.51	Friendly	0.42
Tends to arouse liking and acceptance in people.	0.44	Cooperative	0.40
Interested in establishing relationships.	0.42	Sensitive	0.39
Has warmth; has the capacity for close relationships; compassionate.	0.39	Cheerful	0.36
Is personally charming.	0.35	Considerate	0.35
Behaves in a sympathetic or considerate manner.	0.30	Affectionate	0.35
Arouses nurturing feelings in others.	0.30	Appreciative	0.34
Compares self to others. Is alert to real or fancied differences between self and other people.	0.27	Praising	0.34
Is critical, skeptical, not easily impressed.	-0.43	Trusting	0.33
Is basically distrustful of people in general; questions their motivations.	-0.37	Pleasant	0.33
Has hostility towards others.	-0.37	Generous	0.33
Keeps people at a distance; avoids close interpersonal relationships.	-0.33	Gentle	0.33
Expresses hostile feelings directly.	-0.31	Charming	0.32
Shows condescending behavior in relations with others.	-0.26	Warm	0.32
Is guileful and deceitful, manipulative, opportunistic.	-0.25	Sentimental	0.31
Tends to be rebellious and non-conforming.	-0.25	Sympathetic	0.29
Thinks and associates to ideas in unusual ways; has unconventional thought processes.	-0.24	Quarrelsome	-0.54
		Irritable	-0.41
		Coarse	-0.36
		Unstable	-0.35
		Distrustful	-0.34
		Forceful	-0.34
		Hard-hearted	-0.33
		Stingy	-0.33
		Rigid	-0.31
		Rude	-0.31
		Intolerant	-0.30
		Deceitful	-0.25
		Hostile	-0.23

Table 4.5
Prudence Correlations with CQS and ACL Items

CQS Statements		ACL Adjective	
Has high aspiration level for self.	0.32	Polished	0.35
Is turned to for advice and reassurance.	0.29	Patient	0.31
Genuinely submissive; accepts domination comfortable.	0.24	Poised	0.30
Prides self on being "objective," rational.	0.23	Submissive	0.29
Behaves in an ethically consistent manner; is consistent with own personal standards.	0.23	Conservative	0.27
Tends to be rebellious and non-conforming.	-0.26	Cautious	0.26
Is guileful and deceitful, manipulative, opportunistic.	-0.25	Mild	0.23
Is subtle negativistic; tends to undermine and obstruct or sabotage.	-0.24	Efficient	0.22
Is unpredictable and changeable in behavior and attitudes.	-0.23	Organized	0.22
Extrapunitive; tends to transfer or project blame.	-0.22	Realistic	0.22
		Reckless	-0.34
		Tactless	-0.31
		Unconventional	-0.29
		Infantile	-0.26
		Rebellious	-0.26
		Cruel	-0.25
		Distractible	-0.25
		Absent-minded	-0.24
		Irresponsible	-0.24
		Foolish	-0.23
		Undependable	-0.22

Table 4.6
Inquisitive Correlations with CQS and ACL Items

CQS Statements		ACL Adjective	
Tends to pro-offer advice.	0.26	Tough	0.30
Is experience seeking.	0.25	Interests wide	0.29
Tends toward over-control of needs and impulses; binds tensions excessively; delays gratification unnecessarily.	0.24	Adventurous	0.28
Values own independence and autonomy.	0.24	Enterprising	0.25
Characteristically pushes and tries to stretch limits; sees what he or she can get away with.	0.23	Versatile	0.25
		Artistic	0.23
		Inventive	0.22

Table 4.7
Learning Approach Correlations with CQS and ACL Items

CQS Statements		ACL Adjective	
Tends to pro-offer advice.	0.18*	Complicated	0.33
Is turned to for advice and reassurance.	0.21*	Industrious	0.29
Concerned with own adequacy as a person, either at conscious or unconscious levels.	0.22	Ingenious	0.28
Is critical, skeptical, not easily impressed.	0.22	Rigid	0.28
Is a genuinely dependable and responsible person.	0.22	Shrewd	0.27
Is basically distrustful of people in general; questions their motivation.	0.24	Clever	0.26
Seeks reassurance from others.	-0.24	Deliberate	0.24
		Thorough	0.23
		Trusting	-0.25
Note. *p > .05			

5. Administering the HPI

As publisher of psychological assessments, Hogan Assessment Systems (HAS) provides a state-of-the-art administration platform developed to meet the needs of clients. Since the mid 1990's, the delivery for the HPI has been through a web based assessment platform. The assessment platform was designed and is maintained for security, ease of use, speed, and flexibility. The platform uses leading-edge technologies such as web services, middleware, and XML. The flexibility of these technologies allows customized solutions appropriate for clients of all sizes. An overview of key features of this system is presented below. For further information please contact HAS' Customer Service Department at 1-800-756-0632 or customerservice@hoganassessments.com. Office hours are 8am-5pm and after-hours messages are checked daily.

5.1 Key Features of the Web-Based Platform

It is important that test administrators understand how participants complete an online assessment, are able to address questions or concerns participants may raise, and use test administrator tools. To address these issues, HAS trains administrators in the functionality of the system by Hogan. In the initial training session, an administrator is instructed on how to create participant ID's as well as how to use various other tools on the administrative website. Additional training is available for the creation of participant groups, obtaining reports, changing report options, and specifying report delivery options.

The HAS testing system is fully redundant, using multi-location systems architecture ensuring its constant availability. Clients can access the testing platform 24 hours a day, 7 days a week, from any internet-capable PC. Test results are normally delivered in 90 seconds or less, making results nearly instantaneous. Results are provided to the client via the web or through e-mail as an attached encrypted PDF file. HAS consults with outside security experts to ensure data security; HAS uses 128 bit secure access via password protection when safe guarding clients' and user assessment data.

All HAS web ordering systems allow HAS to tailor the ordering and reporting experience to each user based on a hierarchical system of client and user preferences. Users can select from a wide variety of HPI report options including: simple graphic, data, suitability series, candidate potential series, BASIS, leadership forecast series, performance management series, and group level reports.

Whether a client orders from a single office or numerous locations throughout the US, all orders can flow through a single account. HAS product-level security features allow clients to restrict individual user's ability to order and view reports on a product-by-product basis.

5.2 Completing the HPI Using the Online Internet System

This section provides an example of the participant experience when completing the HPI on line. Testing time for the HPI usually requires twenty minutes, but may vary depending on the test taker's reading speed. Although the inventory is written at a 4.6 grade reading level, it is intended to be used by adults sixteen years and older.

Once a participant receives a User ID from the administrator, he/she logs into the specified website. This is http://www.gotohogan.com or a customized portal designed for Hogan clients. To log on to the website, a minimum version of Microsoft Internet Explorer 4.0 or Netscape Navigator 6.2 is needed. Once at the website, the individual sees a login page similar to the one in Figure 5.1.

Figure 5.1

Hogan Assessment Systems Participant Login Web Page

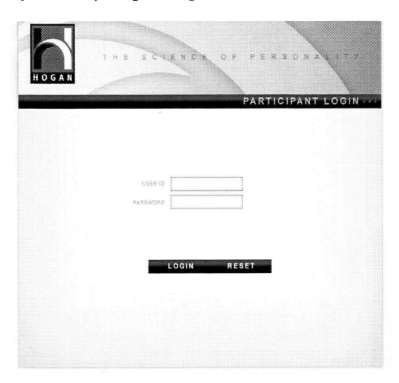

At the login page, the participant is asked to enter his/her assigned User ID and password (e.g., User ID: BB123456; Password = SAMPLE) and then select the Logon button. The participant is prompted to fill out a brief demographics page (see Figure 5.2) and agree to an informed consent clause (see section 5.3). This clause outlines information regarding the purpose, administration, and results of the assessments.

On the Participant Information web page, the participant can insert a string of numbers when asked to input his/her SSN. An administrator may choose to have the individual enter his/her actual social security number, but can also assign an ID designed for internal tracking purposes (e.g., employee ID number). Once the user has logged into the system they will be asked to create a personal password and complete additional information fields. When all fields are complete, the participant must select Submit to continue.

Figure 5.2

Hogan Assessment Systems Participant Information Web Page

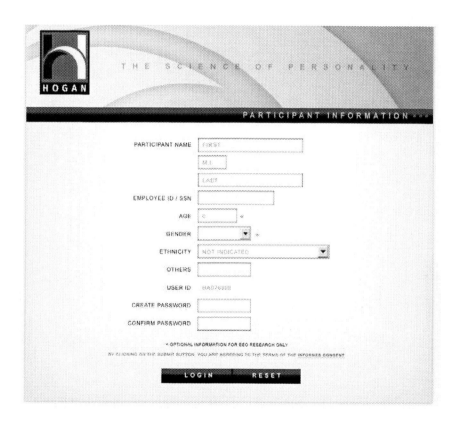

After clicking the Submit button, the user is redirected to the Participant Menu. The Participant Menu displays each assessment they have been assigned to take (see figure 5.3). If the individual is taking multiple assessments, each will be listed. After an assessment is completed, the individual is returned to this menu to select and proceed with additional assessments.

Figure 5.3

Hogan Assessment Systems Participant Menu Web Page

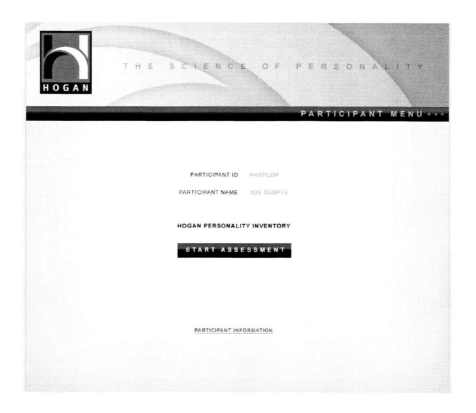

It is important that the administrator emphasize the need to respond to every question. If more than 1/3 of the items on any scale are not answered the test will be invalid. The participant should not spend too much time on any one specific statement; there are no "right" or "wrong" answers. The participant can navigate forward and backward through the assessment. He/she may select the Next button to continue the assessment; the Previous button permits viewing the previous page. Because the assessment does not time out, the participant can stop and start the assessment at will. If at any time the individual discontinues the assessment, all prior submitted information will be retained. The participant can log back into the system with his/her User ID and self-created personal password to continue at any time. Once completed, the assessment is submitted by the participant. Results are processed through a scoring engine that generates and sends the report to an e-mail address(es) designated by the administrator. A sample of an Assessment Questionnaire web page is presented in Figure 5.4.

If the account administrator or the participant experiences a problem, they are encouraged to contact HAS' Customer Service Department at 1-800-756-0632 or customerservice@hoganassessments.com.

Figure 5.4
Hogan Assessment Systems Assessment Questionnaire Web Page

5.3 Participant's Informed Consent

HAS operates under the assumption that all individuals taking assessments have given their informed consent to participate in the assessment process. This is the fundamental concept that underlies all current and anticipated data protection protocols and legislation. In order for individuals taking the assessments to give their informed consent, they must understand the purpose of the assessment, the likely use of the assessment data, and how the data are protected. These protocols are described below and are binding on all HAS clients and individuals taking the assessments. Failure to comply with any of these safeguards will constitute grounds for termination of any data transfer arrangements between HAS and the person(s) or entity(ies) concerned. The Candidate Log-on Entry protocol requires all individuals taking the assessment to give their informed consent before they can complete the assessment process.

Purpose. The assessments on the website were created to provide personal characteristic information and feedback to trained and accredited consultants and HR professionals. These data are primarily used for selection and/or development.

Data Use and Storage. The assessment data only will be used by trained and accredited consultants or HR professionals. HAS will retain individual raw data for a period of three years and, in addition, will use anonymously held (identifying information removed) aggregated data for normative studies. All HAS clients are responsible for complying with national and international protocols covering data use and storage.

Access to Data. HAS will not provide results directly to individuals taking the assessments. The dissemination of results is the sole responsibility of the requesting organization. Individuals taking the assessments are not guaranteed access to their individual results.

Primary Security. In order to safeguard individual results, the website contains only the assessment items, not the assessment programs (which are held by HAS and its clients). It is impossible to process results through the website. Results can only be processed by downloading the raw data, decrypting the raw data, and scoring these data with appropriate programs. Until that time, responses to assessment items are merely encrypted alphanumeric strings with no discernible meaning.

Secondary Security. Individuals taking the assessments are provided a username and password to access the website assessments. In addition, the raw data are encrypted. Each organization using the web site is provided with a secure method of data transfer from the internet to their organization.

5.4 Using International Translations of the HPI

As publisher, HAS undertakes translation and localization initiatives to brand and make available its assessment tools internationally. HPI translations can be accessed in more than twenty languages. A representative listing of current language availability appears in Table 5.1.

Table 5.1

HPI Language Translations

UK English	Swedish
US English	Norwegian
South Africa English	Dutch
Kenya English	Icelandic
French Canadian	Polish
French Parisian	Russian
German	Romanian
Spanish	Czech
Brazilian Portuguese3	Slovak
Danish	Simplified Chinese
Turkish	Traditional Chinese
Italian	
* Please contact HAS for language availability not shown above.	

Translations of the HPI are administered through the HAS web based assessment platform. The administrator can choose to assess participants in multiple languages and also choose to produce HPI reports in various languages. HPI report translations are selected when the User ID is generated from the online system, as illustrated in Figure 5.5

Figure 5.5
Hogan Assessment Systems Report Language Selection

After creating a participant's online User ID for the desired report language, the administrator directs the participant to the Hogan multi-language assessment website. Once the participant logs on to the website, he/she may choose to take the HPI in any of the languages represented by the country flags illustrated in Figure 5.6 by selecting the flag. Then, the login page will appear in the chosen language and the participant is asked to enter his/her assigned User ID and password (e.g., User ID BB123456, Password = SAMPLE) and select the Logon button. The participant is prompted to fill out a brief demographics page and agree to an informed consent clause (see Section 5.3).

Figure 5.6
Hogan Assessment Systems Language Translation Flags

On the Participant Information web page, the participant can insert any string of numbers when asked to input his/her SSN or Employee ID number. Some countries do not use a SSN or have legislation prohibiting the collection of this information. In these cases, the participant should be told what to input into this field by his/her administrator. An administrator may select to have the participant enter his/her employee ID, User ID, or a company assigned ID designed for internal tracking purposes. The remainder of the process follows the procedures previously outlined in sections 5.2 and 5.3.

5.5 Accommodating Individuals with Disabilities

The Americans with Disabilities Act of 1990 (ADA) is the most significant, recent employment law that address-es employers' requirements for fair treatment of disabled individuals. It prohibits employment discrimination against qualified individuals with disabilities in employment. This law has important implications for employers' procedures used in interviewing, testing, and hiring new employees. For pre-employment testing, the ADA speci-fies that employers must provide alternate forms of employment testing that "accurately (assess) the skills, aptitudes, or whatever other factor of such applicant or employee that such test purports to measure, rather than reflecting the impaired sensory, manual or speaking skills of such employee or applicant" Sec. 102(b)(7), 42 U.S.C.A.Sec. 12112. HAS complies with the ADA requirements by working with clients to accommodate in-dividuals with special needs. Large print assessments and screen readers are available from customer service at 1-800-756-0632 or customerservice@hoganassessments.com. In addition, because the HPI is not a timed test, individuals can take as much time as they need to complete the assessment. HAS can make additional accommodations on a case-by-case basis through contacting customer service.

5.6 Frequently Asked Questions

The following are questions participants ask frequently, followed by answers typically given by customer service staff:

Q. I am trying to sign back in to complete the assessments but my user id and password are not working.
A. Please use the new personal password you created when you first accessed the system. (You were requested to change the password on the initial participant information screen).

Q. Can I stop the assessment at any time?
A. Yes, you can select the stop assessment link to end your session. Please make note of your User ID and new personal password in order to log back into the website.

Q. How long will the assessments take?
A. Please allow 15 to 20 minutes to complete the assessment.

Q. Is it a timed assessment?
A. No. You can take as much time as needed to complete the inventory.

Q. Will I receive a copy of my results?
A. We are not at liberty to share or discuss results with candidates. Results are sent to the company that requested your assessments; the company decides whether or not to share results with you.

Q. Will all my data be lost because my system locked up before I completed the assessment?

A. No, your responses are saved after each page is completed.

5.7 Alternative Testing Solutions

Although HAS encourages the use of online testing system, not all assessment situations are conducive to computerized testing formats. HAS can provide paper-and-pencil assessment materials for the HPI. For test security, inventory scores for the HPI are generated by HAS. To calculate the scores, clients must provide answer sheets back by fax or mail for scoring. Alternatively, clients may provide computerized item-level data files back to HAS for scoring. The appropriate data file formats are available by contacting Customer Service at 1-800-756-0632 or customerservice@hoganassessments.com.

6. Compilation Of Norms

6.1 Characteristics of the 2005 HPI Norming Sample

Raw test scores hold very little information without appropriate norms to provide context for their interpretation. According to Nunnally *(1967, p. 244)*, "norms are any scores that provide a frame of reference for interpreting the scores of particular persons." Norms provide context and meaning to individual test scores. Tests report norms as either transformed standard scores or percentiles *(Nunnally, 1967)*. The HPI manual *(R. Hogan & Hogan, 1995)* specifies that the HPI is interpreted using percentile scores. A percentile indicates the percentage of people who score at or below a given raw score on a test. For example, if 85 percent of people have raw score on Adjustment at or below 33, then any person who receives a raw score of 33 is at the 85th percentile of respondents.

The score distributions for all scales on the HPI have changed slightly since the first publication of norms in 1992. Specifically, the scale means increased over time, resulting in a somewhat skewed distribution of scores. Consequently, personnel selection cutoff scores based on the 1992 norms no longer result in the same pass rates that they did in earlier years. This chapter describes the process undertaken to update the HPI norms. To create norms, the intended population for the test (e.g., schoolchildren or working adults) must be specified. Next, a plan for drawing a representative sample from this population is designed. Then using the plan, a representative sample is drawn from the norming population. Test scores from the sample are aggregated to form a final normative database, and these data are used to describe distributions of the test scales and to interpret scores.

Specification of the Population and Sampling Plan. Cronbach *(1984)* noted that the norms for personality inventories are "notoriously inadequate" and emphasized the importance of using appropriate populations when calculating norms. Cronbach listed four standards for developing norms: norming samples must (a) consist of individuals for whom the test was intended and with whom an examinee will be compared; (b) be representative of the population; (c) include a sufficient number of cases; and (d) be appropriately subdivided. The Standards for Educational and Psychological Testing also state this in Standard 4.6 *(AERA, APA, & NCME, 1999, p. 55)*:

> *Reports of norming studies should include precise specification of the population that was sampled, sampling procedures, and participation rates, any weighting of the sample, the dates of testing, and descriptive statistics. The information provided should be sufficient to enable users to judge the appropriateness of the norms for interpreting the scores of local examinees. Technical documentation should indicate the precision of the norms themselves.*

The HPI is intended as a tool for assessing working adults in employee selection and development contexts. The target population for the HPI norms is the US workforce. To create a norming sample appropriate for use in both selection and development, a sampling plan used the following three criteria:

- Selection cases included in the norming sample are representative of the US workforce in terms of both occupation and demographics.

- The proportion of selection and development cases included in the norming sample reflects the Hogan client base using an internet delivery platform.

- The overall sample is demographically representative of the US workforce.

Stratified Sampling of the Norming Population. Using the sampling plan, we drew representative norming samples from the Hogan data warehouse. Beginning with a population (N = 624,856) of working adults, data were collected from on-line testing between June 10, 2003 and June 9, 2005. We eliminated cases from this population based on two rules. First, we removed all cases with an HPI Validity scale raw score of less than 10 (See Chapter 2). Applying this rule eliminated 34,059 cases. Second, we removed cases with excessive missing items. The HPI scoring engine eliminated cases with 33% of items, or 68 items, missing data. Following this logic, we eliminated 4,809 cases. After deletions, the norming population included 585,988 cases.

We applied the three sampling plan criteria and derived the final norming sample using both inductive and deductive approaches. We included a proportionate number of cases from the 23 DoL occupational categories, except in categories where we lacked data (i.e., Farming, Fishing and Forestry Occupations). Additionally, because examinees are not required to provide gender and race data, there were some missing data for these variables, resulting in a slightly disproportionate representation of the US workforce. To achieve proportionate occupational representation in the norming sample, we mapped our test data to DoL categories. Table 6.1 lists the percentage of people in the US workforce by occupational category, as reported in May 2005 *(US Department of Labor, 2006)*.

We followed the DoL classification guidelines by linking jobs in the norming sample to the SOC system *(US DoL, 2001)*. We assigned each case to one of the DoL groups. This ensured that the norming samples represented a realistic distribution of jobs from the US workforce. To increase the accuracy of our classifications, two Hogan psychologists completed the groupings independently. This resulted in 99% classification with the remaining discrepancies resolved through discussion. As seen in Table 6.1, the HPI database contains 14 of the 23 DoL occupational categories, or 84.4 % of the 2005 US occupations.

Table 6.1
HPI Database Classified by DoL Occupations

DoL Occupation	Hogan Archive HPI cases	Percent of Total in HPI Archive	Percent of US Employment	Percent of US Occupations Represented
Management occupations	12,097	5.43%	4.6%	4.2%
Business and financial operations occupations	6,567	2.95%	4.2%	3.7%
Architecture and engineering occupations	1,534	.69%	1.8%	4.4%
Healthcare practitioners and technical occupations	3,241	1.46%	5.0%	6.6%
Protective service occupations	205	.09%	2.3%	2.6%
Food preparation and serving related occupations	329	.15%	8.3%	2.2%
Building and grounds cleaning and maintenance occupations	867	.39%	3.3%	1.2%
Personal care and service occupations	939	.42%	2.4%	4.2%
Sales and related occupations	22,678	10.18%	10.7%	2.7%
Office and administrative support occupations	151,791	68.15%	17.5%	6.9%
Construction and extraction occupations	253	.11%	4.9%	7.4%
Installation, maintenance, and repair occupations	9,565	4.29%	4.1%	6.4%
Production occupations	2,891	1.30%	7.9%	13.7%
Transportation and material moving occupations	9,766	4.38%	7.4%	6.2%
TOTAL	222,723	100.00%	84.4%	72.4%

Compared to the US workforce, some occupations were not represented in the HPI archival data and others were over- represented. In other words, the current HPI archival data set represents the HAS client base, and there are expected differences between the client base and representation of the total US workforce. To control for this inconsistency, yet maintain the best representation of both the US workforce and the HAS client base, we calculated the percent of the total US workforce accounted for by the occupations represented in the HPI archival data (i.e., 84.4%). Then, we used this adjustment to determine the number of cases needed from the HPI archival data set by occupation in the norm sample.

The "Office and Administrative Support Occupation" category showed the largest over-representation. As such, this category was used as the starting point for developing the normative sample. First, 46,163 respondents were randomly selected from this occupation. Second, this occupation was anchored to equal 30.41% of the normative sample. Third, the sample sizes for other occupational categories were determined based on their percentage within the US workforce and the available sample size within the Hogan archive. Finally, we added cases from occupational categories that did not reach the percentage of people in the US workforce. These steps made the resulting normative sample similar to the US workforce and reduced the norming selection sample from 222,723 to 117,095. The final sample by occupational designation appears in Table 6.2. To reflect the HAS client base and balance demographic characteristics (e.g., gender), an additional 10,725 selection cases with unknown occupational categories were added to the norming selection sample.

After populating categories to represent the selection client base, development client cases were added. Although development clients are generally are in upper-level management jobs and fall into the DoL code of "Management Occupations," they remained separate in the norm group, because the examinees' job status may account for some differences in scores and the examinees' motivation for taking the test also could also account for score differences.

Table 6.2

HPI Norming Sample Distribution by Occupation Using Applicants in Selection Contexts

Occupation	Number of cases	Percentage
Management occupations	12,097	10.33%
Business and financial operations occupations	6,567	5.61%
Architecture and engineering occupations	1,534	1.31%
Healthcare practitioners and technical occupations	3,241	2.77%
Protective service occupations	205	.18%
Food preparation and serving related occupations	329	.28%
Building and grounds cleaning and maintenance occupations	867	.74%
Personal care and service occupations	939	.80%
Sales and related occupations	22,678	19.37%
Office and administrative support occupations	46,163	30.41%
Construction and extraction occupations	253	.22%
Installation, maintenance, and repair occupations	9,565	8.17%
Production occupations	2,891	2.47%
Transportation and material moving occupations	9,766	8.34%
TOTAL	117,095	100.00%

To ensure that the correct proportion of development cases were included in the norming samples, we searched the Hogan data warehouse for users' HPI data. The ratio of selection to development examinees for the Hogan System is 9:1. To keep this ratio in our norming group, 15,463 development cases were combined with the selection database. The final distribution of selection and development cases is presented in Table 6.3. Adding the development cases to the selection sample described in Table 6.2 resulted in a total norming sample of approximately 10% development cases and 90% selection cases. To enhance the representation of the norming sample, 13,331 unclassified cases were added as shown in Tables 6.3 and 6.4.

Table 6.3
Final Norming Sample Distribution by Test Purpose

Test Purpose	Number of Cases	Percent of Final Sample
Selection	127,820	81.61%
Development	15,463	9.87%
Not indicated	13,331	8.51%
TOTAL	156,614	100.00%

Table 6.4
Final Norming Sample Distribution by Occupation

Occupation	Number of Cases	Percent of Final Sample
Management occupations	12,097	7.72%
Business and financial operations occupations	6,567	4.19%
Architecture and engineering occupations	1,534	0.98%
Healthcare practitioners and technical occupations	3,241	2.07%
Protective service occupations	205	0.13%
Food preparation and serving related occupations	329	0.21%
Building and grounds cleaning and maintenance occupations	867	0.55%
Personal care and service occupations	939	0.60%
Sales and related occupations	22,678	14.48%
Office and administrative support occupations	46,163	29.48%
Construction and extraction occupations	253	0.16%
Installation, maintenance, and repair occupations	9,565	6.11%
Production occupations	2,891	1.85%
Transportation and material moving occupations	9,766	6.24%
No occupation indicated	10,725	6.85%
Development	15,463	9.87%
Not indicated	13,331	8.51%
TOTAL	156,614	100.00%

6.2 Demographics of the Norming Sample

The final norming sample included 156,614 cases representing various occupational groups within the US workforce. Gender and race/ethnicity information within the US workforce also was used to create the final database (see Tables 6.5 and 6.6).

Table 6.5
Gender Distribution of Final Norming Sample

Gender	Number of Cases	Percent of Final Sample
Male	60,722	38.77%
Female	60,730	38.78%
Not indicated	35,162	22.45%

Table 6.6

Race/Ethnicity Distribution of Final Norming Sample

Race/Ethnicity	Number of Cases	Percent of Final Sample
Black	13,006	8.30%
Hispanic	15,034	9.60%
Asian American/Pacific Islander	5,067	3.24%
American Indian/Alaskan Native	2,208	1.41%
White	72,975	46.60%
Not indicated	48,324	30.86%

Table 6.7
Norming Sample Ethnic Composition by Age and Gender

| Age in Years | Under 40 | | | | 40 and Over | | | |
| Gender | Male | | Female | | Male | | Female | |
Ethnicity	N	%	N	%	N	%	N	%
Black	5,532	3.53	5,528	3.53	1,009	0.64	510	0.33
Hispanic	6,491	4.14	7,494	4.79	502	0.32	237	0.15
Asian American/Pacific Islander	2,462	1.57	2,055	1.31	250	0.16	122	0.08
American Indian/Alaskan Native	984	0.63	981	0.63	144	0.09	68	0.04
White	23,735	15.16	32,900	21.01	8,827	5.64	4,392	2.80
Not indicated	7,308	4.67	4,763	3.04	1,391	0.89	617	0.39
Totals	**46,512**	**29.70**	**53,721**	**34.30**	**12,123**	**7.74**	**5,946**	**3.80**

Note. 34,945 individuals aged less than 40 years old did not identify their gender; 158 individuals Aged 40 years and over did not identify their gender.

6.3 Descriptive Statistics of the Norming Sample

Tables 6.8 through 6.11 present means and standard deviations for the HPI scales categorized by selected demographics. All statistics are computed from the norming sample.

Table 6.8
Norming Sample Scale Means and Standard Deviations

Scales		Black	Hispanic	Asian/P.I.	American Indian/A.N.	White	Not Indicated	Totals
	N	13,006	15,034	5,067	2,208	72,975	48,324	**156,614**
ADJ	M	31.6	31.9	30.5	31.1	31.2	30.8	**31.2**
	SD	4.3	4.0	4.7	4.7	4.7	4.9	**4.7**
AMB	M	26.4	26.1	25.5	25.7	25.8	26.0	**25.9**
	SD	2.8	3.0	3.4	3.4	3.5	3.4	**3.4**
SOC	M	13.1	14.1	14.9	14.6	14.5	14.0	**14.2**
	SD	4.6	4.4	4.3	4.4	4.7	4.7	**4.7**
INP	M	20.4	20.6	20.3	20.5	20.6	20.1	**20.4**
	SD	1.5	1.4	1.7	1.6	1.6	1.9	**1.7**
PRU	M	24.2	24.3	23.6	23.8	23.2	22.7	**23.3**
	SD	3.6	3.6	3.8	3.8	3.9	4.0	**3.9**
INQ	M	16.1	17.2	17.7	17.9	16.5	16.4	**16.6**
	SD	4.4	4.5	4.3	4.3	4.5	4.5	**4.5**
LRN	M	10.7	10.9	10.8	10.9	10.2	9.8	**10.2**
	SD	2.9	2.8	2.8	2.7	3.0	3.1	**3.0**
Validity	M	13.7	13.6	13.5	13.6	13.7	13.7	**13.7**
	SD	0.6	0.7	0.8	0.8	0.6	0.7	**0.6**

Note. P.I. = Pacific Islander, A.N. = Alaskan Native.

Table 6.9
Norming Sample Scale Means and Standard Deviations by Age

Age – Under 40 Years		Black	Hispanic	Asian/P.I.	American Indian/A.N.	White	Not Indicated	Totals
	N	11,310	14,056	4,603	1,979	57,214	46,016	**135,178**
ADJ	M	31.7	31.9	30.6	31.2	31.4	30.8	**31.3**
	SD	4.2	4.0	4.6	4.6	4.6	4.9	**4.7**
AMB	M	26.5	26.1	25.6	25.7	25.9	26.0	**26.0**
	SD	2.7	2.9	3.4	3.3	3.5	3.4	**3.3**
SOC	M	13.3	14.1	15.0	14.8	14.8	14.1	**14.3**
	SD	4.6	4.4	4.3	4.3	4.6	4.7	**4.6**
INP	M	20.5	20.6	20.3	20.5	20.7	20.2	**20.5**
	SD	1.5	1.4	1.6	1.6	1.5	1.9	**1.6**
PRU	M	24.3	24.4	23.6	23.9	23.7	22.7	**23.4**
	SD	3.6	3.6	3.8	3.8	3.9	4.0	**3.9**
INQ	M	16.2	17.2	17.8	18.1	16.7	16.5	**16.7**
	SD	4.4	4.4	4.3	4.2	4.5	4.5	**4.5**
LRN	M	10.9	11.0	10.9	11.1	10.4	9.8	**10.3**
	SD	2.8	2.7	2.7	2.6	2.9	3.1	**2.9**
Validity	M	13.7	13.6	13.5	13.5	13.8	13.7	**13.7**
	SD	0.6	0.7	0.8	0.8	0.5	0.7	**0.6**

Note. P.I. = Pacific Islander, A.N. = Alaskan Native.

Table 6.9 (con't)

Age – 40 Years & Over		Black	Hispanic	Asian/P.I.	American Indian/A.N.	White	Not Indicated	Totals
	N	1,528	740	375	215	13,269	2,100	**18,227**
ADJ	M	31.0	30.8	29.4	30.2	30.3	29.7	**30.3**
	SD	4.4	4.6	5.2	5.3	5.3	5.4	**5.2**
AMB	M	25.9	25.5	24.8	25.1	25.5	25.3	**25.5**
	SD	2.9	3.2	3.5	4.0	3.7	3.8	**3.6**
SOC	M	11.7	12.9	13.1	12.8	13.0	12.5	**12.8**
	SD	4.6	4.6	4.7	4.9	4.9	4.8	**4.8**
INP	M	20.2	20.1	19.1	20.2	20.1	19.7	**20.0**
	SD	1.7	1.8	2.7	2.0	2.1	2.2	**2.1**
PRU	M	23.8	23.6	22.8	22.9	22.5	22.1	**22.6**
	SD	3.7	3.6	3.7	3.8	4.0	4.1	**4.0**
INQ	M	14.9	16.1	16.0	15.6	15.1	15.1	**15.2**
	SD	4.4	4.6	4.5	4.6	4.5	4.4	**4.5**
LRN	M	9.5	9.2	9.6	9.0	9.1	9.1	**9.2**
	SD	3.2	3.2	3.1	3.2	3.2	3.3	**3.2**
Validity	M	13.6	13.6	13.4	13.8	13.7	13.6	**13.7**
	SD	0.7	0.8	0.9	0.5	0.6	0.7	**0.6**

Note. P.I. = Pacific Islander, A.N. = Alaskan Native.

Table 6.10

Norming Sample Scale Means and Standard Deviations by Gender

MALES		Black	Hispanic	Asian/P.I.	American Indian/A.N.	White	Not Indicated	Totals
	N	6,641	7,156	2,763	1,134	34,230	8,798	**60,722**
ADJ	M	31.4	31.9	30.6	31.3	31.2	30.5	**31.2**
	SD	4.2	4.1	4.6	4.6	4.8	5.0	**4.7**
AMB	M	26.5	26.5	26.0	26.2	26.3	26.0	**26.3**
	SD	2.7	2.9	3.3	3.2	3.3	3.4	**3.2**
SOC	M	13.3	14.8	15.4	15.2	14.9	14.2	**14.6**
	SD	4.7	4.4	4.3	4.5	4.8	4.7	**4.7**
INP	M	20.2	20.4	20.1	20.4	20.2	19.8	**20.2**
	SD	1.6	1.5	1.8	1.7	1.8	2.1	**1.8**
PRU	M	24.0	23.9	23.3	23.5	22.7	22.2	**22.9**
	SD	3.7	3.8	3.9	0.4	4.0	4.2	**4.0**
INQ	M	16.6	18.1	18.4	18.6	17.2	16.8	**17.2**
	SD	4.4	4.3	4.2	4.1	4.4	4.3	**4.4**
LRN	M	10.2	10.6	10.7	10.7	9.6	9.5	**9.9**
	SD	3.0	2.9	2.9	2.9	3.1	3.1	**3.1**
Validity	M	13.6	13.6	13.4	13.6	13.7	13.6	**13.6**
	SD	0.7	0.7	0.8	0.7	0.6	0.7	**0.7**

Note. P.I. = Pacific Islander, A.N. = Alaskan Native.

Table 6.10 (con't)

FEMALES		Black	Hispanic	Asian/P.I.	American Indian/A.N.	White	Not Indicated	Totals
	N	6,104	7,806	2,215	1,056	38,115	5,534	**60,730**
ADJ	M	31.8	31.9	30.5	31.0	31.3	29.7	**31.3**
	SD	4.3	4.0	4.7	4.7	4.7	5.5	**4.7**
AMB	M	26.3	25.7	25.0	25.2	25.4	25.5	**25.5**
	SD	2.8	3.0	3.5	3.5	3.6	3.7	**3.5**
SOC	M	13.0	13.4	14.3	14.1	14.3	14.2	**14.0**
	SD	4.5	4.4	4.3	4.3	4.6	4.7	**4.6**
INP	M	20.6	20.7	20.4	20.6	20.9	20.3	**20.8**
	SD	1.4	1.3	1.6	1.5	1.3	1.8	**1.4**
PRU	M	24.5	24.7	23.9	24.2	23.7	22.5	**23.8**
	SD	3.5	3.5	3.6	3.6	3.7	3.9	**3.7**
INQ	M	15.5	16.3	16.9	17.1	15.8	15.5	**15.9**
	SD	4.3	4.5	4.3	4.4	4.6	4.7	**4.6**
LRN	M	11.3	11.2	11.0	11.1	10.7	10.1	**10.8**
	SD	2.6	2.6	2.6	2.6	2.7	2.9	**2.7**
Validity	M	13.7	13.6	13.5	13.5	13.8	13.7	**13.7**
	SD	0.6	0.6	0.8	0.8	0.5	0.6	**0.6**

Note. P.I. = Pacific Islander, A.N. = Alaskan Native.

Table 6.11

Norming Sample Scale Means and Standard Deviations by Age and Gender

MALES < 40 years		Black	Hispanic	Asian/P.I.	American Indian/A.N.	White	Not Indicated	Totals
	N	5,532	6,491	2,462	984	23,735	7,308	**46,512**
ADJ	M	31.5	31.9	30.7	31.5	31.4	30.6	**31.3**
	SD	4.2	4.0	4.6	4.6	4.7	5.0	**4.6**
AMB	M	26.6	26.5	26.0	26.3	26.4	26.1	**26.4**
	SD	2.7	2.9	3.2	3.1	3.2	3.3	**3.1**
SOC	M	13.6	14.9	15.6	15.5	15.3	14.4	**14.9**
	SD	4.6	4.3	4.2	4.3	4.6	4.6	**4.6**
INP	M	20.3	20.5	20.3	20.4	20.3	19.9	**20.3**
	SD	1.5	1.5	1.6	1.7	1.7	2.0	**1.7**
PRU	M	24.0	24.0	23.4	23.6	22.8	22.3	**23.1**
	SD	3.7	3.8	3.9	4.1	4.1	4.2	**4.0**
INQ	M	16.8	18.2	18.6	18.9	17.6	17.0	**17.6**
	SD	4.4	4.2	4.1	4.0	4.2	4.3	**4.3**
LRN	M	10.4	10.7	10.8	11.0	9.9	9.6	**10.1**
	SD	2.9	2.8	2.8	2.8	3.1	3.0	**3.0**
Validity	M	13.6	13.6	13.4	13.6	13.7	13.6	**13.6**
	SD	0.7	0.7	0.8	0.7	0.6	0.7	**0.7**

Note. P.I. = Pacific Islander, A.N. = Alaskan Native.

Table 6.11 (con't)

FEMALES < 40 years		Black	Hispanic	Asian/P.I.	American Indian/A.N.	White	Not Indicated	Totals
	N	5,528	7,494	2,055	981	32,900	4,763	**53,721**
ADJ	M	31.9	31.9	30.5	31.0	31.5	29.7	**31.4**
	SD	4.2	4.0	4.6	4.6	4.6	5.5	**4.6**
AMB	M	26.3	25.7	25.0	25.2	25.5	25.6	**25.6**
	SD	2.8	3.0	3.5	3.4	3.6	3.6	**3.4**
SOC	M	13.0	13.4	14.3	14.2	14.4	14.4	**14.1**
	SD	4.5	4.4	4.2	4.3	4.6	4.7	**4.5**
INP	M	20.6	20.7	20.5	20.6	21.0	20.3	**20.8**
	SD	1.3	1.3	1.5	1.4	1.2	1.8	**1.3**
PRU	M	24.6	24.7	24.0	24.3	23.9	22.5	**23.9**
	SD	3.5	3.5	3.6	3.6	3.6	3.9	**3.7**
INQ	M	15.6	16.4	17.0	17.3	16.0	15.6	**16.0**
	SD	4.3	4.4	4.3	4.3	4.6	4.7	**4.5**
LRN	M	11.4	11.2	11.1	11.2	10.8	10.2	**10.9**
	SD	2.6	2.6	2.6	2.5	2.7	2.9	**2.7**
Validity	M	13.7	13.6	13.5	13.5	13.8	13.7	**13.7**
	SD	0.6	0.6	0.8	0.8	0.5	0.6	**0.6**

Note. P.I. = Pacific Islander, A.N. = Alaskan Native.

Table 6.11 (con't)

MALES ≥ 40 years		Black	Hispanic	Asian/P.I.	American Indian/A.N.	White	Not Indicated	Totals
	N	1,090	502	250	144	8,827	1,391	**12,123**
ADJ	M	30.9	30.8	29.4	30.2	30.4	29.8	**30.3**
	SD	4.2	4.6	5.0	4.9	5.2	5.3	**5.1**
AMB	M	26.1	25.5	25.1	25.4	25.8	25.4	**25.7**
	SD	2.8	3.3	3.5	3.7	3.5	3.7	**3.5**
SOC	M	11.6	13.0	13.5	12.9	13.1	12.5	**12.9**
	SD	4.6	4.6	4.9	5.1	4.9	4.8	**4.8**
INP	M	20.0	19.9	18.8	20.0	19.8	19.5	**19.8**
	SD	1.7	1.9	2.9	2.0	2.2	2.3	**2.2**
PRU	M	23.8	23.4	22.7	22.7	22.4	22.0	**22.5**
	SD	3.7	3.6	3.7	3.8	4.0	4.2	**4.0**
INQ	M	15.2	16.4	16.2	15.9	15.6	15.4	**15.6**
	SD	4.4	4.5	4.4	4.5	4.4	4.3	**4.4**
LRN	M	9.2	9.1	9.3	8.8	8.9	8.8	**8.9**
	SD	3.2	3.2	3.2	3.2	3.3	3.4	**3.3**
Validity	M	13.6	13.5	13.4	13.8	13.7	13.5	**13.6**
	SD	0.7	0.8	0.9	0.5	0.6	0.8	**0.7**

Note. P.I. = Pacific Islander, A.N. = Alaskan Native.

Table 6.11 (con't)

FEMALES ≥ 40 years		Black	Hispanic	Asian/P.I.	American Indian/A.N.	White	Not Indicated	Totals
	N	510	237	122	68	4,392	617	**5,946**
ADJ	M	31.1	30.8	29.4	30.4	30.1	29.7	**30.1**
	SD	4.8	4.7	5.6	5.6	5.5	5.6	**5.4**
AMB	M	25.7	25.5	24.4	24.2	24.8	24.9	**24.9**
	SD	3.0	3.1	3.5	4.4	4.0	3.9	**3.9**
SOC	M	11.9	12.7	12.3	12.3	12.8	12.7	**12.7**
	SD	4.6	4.4	4.4	4.4	4.9	5.0	**4.8**
INP	M	20.5	20.5	19.7	20.7	20.6	20.2	**20.5**
	SD	1.5	1.5	2.2	1.9	1.7	2.0	**1.7**
PRU	M	23.7	24.1	23.1	23.5	22.8	22.3	**22.9**
	SD	3.7	3.5	3.7	3.7	3.8	3.9	**3.8**
INQ	M	14.2	15.4	15.7	14.8	14.2	14.5	**14.3**
	SD	4.3	4.6	4.7	4.9	4.6	4.6	**4.6**
LRN	M	10.1	9.5	10.3	9.5	9.7	9.6	**9.7**
	SD	3.0	3.2	2.6	3.1	3.0	3.1	**3.0**
Validity	M	13.7	13.7	13.4	13.8	13.8	13.7	**13.7**
	SD	0.7	0.7	0.9	0.4	0.5	0.6	**0.6**

Note. P.I. = Pacific Islander, A.N. = Alaskan Native.

References

Ackerman, P. L., & Heggestad, E. D. (1997). Intelligence, personality, and interests: Evidence for overlapping traits. *Psychological Bulletin, 121*, 219-245.

Adler, A. (1939). *Social interest*. New York: Putnam.

Adorno, T. W., Frenkl-Brunswik, E. Levinson, D.J., & Sanford, N. (1950). *The authoritarian personality*. New York: Harper & Row.

Aguinis, H., & Pierce, C. A. (1998). Testing moderator variable hypotheses meta-analytically. *Journal of Management, 24*, 577–592.

Allport, G. (1961). *Patterns and growth in personality*. New York: Wiley.

American Educational Research Association, American Psychological Association, & National Council on Measurement in Education (1999). *Standards for educational and psychological testing*. Washington, DC: American Educational Research Association.

Axford, S. N. (1996). Review of the Hogan Personality Inventory (Revised). In J. C. Impara & J. C. Conoley (Eds.), *The supplement to the twelfth Mental Measurements Yearbook*. Lincoln: The University of Nebraska Press.

Bakan, D. (1966). *The duality of human existence: Isolation and communion in Western man*. Boston: Beacon.

Balma, M. J. (1959). The development of processes for indirect or synthetic validity. *Personnel Psychology, 12*, 395-396.

Bandura, A. (1977). *Social learning theory*, 2nd ed. Englewood Cliffs, NJ: Prentice-Hall.

Barrett, P. T. (2003). Beyond psychometrics: Measurement, non-quantitative structure, and applied numerics. *Journal of Managerial Psychology, 18*, 421-439.

Barrett, P. T. (2005). Person-target profiling. In A. Beauducel, B. Biehl, M. Bosnjak, W. Conrad, G. Schönberger, & D. Wagener (Eds.), *Multivariate research strategies: A festschrift for Werner Wittman* (pp. 63-118). Aachen: Shaker-Verlag.

Barrick, M. R., & Mount, M. K. (1991). The Big Five personality dimensions and job performance: A meta-analysis. *Personnel Psychology, 44*, 1-26.

Barrick, M. R., Mount, M. K., & Strauss, J. P. (1993). Conscientiousness and performance of sales representatives: Test of mediating effects of goal setting. *Journal of Applied Psychology, 78*, 715-722.

Barron, F. (1965). The psychology of creativity. In T. M. Newcomb (Ed.), *New Directions in Psychology* (Vol. II. pp. 1-134). New York: Holt, Reinhart, & Winston.

Bass, B. M. (1990). *Bass & Stogdill's Handbook of Leadership: Theory, research, and managerial applications.* New York: Free Press.

Bennett, G. K. (1992). *Bennett Mechanical Comprehension Test manual.* San Antonio, TX: Harcourt Assessments.

Bentler, P. M., & Wu, E. J. C. (2005). *EQS 6 for Windows user's guide.* Encino, CA: Multivariate Software, Inc.

Block, J. (1961). *The Q-sort method in personality assessment and psychiatric research.* Oxford: Charles C. Thomas.

Borman, W. C., & Motowidlo, S. J. (1993). Expanding the criterion domain to include elements of contextual performance. In N. Schmitt, W. C. Borman, & Associates (Eds.), *Personnel selection in organizations* (pp. 71-98). San Francisco, CA: Jossey-Bass.

Brand, C. R. (1994). Open to experience—closed to intelligence: Why the "Big Five" are really the "Comprehensive Six." *European Journal of Personality, 8*, 299-310.

Brannick, M. T., & Levine, E. L. (2002). Doing a job analysis study. In M.T. Brannick & E.L. Levine (Eds.), *Job analysis: Methods, research, and applications for human resource management in the new millennium* (pp. 265-294). Thousand Oaks, CA: Sage.

Campbell, J. P. (1990). Modeling the performance prediction problem in industrial and organizational psychology. In M. D. Dunnette & L. M. Hough (Eds.), *Handbook of industrial and organizational psychology* (Vol. 1, 2nd ed., pp. 39-74). Palo Alto, CA: Consulting Psychologists Press.

Campbell, J. P., McCloy, R. A., Oppler, S. H., & Sager, C. E. (1993). A theory of performance. In N. Schmitt, W. C. Borman, & Associates (Eds.), *Personnel selection in organizations* (pp. 35-70). San Francisco, CA: Jossey-Bass.

Campbell, J. P., McHenry, J. J., & Wise, L. L. (1990). Modeling job performance in a population of jobs. *Personnel Psychology, 43*, 313-333.

Carson, R. C. (1969). *Interaction concepts of personality.* Chicago: Aldine.

Cattell, R. B., Eber, H. W., & Tatsuoka, N. M. (1970). *Handbook for the 16 Personality Factor Questionnaire* (16PF). Champaign, IL: Institute for Personality and Ability Testing.

Cattell, R. B. (1966). The scree test for number of factors. *Multivariate Behavioral Research, 1*, 245-276.

Chamorro-Premuzic, T., & Furnham, A. (2005). *Personality and intellectual competence.* Mahwah, NJ: Lawrence Erlbaum Associates.

Comrey, A. L. (1995). *Handbook and manual for the interpretation of the Comrey Personality Scales.* San Diego, CA: EdITS Publishers.

Conn, S. R., & Rieke, M. L. (1994). *The 16PF fifth edition technical manual.* Champaign, IL: Institute for Personality and Ability Testing.

Conway, J. M. (1999). Distinguishing contextual performance from task performance for managerial jobs. *Journal of Applied Psychology, 84*, 3-13.

Costa, P. T., Jr., & McCrae, R. R. (1985). *The NEO Personality Inventory manual.* Odessa, FL: Psychological Assessment Resources.

Costa, P. T. Jr., & McCrae, R. R. (1992). *Revised NEO Personality Inventory (NEO-PI-R) and NEO Five-Factor Inventory (NEO-FFI): Professional manual.* Odessa, FL: Psychological Assessment Resources.

Cronbach, L. J. (1951). Coefficient alpha and the internal structure of tests. *Psychometrika, 16*, 297-334.

Cronbach, L. J., & Meehl, P. E. (1955). Construct validity in psychological tests. *Psychological Bulletin, 52*, 281-302.

Cronbach, L. J. (1984). *Essentials of Psychological Testing (4th ed.).* New York: Harper & Row, Publishers.

De Raad, B., & Perugini, M. (Eds.). (2002). *Big Five assessment.* Seattle, WA: Hogrefe & Huber.

Digman, J. M. (1990). Personality structure: Emergence of the Five Factor model. *Annual Review of Psychology, 41*, 417-440.

Digman, J. M. (1997). Higher-order factors of the big five. *Journal of Personality and Social Psychology, 73*, 1246-1256.

Dudek, F. J. (1979). The continuing misinterpretation of the standard error of measurement. *Psychological Bulletin, 86*, 335-337.

Dye, D., & Silver, M. (1999). The origins of O*NET. In N. G. Peterson, M. D. Mumford, W. C. Borman, P. R. Jeanneret, & E. A. Fleishman (Eds.), *An occupation information system for the 21st century: The development of the O*NET* (pp. 9-20). Washington, DC: American Psychological Association.

Ellingson, J. E., Sackett, P. R., & Connelly, B. S. (2007). Personality assessment across selection and development contexts: Insights into response distortion. *Journal of Applied Psychology, 92*, 386-395.

Ellingson, J. E., Sackett, P. R., & Hough, L. M. (1999). Social desirability corrections in personality measurement: Issues of applicant comparison and construct validity. *Journal of Applied Psychology, 84*, 155-166.

Equal Employment Opportunity Commission, Civil Service Commission, Department of Labor, & Department of Justice. (1978). *Uniform guidelines on employee selection procedures.* Federal Register, 43, 38290-38315.

Eysenck, H. J., & Eysenck, S. B.G. (1976). *Manual for the Eysenck Personality Questionnaire.* San Diego, CA: EdITS.

Fiedler, F. E. (1967). *A theory of leadership effectiveness.* New York: McGraw-Hill.

Flanagan, J. C. (1954). The critical incident technique. *Psychological Bulletin, 51*, 327-358.

Fleishman, E. A. (1953). The measurement of leadership attitudes in industry. *Journal of Applied Psychology*, 37, 153-158.

Foa, E. B., & Foa, U. G. (1980). Resource theory. In K. J. Gergen, M. S. Greenberg, & R. H. Willis (Eds.), *Social Exchange: Advances in theory and research* (pp. 77-94). New York: Plenum Press.

Foa, U. G., & Foa, E. B. (1974). *Societal structures of the mind.* Springfield, IL: Thomas.

Gatewood, R. D., & Feild, H. S. (1994). *Human resource selection* (3rd ed.). Orlando, FL: Dryden Press.

Ghiselli, E. E., Campbell, J. P., & Zedeck, S. (1981). *Measurement theory for the behavioral sciences.* San Francisco, CA: W. H. Freeman and Company.

Goldberg, L. R. (1981). Language and individual differences: The search for universals in personality lexicons. In L. W. Wheeler (Ed.), *Review of personality and social psychology* (Vol. 2, pp. 141-165). Beverly Hills, CA: Sage.

Goldberg, L. R. (1992). The development of markers for the Big Five factor structure. *Psychological Assessment, 4,* 26-42.

Goldberg, L. R. (2000). [Hogan Personality Inventory and the NEO-PR-I correlation coefficients]. Unpublished data based on the International Personality Item Pool Project.

Goldberg, L. R. (2005). *Eugene-Springfield community sample: Information available from the research participants* (Tech. Rep., Vol. 45 No. 1). Eugene, OR: Oregon Research Institute.

Goldstein, I. L., Zedeck, S., & Schneider, B. (1993). An exploration of the job analysis-content validity process. In N. Schmitt, W. Borman, & Associates (Eds.), *Personnel selection in organizations* (pp. 3-34). San Francisco: Jossey-Bass.

Gottfredson, G. D., & Holland, J. L. (1996). *Dictionary of Holland occupational codes* (3rd ed.). Odessa FL: Psychological Assessment Resources.

Gottfredson, G. D., & Holland, J. L. (1989). *Dictionary of Holland occupational codes* (2nd ed.). Odessa Fl: Psychological Assessment Resources.

Gough, H. G. (1975). *Manual for the California Psychological Inventory.* Palo Alto, CA: Consulting Psychologists Press.

Gough, H. G. (1996). *CPI manual.* Palo Alto, CA: Consulting Psychologists Press.

Gough, H. G., & Heilbrun, A. B., Jr. (1983). *The Adjective Checklist Manual: 1983 Edition.* Palo Alto, CA: Consulting Psychologists Press.

Grice, J. (2001a). A comparison of factor scores under conditions of factor obliquity. *Psychological Methods, 6,* 67-83.

Grice, J. (2001b). Computing and evaluating factor scores. *Psychological Methods, 6,* 430-450.

Grice, J., & Harris, R. (1998). A comparison of regression and loading weights for the computation of factor scores. *Multivariate Behavioral Research, 33,* 221-247.

Guilford, J. S., Zimmerman, W. S., & Guilford, J P. (1976). *The Guilford-Zimmerman Temperament Survey handbook.* San Diego, CA: Educational and Industrial Testing Service.

Guion, R. M. (1965). Synthetic validity in a small company: A demonstration. *Personnel Psychology, 18,* 40-63.

Hase, H. D., & Goldberg, L. R. (1967). Comparative validities of different strategies of constructing personality inventory scales. *Psychological Bulletin, 67,* 231-248.

Hathaway, S. R., & McKinley, J. C. (1943). *Manual for the Minnesota Multiphasic Personality Inventory.* New York: Psychological Corporation.

Hembree, R. (1988). Correlates, cause, effects, and treatment of test anxiety. *Review of Educational Research, 58,* 47-77.

Hoffman, C. C., Holden, L. M, & Gale, E. (2000). So many jobs, so little "n": Applying expanded validation models to support generalization of cognitive ability. *Personnel Psychology, 53,* 955–991.

Hogan, J., Barrett, P., & Hogan, R. (2007). Personality measurement, faking, and employment selection. *Journal of Applied Psychology.*

Hogan, J., Davies, S., & Hogan, R. (2007). Generalizing personality-based validity evidence. In M. S. McPhail (Ed.), *Alternative validation strategies: Developing new and leveraging existing validity evidence* (pp. 181-229). San Francisco, CA: Jossey-Bass.

Hogan, J., & Hogan, R. (1991). *Levels of analysis in big five theory: The structure of self-description.* Paper presented at the Sixth Annual Conference of the Society for Industrial and Organizational Psychology. St. Louis, MO.

Hogan, J., & Hogan, R. (1996). *Motives, Values, Preferences Inventory manual.* Tulsa, OK: Hogan Assessment Systems.

Hogan, J., & Hogan, R. (1998). Theoretical frameworks for assessment. In P. R. Jeanneret & R. Silzer (Eds.), *Individual psychological assessment* (pp. 27-53). San Francisco, CA: Jossey-Bass.

Hogan, J., & Holland, B. (2003). Using theory to evaluate personality and job-performance relations: A socioanalytic perspective. *Journal of Applied Psychology, 88,* 100-112.

Hogan, J., & Lesser, M. (1996). Selecting personnel for hazardous performance. In J. Driskell & E. Salas (Eds.), *Stress and human performance* (pp. 195-222). Mahwah, NJ: Erlbaum.

Hogan, J., & Rybicki, S. (1997). *Validity of correctional officer selection procedures* (Tech. Rep. No. 119). Tulsa, OK: Hogan Assessment Systems.

Hogan, J., & Rybicki, S. (1998). *Performance Improvement Characteristics job analysis manual.* Tulsa, OK: Hogan Assessment Systems.

Hogan, R. (1983). A socioanalytic theory of personality. In M. M. Page (Ed.), *1982 Nebraska symposium on motivation* (pp. 55-89). Lincoln: University of Nebraska Press.

Hogan, R. (1991). Personality and personality measurement. In M. D. Dunnette & L. M. Hough (Eds.), *Handbook of industrial and organizational psychology* (Vol. 2, 2nd ed., pp. 327-396). Palo Alto, CA: Consulting Psychologists Press.

Hogan, R. (1996). A socioanalytic perspective on the five-factor model. In J. S. Wiggins (Ed.), *The five-factor model of personality* (pp.163-179). New York: Guilford.

Hogan, R., Barrett, P., & Hogan, J. (2007). I. *Hogan Business Reasoning Inventory Technical manual*. Tulsa, OK: Hogan Assessment Systems.

Hogan, R., & Hogan, J. (1995). *Hogan Personality Inventory manual* (2nd ed.). Tulsa, OK: Hogan Assessment Systems.

Hogan, R., & Hogan, J. (1997). *Hogan Development Survey manual*. Tulsa, OK: Hogan Assessment Systems.

Hogan, R., Hogan, J., & Warrenfeltz, R. (2007). *Hogan Assessment inventories: A guide to understanding and interpreting the Hogan Personality Inventory, Motives, Values, Preferences Inventory, and Hogan Development Survey*. Tulsa, OK: Hogan Assessment Systems.

Hogan, R., Jones, W., & Cheek, J. M. (1985). Socioanalytic theory: An alternative to armidillo psychology. In B. R. Schlenker (Ed.), *The self and social life* (pp.175-198). New York: McGraw-Hill.

Hogan, R., & Nicholson, R. (1988). *The meaning of personality test scores. American Psychologist, 43*, 621-626.

Hogan, R., & Shelton, D. (1998). A socioanalytic perspective on job performance. *Human Performance, 11*, 129-144.

Hogan, R., & Warrenfeltz, R. (2003). Educating the modern manager. *Academy of Management Learning and Education, 2*, 74-84.

Holland, J. L. (1985a). *Making vocational choices: A theory of careers*. Englewood Cliffs, NJ: Prentice-Hall.

Holland, J. L. (1985b). *The Self-Directed Search: Professional manual*. Odessa, FL: Psychological Assessment Resources, Inc.

Hough, L. M. (1992). The "Big-Five" personality variables—construct confusion: Description versus prediction. *Human Performance, 5*, 139-156.

Hough, L. M., Eaton, N. K., Dunnette, M. D., Kamp, J. D., & McCloy, R. A. (1990). Criterion-related validities of personality constructs and the effect of response distortion on those validities. *Journal of Applied Psychology, 75*, 581-595.

Hunt, S. T. (1996). Generic work behavior: An investigation into the dimensions of entry-level, hourly job performance. *Personnel Psychology, 49*, 51-83.

Hunter, J. E., & Schmidt, F. L. (1990). *Methods of meta-analysis.* Newbury Park, CA: Sage.

Hunter, J. E., Schmidt, F. L., & Judiesch, M. K. (1990). Individual differences in output variability as a function of job complexity. *Journal of Applied Psychology, 75*, 28-42.

Hurtz, G. M., & Donovan, J. J. (2000). Personality and job performance: The big five revisited. *Journal of Applied Psychology, 85*, 869-879.

Jackson, D. J. (1994). *Jackson Personality Inventory-Revised manual.* Port Huron, MI: Sigma Assessment Systems.

Jeanneret, P. R., & Strong, M. H. (2003). Linking O*Net job analysis information to job requirement predictors: An O*Net application. *Personnel Psychology, 56*, 465-492.

Jennrich, R., & Sampson, P. (1966). Rotation for simple loadings. *Psychometrika, 31*, 313-333.

John, O. P. (1990). The "Big-Five" factor taxonomy: Dimensions of personality in the natural language and in questionnaires. In L. A. Pervin (Ed.), *Handbook of personality theory and research* (pp. 66-100). New York: Guilford.

Johnson, J. A. (1981). The "self-disclosure" and "self-presentation" views of item response dynamics and personality scale validity. *Journal of Personality and Social Psychology, 40*, 761-769.

Johnson, J. W., Carter, G. W., Davison, H. K., & Oliver, D. H. (2001). A synthetic validity approach to testing differential prediction hypotheses. *Journal of Applied Psychology, 86*, 774-780.

Johnson, J. W., Carter, G. W., & Tippins, N. T. (2001, April). *A synthetic validity approach to the development of a selection system for multiple job families.* Paper presented at the 16th Annual Conference of the Society for Industrial and Organizational Psychology, San Diego, CA.

Jung, C. G. (1923). *Psychological types.* New York: Harcourt, Brace, Jovanovich.

Kessler, R. C., Berglund, P., Demler, O., Jin, R., Merikangas, K. R., & Walters, E. E. (2005). Lifetime prevalence and age-of-onset distributions of DSM-IV disorders in the national comorbidity survey replication. *Arch Gen Psychiatry, 62*, 593-602.

Lawshe, C. H. (1952). What can industrial psychology do for small business? (A symposium). *Personnel Psychology, 5,* 31-34.

Leary, T. (1957). *Interpersonal diagnosis of personality.* New York: Ronald Press.

Lobello, S. G. (1996). Review of the Hogan Personality Inventory (Revised). In J. C. Impara & J. C. Conoley (Eds.), *The supplement to the twelfth Mental Measurements Yearbook.* Lincoln: The University of Nebraska Press.

Loevinger, J. (1957). Objective tests as instruments of psychological theory. *Psychological Reports, 3* (Suppl. 9), 635-694.

Mardia, K. V. (1970). Measures of multivariate skewness and kurtosis with applications. *Biometrika, 57,* 519-530.

Mardia, K. V. (1974). Applications of some measures of multivariate skewness and kurtosis in testing normality and robustness studies. *Sankhya B, 36,* 115-128.

Matthews, G., Deary, I., & Whiteman, M. (2003). *Personality traits.* New York: Cambridge University Press.

McAdams, D. P. (1985). *Power, intimacy, and the life story: Psychological inquiries into identity.* Homewood, IL: Dow-Jones-Irwin.

McClelland, D. C. (1985). *Human motivation.* Glenville, IL: Scott-Foresman.

McCloy, R. A. (1994). Predicting job performance scores without performance data. In B. F. Green, & A. S. Mavor (Eds.), *Modeling cost and performance for military enlistment: Report of a workshop.* Washington, DC: National Academy Press.

McCloy, R. A. (2001, April). *Predicting job performance scores in jobs lacking criterion data.* Paper presented at the sixteenth annual conference of the Society for Industrial and Organizational Psychology, San Diego, CA.

McCormick, E. J., DeNisi, A. S., & Shaw, J. B. (1979). Use of the Position Analysis Questionnaire for establishing the job component validity of tests. *Journal of Applied Psychology, 64,* 51-56.

McCrae, R. R., & Costa, P. T., Jr. (1987). Validity of the five-factor model of personality across instruments and observers. *Journal of Personality and Social Psychology, 52,* 81-90.

McDougal, W. (1908). *Social psychology.* London: Methuen.

Michell, J. (1997). Quantitative science and the definition of measurement in psychology. *British Journal of Psychology, 88,* 355-383.

Mills, C. J., & Hogan, R. (1978). A role-theoretical interpretation of personality scale item responses. *Journal of Personality, 46,* 778-785.

Millsap, R. (1997). Invariance in measurement and prediction: their relationship in the single factor case. *Psychological Methods, 2,* 248-260.

Mossholder, K. W., & Arvey, R. D. (1984). Synthetic validity: A conceptual and comparative review. *Journal of Applied Psychology, 69,* 322-333.

Moon, H. (2001). The two faces of conscientiousness: Duty and achievement-striving within evaluation of commitment dilemmas. *Journal of Applied Psychology, 86,* 533-540.

Motowidlo, S. J., Borman, W. C., & Schmit, M. J. (1997). A theory of individual differences in task and contextual performance. *Human Performance, 10,* 71-83.

Mount, M. K., & Barrick, M. R. (1995). The big five personality dimensions: Implications for research and practice in human resources management. In G. R. Ferris (Ed.), *Research in Personnel and Human Resources Management* (Vol. 13, pp. 153-200). Greenwich, CT: JAI Press.

Mount, M. K., & Barrick, M. R. (2001). *Personal Characteristics Inventory manual.* Libertyville, IL: Wonderlic, Inc.

Mount, M. K., Barrick, M. R., & Stewart, G. L. (1998). Five-factor model of personality and performance in jobs involving interpersonal interactions. *Human Performance, 11,* 145-165.

Murphy, K. R., & DeShon, R. (2000). Interrater correlations do not estimate the reliability of job performance ratings. *Personnel Psychology, 53,* 873-900.

Myers, E. B., & McCaulley, M. H. (1985). *Manual: A guide to the development and use of the Myers-Briggs Type Indicator.* Palo Alto, CA: Consulting Psychologists Press, Inc.

Norman, W. T. (1963). Toward an adequate taxonomy of personality attributes: Replicated factor structure in peer nomination personality ratings. *Journal of Abnormal and Social Psychology, 66,* 574-583.

Nunnally, J. C. (1967). *Psychometric theory.* New York: McGraw-Hill.

Nunnally, J.C. (1978). *Psychometric theory* (2nd ed.). New York: McGraw-Hill.

Nunnally, J. C., & Bernstein, I. H. (1994). *Psychometric theory* (3rd ed.). New York: McGraw-Hill.

Ones, D. S., Schmidt, F. L., & Viswesvaran, C. (1994, April). *Examination of construct validity with linear composites and generalizability coefficient corrected correlations.* Paper presented at the ninth annual conference of the Society for Industrial and Organizational Psychology, Nashville, TN.

Ones, D. S., Viswesvaran, C., & Schmidt, F. L. (1993). Comprehensive meta-analysis of integrity test validation: Findings and implications for personnel selection and theories of job performance. *Journal of Applied Psychology, 78,* 679-703.

O*NET OnLine. (2005). *O*NET OnLine – Browse by Job Family.* O*NET 7.0 Database. Retrieved September 22, 2005 from http://online.onetcenter.org/find.

Pearlman, K. (1985). *Validity generalization: From theory to application.* Paper presented at the Center for Human Resources Programs, Institute of Industrial Relations, University of California-Berkeley.

Peterson, N. G., Wise, L. I., Arabian, J., & Hoffman, R. G. (2001). Synthetic validation and validity generalization: When empirical validation is not possible. In J. P. Campbell & D. J. Knapp (Eds.), *Exploring the limits in personnel selection and classification* (pp. 411-451). Mahwah, NJ: Erlbaum.

Primoff, E. S. (1959) Empirical validation of the J-coefficient. *Personnel Psychology, 12,* 413-418.

Rank, O. (1945). *Will therapy and truth and reality.* New York: Knopf.

Raymark, P. H., Schmit, M. J., & Guion, R. M. (1997). Identifying potentially useful personality constructs for employee selection. *Personnel Psychology. 50,* 723-736.

Renaud, H., & Estes, F. (1961). Life history interviews with one hundred normal American males: Pathogenicity of childhood. *American Journal of Orthopyschiatry, 31,* 786-802.

Rosenthal, R., & DiMatteo, M. R. (2001). Meta analysis: Recent developments in quantitative methods for literature reviews. *Annual Review of Psychology, 52,* 59-82.

Rothstein, H. R. (1990). Interrater reliability of job performance ratings: Growth to asymptote level with increasing opportunity to observe. *Journal of Applied Psychology, 75,* 322–327.

Rothstein, M. G., & Goffin, R. D. (2006). The use of personality measures in personnel selection: What does current research support? *Human Resource Management Review, 16,* 155-180.

Rotter, J. (1966). Generalized expectancies for internal vs. external control of reinforcement. *Psychological Monographs. 80* (Whole No. 609).

Ruch, W. W., Weiner, J. A., McKillip, R. H., & Dye, D. A. (1985). *Technical manual for the PSI Basic Skills Test for business, industry, and government.* Glendale, CA: Psychological Services.

Salgado, J. F. (1997). The five factor model of personality and job performance in the European community. *Journal of Applied Psychology, 82*, 36-43.

Salgado, J. F., & Moscoso, S. (1999, May). *Construct validity of two personality inventories based upon the five-factor model (FFM).* Paper presented at the fourteenth annual conference of the Society for Industrial-Organizational Psychology, Inc., Atlanta, GA.

Satorra, A., & Bentler, P. M. (1994). Corrections to test statistics and standard errors in covariance structure analysis. In A. von Eye & C. C. Clogg (Eds.). *Latent Variables Analysis: Applications for Developmental Research* (pp. 399-419). London: Sage.

Satorra, A., & Bentler, P. M. (2002). A scaled difference chi-square test statistic for moment structure analysis. *Psychomctrika, 66*, 507-514.

Saucier, G., & Goldberg, L. R. (1996). The language of personality: Lexical perspectives on the Five-Factor Model. In J. S. Wiggins (Ed.), *The Five-Factor Model of personality* (pp. 21-50). New York: Guilford.

Scherbaum, C. A. (2005). Synthetic validity: Past, present, and future. *Personnel Psychology, 58*, 481-515.

Schmidt, F. L., & Hunter, J. E. (1977). Development of a general solution to the problem of validity generalization. *Journal of Applied Psychology, 62*, 529-54.

Segall, D. O., & Monzon, R. I. (1995). *Equating Forms E and F of the P & &-GATB* (Tech. Report). San Diego, CA: Navy Personnel Research and Development Center.

SHI Group. (2006). *OPQ32: Manual and user's guide.* Thames Ditton, United Kingdom: Author.

Shrout, P. E., & Fleiss, J. L. (1979) Intraclass correlations: Uses in assessing rater reliability. *Psychological Bullctin, 86*, 420-428.

Snyder, M., & Gangestad, S. (1986). On the nature of self-monitoring: Matters of assessment, matters of validity. *Journal of Personality and Social Psychology, 51*, 125-129.

Society for Industrial and Organizational Psychology (2003). *Principles for the validation and use of personnel selection procedures* (4th ed.). Bowling Green, OH: Author.

Stemler, S. E. (2004). A comparison of consensus, consistency, and measurement approaches to estimating interrater reliability. *Practical Assessment, Research & Evaluation, 9*. Retrieved March 18, 2007 from http://pareonline.net/getvn.asp?v=9&n=4.

Sullivan, H. S. (1953). *The interpersonal theory of psychiatry.* New York: Norton.

Tellegen, A. (in press). *MPQ (Multidimensional Personality Questionnaire: Manual for administration, scoring, and interpretation.* Minneapolis, MN: University of Minnesota Press.

Tellegen, A. (1985). Structures of mood and personality and their relevance to assessing Anxiety, with emphasis on self-reports. In A. H. Tuma & D. J. Masser (Eds.), *Anxiety and anxiety disorders* (pp. 681-706). Hillsdale, NJ: Erlbaum.

Tett, R. P., Guterman, H. A., Bleier, A., & Murphy, P. J. (2000). Development and content validation of a "hyperdimensional" taxonomy of managerial competence. *Human Performance, 13,* 205-251.

Tett, R. P., Jackson, D. N., & Rothstein, M. (1991). Personality measures as predictors of job performance: A meta-analytic review. *Personnel Psychology, 44,* 703-742.

Thurstone, L. L. (1934). The vectors of mind. *Psychological Review, 41,* 1-32.

Thurstone, L.L. (1935). *The vectors of the mind.* Chicago: University of Chicago Press.

Tupes, E. C., & Christal, R. E. (1961). *Recurrent personality factors based on trait ratings* (Tech. Rep. No. ASD-TR-61-97). Lackland Air Force Base, TX: Aeronautical Systems Division, Personnel Laboratory.

US Department of Defense. (1984). *Manual for the Armed Services Vocational Aptitude Battery.* North Chicago, IL: U. S. Military Entrance Processing Command.

US Department of Labor, Bureau of Labor Statistics (2006, May 24). *News.* Washington, DC: Author

US Department of Labor (2001). *Standard Occupational Classification.* Retrieved September 22, 2005 from http://stats.bls.gov/soc/soc_majo.htm.

US Department of Labor (1991). *Dictionary of occupational titles.* Washington, DC: US Government Printing Office.

US Department of Labor (1970). *Manual for the USES General Aptitude Test Battery, Section III: Development.* Washington, DC: US Department of Labor.

Vinchur, A., Schippmann, J., & Switzer, F. (1998). A meta-analytic review of predictors of job performance for salespeople. *Journal of Applied Psychology, 83,* 586-597.

Warrenfeltz, R. B. (1995, May). *An executive-level validation of the Borman and Brush taxonomy.* Paper presented at the tenth annual conference of the Society for Industrial and Organizational Psychology, Orlando, FL.

Watson, D., Hubbard, B., & Wiese, D. (2000). Self-other agreement in personality and affectivity: The role of acquaintanceship, trait visibility, and assumed similarity. *Journal of Personality and Social Psychology, 78,* 546-558.

Watson, G., & Glaser, E. M. (2002). *Watson-Glaser Critical Thinking Appraisal manual.* San Antonio, TX; Harcourt Assessments.

Wiggins, J. S. (1979). A psychological taxonomy of trait-descriptive terms: The interpersonal domain. *Journal of Personality and Social Psychology, 37,* 395-412.

Wiggins, J. S. (1991). *Manual for the Interpersonal Adjective Scales.* Odessa, FL: Psychological Assessment Resources.

Wiggins, J. S., & Trapnell, P. D. (1996). A dyadic-interactional perspective on the Five-Factor model. In J. S. Wiggins (Ed.), *The Five-Factor model of personality* (pp. 88-162). New York: Guilford.

Zonderman, A. B. (1980). *Inventory construction by the method of homogenous item composites.* Unpublished manuscript, The Johns Hopkins University, Baltimore, MD.

Appendix A: 2005 HPI Norming Sample Scale Scores

Table A.1

Norms for the Total Sample (N = 156,614)

Scores	HPI Scales						
	ADJ	AMB	SOC	INP	PRU	INQ	LRN
Raw	Norms	Norms	Norms	Norms	Norms	Norms	Norms
0	0	0	0	0	0	0	0
1	0	0	0	0	0	0	1
2	0	0	1	0	0	0	1
3	0	0	1	0	0	0	3
4	0	0	2	0	0	1	5
5	0	0	4	0	0	1	8
6	0	0	6	0	0	2	13
7	0	0	9	0	0	3	19
8	0	0	13	0	0	5	26
9	0	0	17	0	0	7	36
10	0	0	22	0	0	11	47
11	0	0	28	0	0	15	60
12	0	0	34	0	1	19	73
13	0	1	42	1	1	25	86
14	1	1	49	1	2	31	100
15	1	1	58	2	4	39	
16	1	2	66	3	5	47	
17	2	3	73	6	8	55	
18	2	4	80	10	12	63	
19	3	6	86	20	17	71	
20	4	8	91	40	23	79	
21	5	11	95	73	30	86	
22	6	14	98	100	39	91	
23	8	19	100		49	96	
24	10	25	100		59	98	
25	12	33			69	100	
26	15	44			78		
27	19	57			86		
28	23	76			93		
29	28	100			97		
30	35				99		
31	43				100		
32	51						
33	62						
34	73						
35	85						
36	95						
37	100						

Note. ADJ = Adjustment, AMB = Ambition, SOC = Sociability, INP = Interpersonal Sensitivity, PRU = Prudence, INQ = Inquisitive, LRN = Learning Approach.

Table A.2
Stratified Norms of Validity Scale

Validity	Gender		Race/EthnicityAge					Age	
Score	M	F	B	H	A/P.I.	A./A.N.	W	< 40	≥40
0	.0	.0	.0	.0	.0	.0	.0	.0	.0
1	.0	.0	.0	.0	.0	.0	.0	.0	.0
2	.0	.0	.0	.0	.0	.0	.0	.0	.0
3	.0	.0	.0	.0	.0	.0	.0	.0	.0
4	.0	.0	.0	.0	.0	.0	.0	.0	.0
5	.0	.0	.0	.0	.0	.0	.0	.0	.0
6	.0	.0	.0	.0	.0	.0	.0	.0	.0
7	.0	.0	.0	.0	.0	.0	.0	.0	.0
8	.0	.0	.0	.0	.0	.0	.0	.0	.0
9	.0	.0	.0	.0	.0	.0	.0	.0	.0
10	.4	.2	.4	.4	.6	.8	.2	.4	.4
11	1.6	.8	1.4	1.9	3.1	2.9	.7	1.3	1.5
12	6.3	4.0	5.6	7.1	11.9	9.0	3.6	5.4	5.9
13	27.9	20.8	26.1	30.5	38.0	30.2	20.7	26.0	24.2
14	100.0	100.0	100.0	100.0	100.0	100.0	100.0	100.0	100.0

Note. M = Male, F = Female, B = Black, H = Hispanic, A./P.I. = Asian American/Pacific Islander, A./A.N. = AmericanIndian/Alaskan Native, W = White, <40 = Less Than 40 Years, > 40 = Greater Than or Equal to 40 Years.

Table A.3
Stratified Norms of Adjustment Scale

Adjustment	Gender		Race/Ethnicity					Age	
Score	M	F	B	H	A./P.I.	A./A.N.	W	< 40	≥40
0	.0	.0	.0	.0	.0	.0	.0	.0	.0
1	.0	.0	.0	.0	.0	.0	.0	.0	.0
2	.0	.0	.0	.0	.0	.0	.0	.0	.0
3	.0	.0	.0	.0	.0	.0	.0	.0	.0
4	.0	.0	.0	.0	.0	.0	.0	.0	.0
5	.0	.0	.0	.0	.0	.0	.0	.0	.0
6	.0	.0	.0	.0	.0	.0	.0	.0	.0
7	.0	.0	.0	.0	.0	.0	.0	.0	.1
8	.1	.1	.0	.0	.1	.0	.1	.1	.1
9	.1	.1	.0	.0	.1	.0	.1	.1	.2
10	.1	.2	.1	.0	.2	.1	.2	.2	.3
11	.2	.2	.1	.1	.3	.2	.2	.2	.4
12	.3	.3	.2	.1	.4	.3	.4	.3	.6
13	.4	.5	.2	.2	.4	.5	.5	.5	.8
14	.6	.7	.3	.3	.7	.8	.7	.6	1.1
15	.9	1.0	.6	.4	1.1	1.1	1.0	.9	1.6
16	1.2	1.3	.7	.5	1.3	1.3	1.3	1.1	2.1
17	1.6	1.7	.9	.7	1.6	1.7	1.7	1.5	2.8
18	2.1	2.2	1.4	1.0	2.2	2.0	2.2	2.0	3.6
19	2.8	2.7	1.9	1.3	3.0	2.6	2.9	2.6	4.5
20	3.6	3.5	2.4	1.9	3.9	3.6	3.7	3.4	5.7
21	4.6	4.5	3.1	2.7	5.0	4.5	4.7	4.4	7.1
22	6.0	5.8	4.1	3.5	6.8	5.9	6.0	5.7	9.0
23	7.6	7.3	5.4	4.5	8.6	7.8	7.6	7.3	11.2
24	9.6	9.2	6.8	6.0	11.1	9.4	9.6	9.1	13.9
25	12.0	11.6	9.0	7.8	13.8	12.1	12.0	11.5	16.8
26	14.9	14.5	11.9	10.1	17.3	15.0	14.8	14.4	20.5
27	18.6	18.1	15.2	13.2	21.5	19.2	18.4	18.0	25.0
28	23.1	22.2	19.6	17.1	26.5	24.0	22.7	22.3	30.1
29	28.5	27.5	25.0	22.0	32.8	29.8	27.9	27.6	36.2
30	35.0	33.7	31.6	28.1	40.8	35.3	34.1	34.0	42.7
31	42.9	41.4	39.5	36.2	49.3	42.6	41.6	41.7	50.3
32	51.9	50.2	48.7	45.6	59.6	51.3	50.3	50.5	59.0
33	62.3	60.7	59.9	57.4	69.8	62.6	60.5	61.0	68.2
34	73.5	72.5	72.0	71.1	80.4	73.8	71.9	72.5	77.4
35	84.8	84.7	84.3	84.6	90.5	85.6	83.8	84.4	86.7
36	94.7	95.0	94.6	95.0	97.3	94.8	94.5	94.7	95.0
37	100.0	100.0	100.0	100.0	100.0	100.0	100.0	100.0	100.0

Note. M = Male, F = Female, B = Black, H = Hispanic, A./P.I. = Asian American/Pacific Islander, A./A.N. = American Indian/Alaskan Native, W = White, <40 = Less Than 40 Years, > 40 = Greater Than or Equal to 40 Years.

Table A.4

Stratified Norms of Ambition Scale

Ambition	Gender		Race/Ethnicity					Age	
Score	M	F	B	H	A./P.I.	A./A.N.	W	< 40	≥ 40
0	.0	.0	.0	.0	.0	.0	.0	.0	.0
1	.0	.0	.0	.0	.0	.0	.0	.0	.0
2	.0	.0	.0	.0	.0	.0	.0	.0	.0
3	.0	.0	.0	.0	.0	.0	.0	.0	.0
4	.0	.0	.0	.0	.0	.0	.0	.0	.0
5	.0	.0	.0	.0	.0	.0	.0	.0	.0
6	.0	.0	.0	.0	.0	.0	.0	.0	.0
7	.0	.1	.0	.0	.0	.0	.1	.1	.1
8	.1	.1	.1	.0	.1	.0	.1	.1	.1
9	.1	.1	.1	.0	.1	.1	.1	.1	.2
10	.2	.2	.1	.1	.2	.1	.2	.2	.3
11	.3	.3	.1	.1	.3	.3	.4	.3	.4
12	.4	.5	.1	.2	.4	.4	.5	.4	.6
13	.5	.8	.2	.3	.7	.5	.8	.7	1.0
14	.8	1.2	.3	.5	.9	1.1	1.2	1.0	1.4
15	1.2	1.8	.6	.7	1.5	1.6	1.7	1.4	2.1
16	1.7	2.5	.8	1.2	2.4	2.1	2.4	2.0	3.0
17	2.4	3.6	1.3	1.7	3.6	2.9	3.5	2.8	4.3
18	3.4	5.1	1.9	2.5	4.9	4.2	4.9	4.1	5.8
19	4.7	6.9	2.8	3.7	6.6	5.8	6.5	5.5	8.0
20	6.5	9.4	4.1	5.6	8.8	8.4	8.8	7.6	10.8
21	8.8	12.6	6.1	8.2	12.3	11.6	11.6	10.3	13.9
22	12.0	16.9	9.2	12.0	16.6	16.1	15.4	13.9	18.2
23	16.0	22.3	13.2	16.8	21.7	22.1	20.2	18.7	23.4
24	21.2	29.3	19.3	23.4	29.7	29.5	26.1	24.6	30.0
25	28.5	38.4	27.8	32.9	38.9	37.0	33.9	32.8	38.6
26	38.2	49.9	39.7	44.3	50.2	47.4	44.1	43.2	49.2
27	51.9	63.4	54.6	59.6	64.3	60.7	57.2	56.9	62.5
28	72.1	80.3	75.7	78.9	82.2	80.1	75.2	75.6	80.3
29	100.0	100.0	100.0	100.0	100.0	100.0	100.0	100.0	100.0

Note. M = Male, F = Female, B = Black, H = Hispanic, A./P.I. = Asian American/Pacific Islander, A./A.N. = American Indian/Alaskan Native, W = White, <40 = Less Than 40 Years, > 40 = Greater Than or Equal to 40 Years.

Table A.5

Stratified Norms of Sociability Scale

Sociability	Gender		Race/Ethnicity					Age	
Score	M	F	B	H	A./P.I.	A./A.N.	W	< 40	≥ 40
0	.0	.1	.0	.0	.0	.0	.0	.1	.1
1	.2	.3	.3	.2	.1	.3	.3	.2	.5
2	.6	.8	.9	.5	.3	.6	.7	.6	1.3
3	1.2	1.5	1.7	1.1	0.7	1.3	1.4	1.3	2.6
4	2.2	2.6	3.2	2.0	1.2	2.0	2.4	2.3	4.5
5	3.8	4.3	5.7	3.5	2.4	3.4	4.0	3.8	7.3
6	5.7	6.5	8.4	5.4	3.9	4.9	6.0	5.7	11.0
7	8.4	9.4	12.5	8.2	5.9	7.0	8.6	8.4	15.6
8	11.6	12.9	17.2	11.7	8.3	9.8	11.8	11.7	20.5
9	15.5	17.3	22.5	16.3	11.4	13.5	15.7	15.9	26.1
10	20.1	22.3	28.9	21.5	15.9	17.9	20.1	20.8	32.2
11	25.5	28.5	35.7	27.9	21.2	23.1	25.5	26.6	38.9
12	31.7	35.5	43.8	35.2	28.1	29.1	31.8	33.2	46.3
13	38.6	43.2	51.6	43.0	35.6	36.0	38.8	40.6	54.2
14	46.1	51.4	59.5	51.7	43.9	44.8	46.4	48.5	61.9
15	54.0	59.9	67.8	60.5	53.4	54.5	54.4	56.8	69.2
16	61.9	68.1	74.8	68.9	61.7	63.4	62.5	65.0	76.1
17	69.7	75.7	81.6	76.6	70.1	72.5	70.4	72.9	81.8
18	77.1	82.6	87.3	83.4	77.7	79.9	77.9	80.1	86.8
19	83.7	88.2	91.5	88.8	84.9	86.1	84.5	86.2	91.1
20	89.7	92.8	94.9	93.2	91.0	91.6	90.2	91.3	94.6
21	94.4	96.3	97.4	96.5	95.3	95.9	94.7	95.4	97.2
22	97.7	98.5	99.0	98.5	98.1	98.4	97.9	98.1	99.0
23	99.5	99.6	99.7	99.7	99.6	99.6	99.5	99.5	99.8
24	99.5	99.6	100.0	100.0	100.0	100.0	100.0	100.0	100.0

Note. M = Male, F = Female, B = Black, H = Hispanic, A./P.I. = Asian American/Pacific Islander, A./A.N. = American Indian/Alaskan Native, W = White, <40 = Less Than 40 Years, > 40 = Greater Than or Equal to 40 Years.

Table A.6
Stratified Norms of Interpersonal Sensitivity Scale

Interpersonal Sensitivity	Gender		Race/Ethnicity					Age	
Score	M	F	B	H	A./P.I.	A./A.N.	W	< 40	≥ 40
0	.0	.0	.0	.0	.0	.0	.0	.0	.0
1	.0	.0	.0	.0	.0	.0	.0	.0	.0
2	.0	.0	.0	.0	.0	.0	.0	.0	.0
3	.0	.0	.0	.0	.0	.0	.0	.0	.0
4	.0	.0	.0	.0	.0	.0	.0	.0	.0
5	.0	.0	.0	.0	.0	.0	.0	.0	.0
6	.0	.0	.0	.0	.0	.0	.0	.0	.1
7	.1	.0	.0	.0	.0	.0	.0	.0	.1
8	.1	.0	.0	.0	.1	.0	.1	.1	.2
9	.1	.1	.1	.0	.1	.0	.1	.1	.3
10	.2	.1	.1	.0	.2	.0	.1	.2	.4
11	.4	.1	.1	1	.3	.1	.2	.3	.6
12	.7	.2	.2	.1	.6	.2	.4	.4	1.0
13	1.0	.3	.3	.3	.9	.5	.6	.7	1.6
14	1.7	.5	.5	.5	1.4	1.0	1.0	1.1	2.5
15	2.7	.8	1.0	1.0	2.3	1.7	1.7	1.8	4.1
16	4.4	1.4	2.1	1.7	3.7	2.9	2.7	2.9	6.3
17	7.2	2.8	4.0	3.5	6.6	4.7	4.6	5.1	10.1
18	12.8	5.8	9.2	7.5	12.1	9.7	8.3	9.5	16.7
19	24.1	13.2	20.9	16.8	23.1	20.0	16.5	19.0	28.2
20	46.0	30.7	42.9	38.2	44.5	38.8	35.2	39.1	48.3
21	79.1	64.5	76.2	72.6	79.0	70.3	69.0	72.4	76.9
22	100.0	100.0	100.0	100.0	100.0	100.0	100.0	100.0	100.0

Note. M = Male, F = Female, B = Black, H = Hispanic, A./P.I. = Asian American/Pacific Islander, A./A.N. = American Indian/Alaskan Native, W = White, <40 = Less Than 40 Years, > 40 = Greater Than or Equal to 40 Years.

Table A.7
Stratified Norms of Prudence Scale

Prudence	Gender		Race/Ethnicity					Age	
Score	M	F	B	H	A./P.I.	A./A.N.	W	< 40	≥ 40
0	.0	.0	.0	.0	.0	.0	.0	.0	.0
1	.0	.0	.0	.0	.0	.0	.0	.0	.0
2	.0	.0	.0	.0	.0	.0	.0	.0	.0
3	.0	.0	.0	.0	.0	.0	.0	.0	.0
4	.0	.0	.0	.0	.0	.0	.0	.0	.0
5	.0	.0	.0	.0	.0	.0	.0	.0	.0
6	.0	.0	.0	.0	.0	.0	.0	.0	.0
7	.1	.0	.0	.0	.0	.0	.0	.0	.1
8	.1	.0	.0	.0	.0	.0	.1	.1	.1
9	.2	.0	.0	.0	.1	.1	.2	.1	.2
10	.4	.1	.1	.1	.2	.2	.3	.2	.4
11	.7	.2	.2	.2	.3	.3	.5	.4	.7
12	1.1	.4	.3	.4	.5	.8	.8	.8	1.2
13	1.8	.8	.6	.6	.8	1.1	1.3	1.3	1.9
14	2.9	1.3	1.0	.9	1.4	1.6	2.2	2.1	3.0
15	4.4	2.2	1.7	1.7	2.6	3.1	3.5	3.4	4.8
16	6.7	3.5	2.8	2.9	4.3	4.8	5.4	5.2	7.1
17	9.9	5.7	4.7	4.4	6.9	6.7	8.2	7.9	10.6
18	13.9	8.6	7.0	6.7	10.6	9.1	12.0	11.5	14.8
19	19.3	12.7	10.5	10.3	15.1	13.2	17.0	16.2	21.0
20	25.9	18.2	15.5	15.0	21.0	18.3	23.3	22.2	28.0
21	33.5	25.1	22.0	20.8	27.6	25.4	30.8	29.4	36.2
22	42.4	33.5	29.6	28.5	36.1	33.2	39.6	38.0	45.6
23	51.8	42.9	38.6	37.9	45.3	42.2	49.1	47.5	55.2
24	61.6	53.5	48.9	48.1	56.5	52.9	59.3	57.7	65.3
25	71.2	64.3	59.4	59.0	67.2	64.0	69.5	67.8	74.8
26	80.2	74.5	70.5	69.9	76.7	74.1	78.9	77.4	83.2
27	87.5	83.8	80.4	79.8	84.9	82.9	86.9	85.6	90.0
28	93.3	90.9	88.5	88.4	91.4	90.6	93.1	92.1	95.1
29	97.1	96.0	94.8	94.6	95.8	95.3	97.1	96.5	98.0
30	99.2	98.9	98.5	98.5	98.8	98.6	99.2	99.1	99.5
31	100.0	100.0	100.0	100.0	100.0	100.0	100.0	100.0	100.0

Note. M = Male, F = Female, B = Black, H = Hispanic, A./P.I. = Asian American/Pacific Islander, A./A.N. = American Indian/Alaskan Native, W = White, <40 = Less Than 40 Years, > 40 = Greater Than or Equal to 40 Years.

Table A.8
Stratified Norms of Inquisitive Scale

Inquisitive	Gender		Race/Ethnicity					Age	
Score	M	F	B	H	A./P.I.	A./A.N.	W	< 40	≥40
0	.0	.0	.0	.0	.0	.0	.0	.0	.0
1	.0	.0	.0	.0	.0	.0	.0	.0	.0
2	.1	.1	.1	.0	.0	.0	.1	.1	.1
3	.2	.3	.2	.2	.1	.2	.3	.2	.4
4	.4	.7	.4	.3	.2	.4	.6	.5	.9
5	.7	1.3	.9	.7	.4	.7	1.1	.9	1.9
6	1.3	2.4	1.8	1.2	.9	1.1	2.1	1.7	3.3
7	2.2	4.1	3.1	2.1	1.6	1.9	3.5	2.9	5.4
8	3.5	6.4	5.2	3.6	2.5	2.9	5.3	4.7	8.1
9	5.4	9.4	7.9	5.8	4.4	4.6	7.8	7.0	11.8
10	7.9	13.2	11.6	8.4	6.6	6.7	11.1	10.0	16.3
11	11.1	18.0	16.0	12.0	9.3	9.0	15.2	13.8	21.3
12	15.1	23.6	21.3	16.2	12.7	12.1	20.1	18.5	27.8
13	20.0	30.0	27.9	21.1	17.4	16.4	25.7	23.9	35.0
14	25.7	37.0	35.2	27.0	22.9	21.7	32.1	30.3	42.5
15	32.5	44.7	43.1	33.9	29.6	27.7	39.4	37.3	51.1
16	40.2	52.6	51.8	41.5	36.2	34.2	47.1	45.2	59.4
17	48.5	60.6	60.4	49.3	44.1	41.5	55.3	53.4	67.7
18	57.4	68.6	69.0	57.7	52.5	50.3	63.6	62.0	75.4
19	66.2	76.1	76.4	66.1	61.3	59.5	71.9	70.3	82.4
20	74.8	83.0	83.1	74.1	70.4	68.6	79.6	78.1	87.8
21	82.4	88.9	88.7	81.7	78.3	77.5	86.3	85.0	92.3
22	89.1	93.5	93.1	88.4	85.9	86.3	91.8	90.8	95.8
23	94.3	96.8	96.4	94.0	92.9	93.5	95.8	95.2	98.1
24	98.1	99.0	98.8	97.9	97.6	97.5	98.7	98.3	99.4
25	100.0	100.0	100.0	100.0	100.0	100.0	100.0	100.0	100.0

Note. M = Male, F = Female, B = Black, H = Hispanic, A./P.I. = Asian American/Pacific Islander, A./A.N. = American Indian/Alaskan Native, W = White, <40 = Less Than 40 Years, > 40 = Greater Than or Equal to 40 Years.

Table A.9
Stratified Norms of Learning Approach Scale

Learning Approach Score	Gender		Race/Ethnicity						Age	
	M	F	B	H	A./P.I.	A./A.N.	W	< 40	≥40
0	.2	.1	.1	.1	.1	.0	.2	.1	.5
1	.8	.3	.3	.2	.2	.3	.6	.5	1.4
2	2.0	.7	.9	.7	.6	.6	1.5	1.3	3.2
3	3.8	1.4	2.0	1.5	1.5	1.4	2.9	2.5	5.8
4	6.6	2.8	3.7	2.8	2.9	2.9	5.1	4.6	9.8
5	10.4	5.1	6.2	5.0	5.2	5.0	8.3	7.6	14.9
6	15.4	8.4	9.8	8.3	8.9	8.3	12.7	11.8	21.2
7	21.9	13.2	14.7	12.8	13.3	12.9	18.6	17.4	29.0
8	29.9	19.6	21.0	18.8	20.1	18.5	26.0	24.6	38.2
9	40.0	28.3	29.2	27.0	28.5	26.4	35.7	34.0	49.0
10	51.7	39.5	40.0	37.8	38.8	36.9	47.3	45.3	60.8
11	65.0	53.1	52.7	51.3	51.7	50.6	61.0	58.8	73.0
12	77.2	67.1	65.8	65.1	66.7	64.2	74.0	71.9	83.3
13	88.6	82.4	81.5	80.9	82.0	81.6	86.8	85.4	92.4
14	100.0	100.0	100.0	100.0	100.0	100.0	100.0	100.0	100.0

Note. M = Male, F = Female, B = Black, H = Hispanic, A./P.I. = Asian American/Pacific Islander, A./A.N. = American Indian/Alaskan Native, W = White, <40 = Less Than 40 Years, > 40 = Greater Than or Equal to 40 Years.

Appendix B: 1995 HPI Norms (N=21,573)

	Personality Scales						
	ADJ	AMB	SOC	INP	PRU	INQ	LRN
Raw	Norms	Norms	Norms	Norms	Norms	Norms	Norms
0	0	0	0	0	0	0	0
1	0	0	1	0	0	0	2
2	0	0	1	0	0	1	4
3	0	0	2	0	0	1	8
4	0	0	4	0	0	2	13
5	0	0	7	0	0	3	19
6	0	1	10	0	0	5	27
7	1	1	14	0	1	8	36
8	1	1	19	0	1	12	46
9	2	2	25	1	2	17	58
10	2	2	31	1	3	22	69
11	3	3	38	2	4	27	79
12	4	4	44	2	6	32	88
13	5	5	52	3	9	39	95
14	6	6	59	5	12	46	100
15	8	8	66	7	16	54	
16	9	10	73	11	21	62	
17	12	13	79	16	27	69	
18	14	16	85	26	34	76	
19	16	19	89	39	42	83	
20	19	24	93	60	50	88	
21	23	28	96	83	58	91	
22	26	33	98	100	67	95	
23	30	40	100		75	98	
24	34	47	100		82	99	
25	39	55			88	100	
26	44	64			92		
27	49	74			96		
28	55	87			98		
29	60	100			99		
30	66				100		
31	72				100		
32	78						
33	84						
34	89						
35	94						
36	98						
37	100						

Note. ADJ = Adjustment, AMB = Ambition, SOC = Sociability, INP = Interpersonal Sensitivity, PRU = Prudence, INQ = Inquisitive, LRN = Learning Approach.

Appendix C: References For Transportability Of Validity Within Job Families

Table C.1
Research References Contributing HPI Validity Data for Seven Job Families

Tech Rep. Number	Citation
349	Leckband, M. M. (2005). *Development of a personality profile of firefighters* (Tech Rep. No 349). Unpublished doctoral dissertation. Miami, FL: Florida International University.
330	Burnett, D., Facteau, J., Hogan, J., & Holland, B. (2004). V*alidity of the Hogan Personality Inventory, Hogan Development Survey, and Bennett Mechanical Comprehension Test for entry-level factory workers* (Tech. Rep. No. 330). Tulsa, OK: Hogan Assessment Systems.
326	Lock, J., Jerden, E., & Bourdeau, N. (2004). *Validity of the Hogan Personality Inventory and FS Situational Judgment Inventory for selecting financial specialist employees: Documentation of evidence for validity generalization, transportability and synthetic validity, and criterion-related validity* (Tech. Rep. No. 326). Tulsa, OK: Hogan Assessment Systems.
325	Moros, A. (2004). *Validity of the Hogan Personality Inventory and Motives, Values, Preferences Inventory for selecting sales representatives* (Tech. Rep. No. 325). Tulsa, OK: Hogan Assessment Systems.
324	Moros, A. (2003). *Validity of the Hogan Personality Inventory, the Hogan Development Survey, and the UPS Multi-Rater Tool for selecting management-level employees: Documentation of evidence for criterion-related validity* (Tech. Rep. No. 324). Tulsa, OK: Hogan Assessment Systems.
323	Moros, A. (2003). V*alidity of the Hogan Personality Inventory for selecting truck drivers: Documentation of evidence for job analysis, validity generalization, transportability and synthetic validity, and criterion-related validity* (Tech. Rep. No. 323). Tulsa, OK: Hogan Assessment Systems.
320	Burnett, D. (2004). *Validity of the Hogan Personality Inventory and the Motives, Values, Preferences Inventory for selecting assistant project managers: Documentation of evidence for job analysis, validity generalization, transportability and synthetic validity, and criterion-related validity* (Tech. Rep. No. 320). Tulsa, OK: Hogan Assessment Systems.
319	Shin, H., & Holland, B. (2003). *Validity of the Hogan Personality Inventory and the Motives, Values, Preferences Inventory for selecting managers and sales representatives: Documentation of evidence for validity generalization and criterion-related validity* (Tech. Rep. No. 319). Tulsa, OK: Hogan Assessment Systems.
311	Fleming, B. (2003). *Validity of the Hogan Personality Inventory for selecting truck drivers: Documentation of evidence for validity generalization, synthetic validity, and criterion-related validity* (Tech. Rep. No. 311). Tulsa, OK: Hogan Assessment Systems.
310	Moros, A. (2003). *Validity of the Hogan Personality Inventory and the Hogan Development Survey for selecting account managers: Documentation of evidence for job analysis, validity generalization, transportability and synthetic validity, and criterion-related validity.* (Tech. Rep. No. 310). Tulsa, OK: Hogan Assessment Systems.
309	Van Landuyt, C. (2003). *Validity of the Hogan Personality Inventory for selecting management-level employees: Documentation of evidence for validity generalization, transportability, synthetic validity, and criterion-related validity.* (Tech. Rep. No. 309). Tulsa, OK: Hogan Assessment Systems.
304	Van Landuyt, C., & Holland, B. (2002). *Validity of the Hogan Personality Inventory for selecting entry-level employees for supermarkets: Documentation of evidence for validity generalization, synthetic validity, and criterion-related validity* (Tech. Rep. No. 304). Tulsa, OK: Hogan Assessment Systems.

Tech Rep. Number	Citation
301	Fleming, B., & Holland, B. (2003). *Validity of the Hogan Personality Inventory for selecting loan officers and branch managers: Documentation of evidence for validity generalization, transport, synthetic, and criterion-related validity* (Tech. Rep. No. 301). Tulsa, OK: Hogan Assessment Systems.
297	Fleming, B., & Holland, B. (2002). *Validity of the Hogan Personality Short Form for selecting NBA sales, consumer sales, and care employees: Generalizability, transportability, synthetic, and criterion validation evidence* (Tech. Rep. No. 297). Tulsa, OK: Hogan Assessment Systems.
291	Van Landuyt, C., & Holland, B. (2002). T*he Validity of the Hogan Personality Inventory for selecting dispatchers and supervisors: Documentation of evidence for validity generalization, transportability, synthetic validity, and criterion-related validity* (Tech. Rep. No. 291). Tulsa, OK: Hogan Assessment Systems.
288	Van Landuyt, C., Fleming, B., & Holland, B. (2002). *Validity of the Hogan Personality Inventory in selecting field service technicians and delivery service representatives* (Tech. Rep. No. 288). Tulsa, OK: Hogan Assessment Systems.
287	Marrs, L., Borich, J., & Holland, B. (2002). *The Validity of the Hogan Personality Inventory for selecting cashiers/customer service representatives:Documentation of evidence for validity generalization, transportability, synthetic validity, and criterion-related validity* (Tech. Rep. No. 287). Tulsa, OK: Hogan Assessment Systems.
284	Lock, J. (2000). *Validity of the Hogan Personality Inventory for selecting correctional officers* (Tech. Rep. No. 284). Tulsa, OK: Hogan Assessment Systems.
280	Fleming, B., Marrs, L., & Holland, B. (2002). *Validity of the Hogan Personality Inventory for selecting regional drivers: Generalizability, transportability, synthetic validation, and criterion evidence* (Tech. Rep. No. 280). Tulsa, OK: Hogan Assessment Systems.
278	Marrs, L., Van Landuyt, C., & Holland, B. (2002). V*alidity of the Hogan Personality Inventory for selecting crew members and restaurant managers: Documentation of evidence for validity generalization, transportability, and synthetic validity and criterion-related validity* (Tech. Rep. No. 278). Tulsa, OK: Hogan Assessment Systems.
276	Marrs, L., & Holland, B. (2002). *Preliminary HPI, HDS, and MVPI validity study for customer operators* (Tech. Rep. No. 276). Tulsa, OK: Hogan Assessment Systems.
275	Marrs, L., & Holland, B. (2002). *Preliminary HPI validity study for auto maker employees* (Tech. Rep. No. 275). Tulsa, OK: Hogan Assessment Systems.
274	Marrs, L. (2002). *Preliminary HPI validity study for executive directors* (Tech. Rep. No. 274). Tulsa, OK: Hogan Assessment Systems.
270	Hogan, R., & Michel, R. (1996). *Preemployment testing for owner operators* (Tech. Rep. No. 270). Tulsa, OK: Hogan Assessment Systems.
267	Oh, K., & Holland, B. (2002). *Validity of the Hogan Personality Inventory for selecting police officers* (Tech. Rep. No. 267). Tulsa, OK: Hogan Assessment Systems.
265	Shin, H., & Holland, B. (2001). *Validity of the Hogan Personality Inventory for selecting farm marketing representatives* (Tech. Rep. No. 265). Tulsa, OK: Hogan Assessment Systems.
263	Hogan, J. & Brinkmeyer, K. (1994). *Validity of the Hogan Personality Inventory for selecting telephone sales representatives* (Tech. Rep. No. 263). Tulsa, OK: Hogan Assessment Systems.
256	Shin, H., Van Landuyt, C., & Holland, B. (2001). *Validity of the Hogan Personality Inventory for selecting telephone sales representatives and telemarketing supervisors* (Tech. Rep. No. 256). Tulsa, OK: Hogan Assessment Systems.
247	Van Landuyt, C., Philp, T., & Holland, B. (2001). *Validity of the Hogan Personality Inventory for selecting field service technicians and delivery service representatives* (Tech. Rep. No. 247). Tulsa, OK: Hogan Assessment Systems.
244	Abalos, A., & Shin, H. (2001). V*alidity of the Hogan Personality Inventory for selecting surfacing and coating employees* (Tech. Rep. No. 244). Tulsa, OK: Hogan Assessment Systems.

Tech Rep. Number	Citation
242	Hogan, R., & Holland, B. (1999). *Validity of the Hogan Personality Inventory for selecting drivers* (Tech. Rep. No. 242). Tulsa, OK: Hogan Assessment Systems
241	Van Landuyt, C., & Holland, B. (2001). *Validity of the Hogan Personality Inventory for selecting mechanics* (Tech. Rep. No. 241). Tulsa, OK: Hogan Assessment Systems.
221	McDonald, D. G., Beckett, M. B., & Hodgdon, J. A. (1988). *Psychological predictors of fitness and performance in active duty* (Tech. Rep. No. 221). San Diego, California: Naval Health Research Center.
220	Shanks, D. (2000). *Can personality be used to identify officer potential in the fire brigade?* (Tech. Rep. No. 220). Unpublished master's thesis, University of Aberdeen, London UK.
219	McDaniel, S. (2000). *[Validity of the Hogan Personality Inventory for field sales, salaried professional, and managerial jobs]* (Tech. Rep. No. 219). Unpublished raw data. Tulsa, OK: Hogan Assessment Systems.
216	Shin, H. C., Holland, B., & Hogan, R. (2000). *Validity of the Hogan Personality Inventory for selecting sales people* (Tech. Rep. No. 216). Tulsa, OK: Hogan Assessments Systems.
214	Barnett, G., Shin, H. C., & Holland, B. (2000). *Validity of the Hogan Personality Inventory for selecting crewmen* (Tech. Rep. No. 214). Tulsa, OK: Hogan Assessment Systems.
213	Barnett, G., & Lock, J. (2000). *Validity of the Hogan Personality Inventory for selecting bank tellers* (Tech. Rep. No. 213). Tulsa, OK: Hogan Assessment Systems.
209	Hogan, R., & Holland B. (1998). *Validity of the Hogan Personality Inventory for selecting drivers* (Tech. Rep. No. 209). Tulsa, OK: Hogan Assessment Systems.
203	Abalos, A., McDaniel, S., & Kisner, R. F. (2000). *Validity of the Hogan Personality Inventory for selecting bus operators* (Tech. Rep. No. 203). Tulsa, OK: Hogan Assessment Systems.
200	Shelton, D., Holland, B., & Hogan, J. (1999). *Selecting terminal managers using the Hogan Personality Inventory, the Hogan Development Survey, and the Motives, Values, Preferences Inventory* (Tech. Rep. No. 200). Tulsa, OK: Hogan Assessment Systems.
199	Lock, J. (1997). *Development and validation of selection procedures for the information technology department* (Tech. Rep. No. 199). Houston, TX: Jeanneret & Associates, Inc.
196	Brinkmeyer, K. R. (1999). *Sales representative profiling and validity study using the Hogan Personality Inventory, the Hogan Development Survey, and the Motives, Values, Preferences Inventory* (Tech. Rep. No. 196). Tulsa, OK: CDR Assessment Group.
194	Ryan, A. M., & Ployhart, R. E. (1995). *A criterion-related validation study of the Hogan Personality Inventory for police officers* (Tech. Rep. No. 194). Perrysburg, OH: AMR, Inc.
193	Connolly, P. M. (1996). *[Relations between Overseas Assignment Inventory ratings and Hogan Personality Inventory scores]* (Tech. Rep. No. 193). Unpublished raw data. Old Saybrook, CT: Performance Programs.
192	Shelton, D., Holland, B., & Hogan, J. (2000). *Validity of the Hogan Personality Inventory for selecting managers* (Tech. Rep. No. 192). Tulsa, OK: Hogan Assessment Systems.
190	Shin, H. C., Holland, B., & Hogan, R. (2000). *Validity of Hogan Personality Inventory for selecting customer service operators* (Tech. Rep. No. 190). Tulsa, OK: Hogan Assessment Systems.
185	Hogan, J., Hogan, R., & Klippel, D. (2000). *Validity of the Hogan Personality Inventory for selecting locomotive engineer trainees* (Tech. Rep. No. 185). Tulsa, OK: Hogan Assessment Systems.
182	Holland, B., Shin, H., & Hogan, J. (2000). *Selecting Project Managers, Superintendents, and Estimators using the Hogan Personality Inventory, Hogan Development Survey, and Motives, Values, Preferences Inventory* (Tech. Rep. No. 182). Tulsa, OK: Hogan Assessment Systems.
181	Personnel Assessment, Inc. (1999). *Validity of the Hogan Personality Inventory for Selecting Drivers* (Tech. Rep. No. 181). Tulsa, OK: Hogan Assessment Systems.

Tech Rep. Number	Citation
179	Holland, B., & Hogan, J. (1999). *Validity of Hogan Personality Inventory for selecting outside sales associates* (Tech. Rep. No. 179). Tulsa, OK: Hogan Assessment Systems.
175	Ross, R., & Hogan, J. (1999). *Validity of the Hogan Personality Inventory for selecting store managers* (Tech. Rep. No. 175). Tulsa, OK: Hogan Assessment Systems.
174	Kisner, R. F., Holland, B., & Hogan, J. (1999). *Validity of the Hogan Personality Inventory for trading assistants* (Tech. Rep. No. 174). Tulsa, OK: Hogan Assessment Systems.
173	Kisner, R. F., & McDaniel, S. (1999). *Validity of the Hogan Personality Inventory for selecting termite inspectors* (Tech. Rep. No. 173). Tulsa, OK: Hogan Assessment Systems.
172	Hogan, R., & Holland, B. (1998). *Validity of the Hogan Personality Inventory for selecting auditors* (Tech. Rep. No. 172). Tulsa, OK: Hogan Assessment Systems.
171	Rybicki, S. (2000). *[Validity of the Hogan Personality Inventory for customer service representatives]* (Tech. Rep. No. 171). Unpublished raw data. Tulsa, OK: Hogan Assessment Systems.
170	Hogan, J., Holland, B., & Hogan, R. (1998). *Validity of the Hogan Personality Inventory for selecting emergency communications officers* (Tech. Rep. No. 170). Tulsa, OK: Hogan Assessment Systems.
169	Hogan, J., Holland, B., & Hogan, R. (1998). *Validity of the Hogan Personality Inventory for selecting mechanics* (Tech. Rep. No. 169). Tulsa, OK: Hogan Assessment Systems.
168	Holland, B., & Hogan, J. (1999). *Validity of the Hogan Personality Inventory for selecting recreation leaders* (Tech. Rep. No. 168). Tulsa, OK: Hogan Assessment Systems.
167	Holland, B., & Hogan, J. (1999). *Validity of the Hogan Personality Inventory for selecting clerical support aides II and III* (Tech. Rep. No. 167). Tulsa, OK: Hogan Assessment Systems.
166	McDaniel, S. (1999). *Validity of the Hogan Personality Inventory for selecting sheriff's deputies* (Tech. Rep. No. 166). Tulsa, OK: Hogan Assessment Systems.
165	Brinkmeyer, K., & Hogan, R. (1996). *Preemployment screening for customer service representatives* (Tech. Rep. No. 165). Tulsa, OK: Hogan Assessment Systems.
164	Brinkmeyer, K. R. (1999). *Customer service employee profiling & validity study using the Hogan Personality Inventory, the Hogan Development Survey, & the Motives, Values, Preferences Inventory* (Tech. Rep. No. 164). Tulsa, OK: CDR Assessment Group.
162	Holland, B., Kisner, R. F., & McDaniel, S. (1999). *Predicting turnover using the Hogan Personality Inventory for customer service representatives, driver/delivery and installation personnel, and service personnel* (TechRep. No. 162). Tulsa, OK: Hogan Assessments System.
158	Hogan, J., Najar, M., & Holland, B. (1999). *Validity of the Hogan Personality Inventory of selecting managers* (Tech. Rep. No. 158). Tulsa, OK: Hogan Assessment Systems.
157	Gregg, M., & Rudolph, L. (1998). *Using personality assessment as the basis for selecting business managers* (Tech. Rep. No. 157). Southampton, Hampshire: Ramsey Hall/Lloyds UDT.
155	McDaniel, S. & Hogan, J. (1998). *Using the Hogan Personality Inventory to select jeffboat supervisors* (Tech. Rep. No. 155). Tulsa, OK: Hogan Assessment Systems.
152	Rybicki, S., & Hogan, R. (1997). *Personality profiles of a sales group* (Tech. Rep. No. 152). Tulsa, OK: Hogan Assessment Systems.
151	McDaniel, S. (1998). *Validity of Hogan Personality Inventory for selecting supervisors* (Tech. Rep. No. 151). Tulsa, OK: Hogan Assessment Systems.
149	Brinkmeyer, K., & Hogan, R. (1998). *Validity of the Hogan Personality Inventory for selecting customer service representatives* (Tech. Rep. No. 149). Tulsa, OK: Hogan Assessment Systems.
148	Hogan, R., & Powell, J. (1998). *Validity of the Hogan Personality Inventory for selecting drivers* (Tech. Rep. No. 148). Tulsa, OK: Hogan Assessment Systems.
142	Ross, R., Rybicki, S., & Hogan, J. (1997). *Validity of the Hogan Personality Inventory for selecting office clerks and office managers* (Tech. Rep. No. 142). Tulsa, OK: Hogan Assessment Systems.

Tech Rep. Number	Citation
140	Hogan, R., & Heidelberg, H. (1998). *Validity of the Hogan Personality Inventory for selecting drivers* (Tech. Rep. No. 140). Tulsa, OK: Hogan Assessment Systems.
138	Lock, J. (1995). *Using Hogan Personality Inventory for Selecting Customer & Policy Service Representatives, Data Entry Operators, and Document Processors* (Tech. Rep. No. 138). Tulsa, OK: Hogan Assessment Systems.
137	Hogan, J., Michel, R. & Hogan, R. (1997). *Validity of personality measures for entry level jobs: Final report* (Tech. Rep. No. 137). Tulsa, OK: Hogan Assessment Systems.
136	Brinkmeyer, K., Hogan, R., & Heidelberg, H. (1997). *Validity of the Hogan Personality Inventory for selecting pipe manufacturing workers* (Tech. Rep. No. 136). Tulsa, OK: Hogan Assessment Systems.
135	Brinkmeyer, K., & Hogan, R. (1997). *Validity of the Hogan Personality Inventory for selecting telemarketers* (Tech. Rep. No. 135). Tulsa, OK: Hogan Assessment Systems.
134	Hogan, R., & Brinkmeyer, K. (1996). *Preemployment screening for drivers* (Tech. Rep. No. 134). Tulsa, OK: Hogan Assessment Systems.
131	Brinkmeyer, K., & Hogan, R. (1996). *Preemployment screening for customer service representatives* (Tech. Rep. No. 131). Tulsa, OK: Hogan Assessment Systems.
130	Hogan, R., & Heidelberg, H. (1998). *Validity of the Hogan Personality Inventory for selecting dockworkers* (Tech. Rep. No. 130). Tulsa, OK: Hogan Assessment Systems.
129	Hogan, R., & Heidelberg, H. (1998). *Validity of the Hogan Personality Inventory for selecting drivers* (Tech. Rep. No. 129). Tulsa, OK: Hogan Assessment Systems.
127	Hogan, R., & Shelton, D. (1997). *Validity of the Hogan Personality Inventory for selecting certified nursing assistants* (Tech. Rep. No. 127). Tulsa, OK: Hogan Assessment Systems.
126	Hogan, J., Rybicki, S., Heidelberg, H., & Shelton, D. (1997). *Validity of the Hogan Personality Inventory for selecting offshore anchor handlers* (Tech. Rep. No. 126). Tulsa, OK: Hogan Assessment Systems.
125	Hogan, J., Rybicki, S., & Shelton, D. (1997). *Validity of the Hogan Personality Inventory for selecting international relocation consultants and international relocation assistants* (Tech. Rep. No. 125). Tulsa, OK: Hogan Assessment Systems.
124	Hogan, R., & Shelton, D. (1997). *Preemployment screening for road drivers, city drivers, mechanics, and jockeys* (Tech. Rep. No. 124). Tulsa, OK: Hogan Assessment Systems.
123	Shelton, D. (1997). *Validation study using the Hogan Personality Inventory for service operations coordinators* (Tech. Rep. No. 123). Tulsa, OK: Hogan Assessment Systems.
122	Sinangil, H. K., Ones, D. S., & Cemalcilar, Z. (1997, July). *Personality characteristics of expatriate managers working in Turkey* (Tech. Rep. No. 122). Paper presented at the 5th European Congress of Psychology, Dublin, Ireland.
121	Rybicki, S., & Hogan, R. (1996). *Validity of the Hogan Personality Inventory for selecting sales/service technicians* (Tech. Rep. No. 121). Tulsa, OKHogan Assessment Systems.
120	Rybicki, S., & Hogan, J. (1997). *Validity of the Hogan Personality Inventory Form-S for selecting correctional deputy sheriffs* (Tech. Rep. No. 120). Tulsa, OK: Hogan Assessment Systems.
119	Hogan, J., & Rybicki, S. (1997). *Validity of correctional officer selection procedures* (Tech. Rep. No. 119). Tulsa, OK: Hogan Assessment Systems.
118	Rybicki, S., & Hogan, R. (1997). *Validity of the Hogan Personality Inventory for selecting facility administrators* (Tech. Rep. No. 118). Tulsa, OK: Hogan Assessment Systems.
117	Hogan, R., & Shelton, D. (1997). *Validity of the Hogan Personality Inventory for selecting mechanics* (Tech. Rep. No. 117). Tulsa, OK: Hogan Assessment Systems.
116	Hogan, R., & Shelton, D. (1997). *Validity of the Hogan Personality Inventory for selecting truck drivers* (Tech. Rep. No. 116). Tulsa, OK: Hogan Assessment Systems.
115	Hogan, R., & Shelton, D. (1997). *Validity of the Hogan Personality Inventory for selecting conservation officers* (Tech. Rep. No. 115). Tulsa, OK: Hogan Assessment Systems.

Tech Rep. Number	Citation
114	Hogan, R., & Shelton, D. (1997). *Preemployment screening for quality management, administrative, and clerical personnel* (Tech. Rep. No. 114). Tulsa, OK: Hogan Assessment Systems.
112	Hogan, R., & Shelton, D. (1997). V*alidity of the Hogan Personality Inventory for selecting freight handlers* (Tech. Rep. No. 112). Tulsa, OK: Hogan Assessment Systems.
111	Hogan, R., & Shelton, D. (1997). *Validity of the Hogan Personality Inventory for selecting drivers* (Tech. Rep. No. 111). Tulsa, OK: Hogan Assessment Systems.
110	Hogan, R., & Shelton, D. (1997). *Validity of the Hogan Personality Inventory for selecting drivers* (Tech. Rep. No. 110). Tulsa, OK: Hogan Assessment Systems.
109	Rioux, S. (1997). *Validation study of personality with customer service representatives* (Tech. Rep. No. 109). Talahassee, FL: Florida Power Corporation.
107	Brinkmeyer, K. R., & Hogan, R. (1997). *Validity of the Hogan Personality Inventory for selecting field representatives* (Tech. Rep. No. 107). Tulsa, OK: Hogan Assessment Systems.
106	Brinkmeyer, K., & Hogan R. (1996). *Validity of the Hogan Personality Inventory for the selection of reservation sales representatives* (Tech. Rep. No. 106). Tulsa, OK: Hogan Assessment Systems.
104	Stovall, D., & Hogan, R. (1997). *Validity of the Hogan Personality Inventory for selecting drivers* (Tech. Rep. No. 104). Tulsa, OK: Hogan Assessment Systems.
103	Stovall, D., Rybicki, S., Hogan, R., & Hauxwell, R. (1997). *Preemployment screening for cashiers* (Tech. Rep. No. 103). Tulsa, OK: Hogan Assessment Systems.
102	Rybicki, S., Brinkmeyer, K., & Hogan, R. (1997). *Validity of the Hogan Personality Inventory for selecting customer service representatives, drivers, and delivery and installation/service employees* (Tech. RepNo. 102). Tulsa, OK: Hogan Assessment Systems.
101	Rybicki, S., & Hogan, J. (1996). *Validity of the Hogan Personality Inventory and the Motives, Values, Preferences Inventory for selecting small business bankers* (Tech. Rep. No. 101). Tulsa, OK: Hogan Assessment Systems.
99	Rybicki, S. & Hogan, R. (1996). V*alidity of the Hogan Personality Inventory for selecting of sales* (Tech. Rep. No. 99). Tulsa, OK: Hogan Assessment Systems.
96	Hogan, R., & Brinkmeyer, K. (1996). *Preemployment screening for drivers* (Tech. Rep. No. 96). Tulsa, OK: Hogan Assessment Systems.
95	Rybicki, S., & Hogan, R. (1996). *Validity of the Hogan Personality Inventory for selecting sales/service technicianss.* (Tech. Rep. No. 95). Tulsa, OK: Hogan Assessment Systems.
94	Brinkmeyer, K. (1996). *Validation study for drivers* (Tech. Rep. No. 94). Tulsa, OK: Hogan Assessment Systems.
92	McDaniel, S., & Hogan, R. (1997). [Correlation coefficients between HPI and performance scores of flight attendants] (Tech. Rep. No. 92). Unpublished raw data. Tulsa, OK: Hogan Assessment Systems.
91	Hogan, J., Rybicki, S., & Hogan, R. (1996). *Validity of the Hogan Personality Inventory for selecting drivers and customer service representatives* (Tech. Rep. No. 91). Tulsa, OK: Hogan Assessment Systems.
90	Hogan, R., & Brinkmeyer, K. (1996). *Preemployment screening for drivers* (Tech. Rep. No. 90). Tulsa, OK: Hogan Assessment Systems.
88	Hogan, R., & Brinkmeyer, K. (1996). Preemployment screening for telemarketers (Tech. Rep. No. 88). Tulsa, OK: Hogan Assessment Systems.
87	Borman, W. C., Logan, K. K., Hedge, J. W., Hanson, M. A., Bruskiewicz, K. T., Schneider, R. J., & Houston, J. S. (1996). *Basic research evaluating reliability of the situational test of aircrew response styles and its ability, personality, and leadership correlates.* (Tech. Rep. No. 87). Tampa, FL: Personnel Decisions Research Institutes.
86	Hogan, J., & Stovall, D. (1996). *Validity of the Hogan Personality Inventory for selecting customer operations representatives* (Tech. Rep. No. 86). Tulsa, OK: Hogan Assessment Systems.

Tech Rep. Number	Citation
85	Hogan, J., & Michel, R. (1996). *Validity of the Hogan Personality Inventory for the selection of cashiers* (Tech. Rep. No. 85). Tulsa, OK: Hogan Assessment Systems.
84	Hogan, R., Hogan, J., & Stovall, D. (1996). *Validity of the Hogan Personality Inventory for selecting trading assistants* (Tech. Rep. No. 84). Tulsa, OK: Hogan Assessment Systems.
83	Hogan, R., Hogan, J., Stovall, D., & Brinkmeyer, K. (1995). *Validity of the Hogan Personality Inventory for employee selection* (Tech. Rep. No. 83). Tulsa, OK: Hogan Assessment Systems.
81	Landy, F. (1995). *Validity study results for using the Hogan Personality Inventory to select police officers* (Tech. Rep. No. 81). Spring, CO: Landy, Jacobs and Associates.
80	Hogan, R., Hogan, J., & Stovall, D. (1995). *Validity of the Hogan Personality Inventory for selecting bank tellers* (Tech. Rep. No. 80). Tulsa, OK: Hogan Assessment Systems.
79	Hayes, T. L., Roehm, H. A., & Castellano, J. P. (1994). *Personality correlates of success in total quality manufacturing* (Tech. Rep. No. 79). Journal of Business and Psychology, 8, 397-411.
78	Muchinsky, P. M. (1993). *Validation of personality constructs for the selection of insurance industry employees* (Tech. Rep. No. 78). Journal of Business and Psychology, 7, 475-482.
77	Hogan, J., Hogan, R., & Rybicki, S. (1995). *Validity of the Hogan Personality Inventory and the Inventory of Personal Motives for selecting marketing personnel* (Tech. Rep. No. 77). Tulsa, OK: Hogan Assessment Systems.
76	Hogan, R., Hogan, J., & Stovall, D. (1995). *Validity of the Hogan Personality Inventory for selecting drivers* (Tech. Rep. No. 76). Tulsa, OK: Hogan Assessment Systems.
75	Hogan, R., & Hogan, J. (1995). *Validity of the Hogan Personality Inventory for selecting salespeople* (Tech. Rep. No. 75). Tulsa, OK: Hogan Assessment Systems.
73	Hogan, R., Hogan, J., & Stovall, D. (1995). *Validity of the Hogan Personality Inventory for the selection of sales representatives* (Tech. Rep. No. 73). Tulsa, OK: Hogan Assessment Systems.
72	Brinkmeyer, K., & Hogan, J. (1995). *Validity of the Hogan Personality Inventory for selecting police communications operators* (Tech. Rep. No. 72). Tulsa, OK: Hogan Assessment Systems.
71	Hogan, J., & Stovall, D. (1995). *Validity of the Hogan Personality Inventory for selecting licensed practical nurses* (Tech. Rep. No. 71). Tulsa, OK: Hogan Assessment Systems.
70	Hogan, R., Hogan, J., & Brinkmeyer, K. (1995). *Validity of the Hogan Personality Inventory for selecting service operations coordinators* (Tech. Rep. No. 70). Tulsa, OK: Hogan Assessment Systems.
69	Hogan, R., Brinkmeyer, K., & Kidwell, D. (1995). *Validity of the Hogan Personality Inventory for selecting installers/assemblers* (Tech. Rep. No69). Tulsa, OK: Hogan Assessment Systems.
67	Hogan, R., & Gerhold, C. (1995). *Validity of the Hogan Personality Inventory for selecting managers and assistant managers* (Tech. Rep. No. 67). Tulsa, OK: Hogan Assessment Systems.
66	Hogan, R., & Gerhold, C. (1995). *Validity of the Hogan Personality Inventory for selecting financial consultants* (Tech Rep. No. 66). Tulsa, OK: Hogan Assessment Systems.
65	Hogan, J., Brinkmeyer, K., & Kidwell, D. (1994). *Validity of the Hogan Personality Inventory for selecting machine operators* (Tech. Rep. No. 65). Tulsa, OK: Hogan Assessment Systems.
64	Hogan, R., Hogan, J., & Brinkmeyer, K. (1994). *Validity of the Hogan Personality inventory for selecting drivers* (Tech. Rep. No. 64). Tulsa, OK: Hogan Assessment Systems.
63	Hogan, R., & Gerhold, C. (1994). *Validity of the Hogan Personality Inventory for selecting certified nursing assistants* (Tech. Rep. No. 63). Tulsa, OK: Hogan Assessment Systems.
62	Hogan, J., Brinkmeyer, K., & Kidwell, D. (1994). *Validity of the Hogan Personality Inventory for selecting drivers* (Tech. Rep. No. 62) Tulsa, OK: Hogan Assessment Systems.
61	Hogan, R., Hogan, J., Lock, J., & Brinkmeyer, K. (1994). *Validity of the Hogan Personality Inventory for selecting managers* (Tech. Rep. No. 61). Tulsa, OK: Hogan Assessment Systems.
60	Hogan, R., Brinkmeyer, K., & Hogan, J. (1994). *Validity of the Hogan Personality Inventory for employee selection* (Tech. Rep. No. 60). Tulsa, OK: Hogan Assessment Systems.

Tech Rep. Number	Citation
58	Hogan, R., Hogan, J., & Brinkmeyer, K. (1993). *Validity of Hogan Personality Inventory for selecting drivers* (Tech. Rep. No. 58). Tulsa, OK: Hogan Assessment Systems.
56	Hogan, J., & Hogan, R. (1993). *Validity of Hogan Inventory for selecting drivers* (Tech. Rep. No. 56). Tulsa, OK: Hogan Assessment Systems.
37	Arneson, S., Hogan, J., Hogan, R., & Petersons, A. V. (1989). *Development and validation of a clerical associates selection inventory* (Tech. Rep. No. 37). Tulsa, OK: Hogan Assessment Systems.
33	Arneson, S., Millikin-Davies, M., & Hogan, J. (1989). *Development and validation of the claims examiner selection inventory* (Tech. Rep. No. 33). Tulsa, OK: Hogan Assessment Systems.
32	Salas, E., Hogan, J., Driskell, J. E., & Hoskins, B. J. (1988). *Individual differences in technical training: Contributions of noncognitive measures* (Tech. Rep. No. 32). Orlando, FL: Naval Training Systems Center.
20	Hogan, R., Jacobson, G., Hogan, J., & Thompson, B. (1987). *Development and validation of a service operations dispatcher selection inventory* (Tech. Rep. No. 20). Tulsa, OK: Hogan Assessment Systems.
19	Arneson, S., & Hogan, R. (1987). *Development and validation of personnel selection tests for telemarketers and account executives* (Tech. Rep. No. 19). Tulsa, OK: Hogan Assessment Systems.
14	Hogan, R., & Hogan, J. (1986). *Development and validation of an organizational leadership index* (Tech. Rep. No. 14). Tulsa, OK: Hogan Assessment Systems.
11	Hogan, J., Peterson, S., Hogan, R., & Jones, S. (1985). *Development and validation of a line haul driver selection inventory* (Tech. Rep. No. 11). Tulsa, OK: University of Tulsa.
10	Hogan, J., Hogan, R., & Griffith, S. (1985). *Development and validation of a management potential inventory* (Tech. Rep. No. 10). Tulsa, OK: University of Tulsa.
8	Hogan, J., Peterson, S., Hogan, R., & Griffith, S. (1985). *Development and validation of a mechanic selection inventory* (Tech. Rep. No. 8). Tulsa, OK: University of Tulsa.
7	Hogan, J., & Hogan, R. (1984). *Development and validation of a sales representative selection inventory* (Tech. Rep. No. 7). Tulsa, OK: University of Tulsa.
2	Hogan, J., Hogan, R., & Busch, C. (1981) *Development and validation of the nursing aide inventory* (Tech. Rep. No. 2). Baltimore, MD: Johns Hopkins University.

Appendix D: Correlations of HPI Scales With Adjectival Descriptions By Observers

Table D.1

HPI Scale Correlations with Adjective Checklist Items

	ADJ	AMB	SOC	INP	PRU	INQ	LRN
Absent-minded	-0.11	-0.07	0.02	-0.01	**-0.24**	-0.01	-0.13
Active	**0.34**	**0.27**	**0.29**	**0.25**	0.10	0.09	0.12
Adaptable	**0.22**	0.12	0.12	**0.25**	0.17	0.13	0.06
Adventurous	0.21	0.13	**0.37**	0.18	-0.02	**0.28**	**0.35**
Affected	-0.09	**-0.24**	0.06	0.08	-0.12	-0.06	-0.10
Affectionate	-0.08	-0.08	0.13	**0.35**	0.20	0.00	-0.03
Aggressive	-0.08	0.05	0.12	-0.19	-0.04	0.16	0.11
Alert	**0.23**	0.06	0.02	0.03	0.09	0.10	-0.02
Aloof	0.02	-0.06	0.00	0.01	-0.12	0.16	-0.03
Ambitious	**0.23**	0.18	0.13	0.15	0.16	0.01	0.02
Anxious	-0.20	-0.17	-0.02	0.03	0.03	-0.19	0.08
Apathetic	**-0.22**	-0.16	0.02	-0.07	-0.17	-0.07	**-0.22**
Appreciative	0.12	0.02	0.18	**0.34**	0.09	-0.03	-0.03
Argumentative	-0.03	0.12	0.01	**-0.22**	-0.09	0.04	0.15
Arrogant	-0.03	0.15	0.06	-0.17	-0.18	0.17	0.00
Artistic	-0.12	-0.16	0.05	0.11	0.00	**0.23**	0.16
Assertive	**-0.23**	0.05	-0.04	**-0.23**	-0.12	0.04	0.08
Attractive	-0.12	0.02	0.11	0.09	0.16	-0.18	-0.17
Autocratic	0.10	0.01	0.14	-0.13	-0.20	0.15	0.07
Awkward	-0.04	-0.20	0.04	-0.05	-0.18	-0.02	-0.04
Bitter	**-0.27**	-0.15	-0.08	**-0.30**	-0.17	0.03	0.03
Blustery	0.01	0.09	0.19	-0.03	-0.19	0.14	-0.13
Boastful	0.04	0.11	0.11	0.05	0.02	0.14	0.11
Bossy	-0.13	0.08	0.10	**-0.25**	-0.02	0.17	0.14
Calm	0.18	-0.02	-0.03	**0.27**	0.17	-0.05	-0.01
Capable	0.14	0.07	0.14	0.11	0.06	0.14	-0.12
Careless	-0.04	0.05	0.04	**-0.24**	-0.18	0.12	0.02
Cautious	0.18	-0.04	**-0.24**	0.13	**0.26**	0.12	0.15
Changeable	-0.02	**-0.25**	-0.13	0.03	0.03	-0.01	0.01
Charming	0.11	0.08	0.21	**0.32**	**0.22**	-0.03	-0.01
Cheerful	0.18	0.07	**0.24**	**0.36**	**0.27**	-0.05	0.02
Civilized	0.16	0.05	-0.06	0.07	0.21	0.05	0.11
Clear-Thinking	0.11	-0.07	-0.09	-0.06	0.19	-0.12	0.09

	ADJ	AMB	SOC	INP	PRU	INQ	LRN
Clever	0.14	0.06	0.07	0.19	**0.23**	0.16	**0.26**
Coarse	**-0.24**	-0.15	-0.09	**-0.36**	-0.19	-0.07	0.03
Cold	-0.10	0.00	-0.08	-0.25	**-0.23**	-0.06	-0.03
Commonplace	0.05	-0.20	-0.08	0.02	0.00	-0.07	-0.05
Complaining	-0.14	-0.01	-0.10	-0.08	0.17	0.04	0.10
Complicated	0.08	0.12	0.07	-0.12	-0.06	0.13	**0.33**
Conceited	0.09	0.01	0.16	0.02	-0.10	0.16	0.12
Confident	**0.26**	**0.25**	0.05	-0.07	0.14	**0.30**	0.06
Confused	-0.06	-0.13	0.02	0.00	-0.12	-0.01	-0.08
Conscientious	**0.24**	0.11	0.18	**0.32**	0.21	0.21	0.09
Conservative	0.18	-0.01	0.00	0.12	**0.27**	-0.03	0.00
Considerate	**0.22**	0.18	**0.27**	**0.35**	**0.24**	0.19	0.12
Contented	0.08	-0.03	-0.06	-0.01	0.14	0.03	0.07
Conventional	**0.26**	-0.01	0.08	0.17	0.21	0.05	0.00
Cool	0.13	0.05	**0.27**	0.19	-0.01	-0.02	0.05
Cooperative	**0.31**	0.13	0.26	**0.40**	0.19	0.05	-0.09
Courageous	0.12	0.18	0.11	-0.02	0.03	0.09	0.09
Cowardly	-0.03	-0.15	-0.10	0.05	-0.03	-0.12	-0.11
Cruel	0.08	0.00	0.04	**-0.22**	**-0.25**	0.04	-0.06
Curious	0.05	0.00	0.18	0.15	0.07	0.13	0.16
Cynical	**-0.23**	-0.13	-0.06	**-0.29**	**-0.23**	0.04	0.05
Daring	0.00	-0.03	0.16	-0.11	-0.16	0.21	0.10
Deceitful	-0.08	**-0.22**	-0.17	-0.25	-0.13	-0.04	-0.01
Defensive	**-0.22**	-0.15	0.05	-0.11	-0.12	0.12	-0.01
Deliberate	0.04	-0.04	-0.16	-0.19	-0.01	0.09	0.24
Demanding	-0.09	0.14	0.05	-0.18	-0.04	-0.05	0.02
Dependable	0.08	-0.06	0.07	-0.03	0.13	-0.02	0.13
Dependent	0.04	-0.10	0.00	-0.02	0.13	0.06	-0.06
Despondent	0.04	-0.01	-0.01	-0.09	-0.14	0.11	0.05
Determined	0.04	0.11	0.07	-0.03	0.11	0.09	0.03
Dignified	0.17	0.02	0.01	0.10	0.09	0.05	0.01
Discreet	-0.06	-0.17	**-0.28**	-0.13	0.08	0.00	0.00
Disorderly	0.05	0.02	0.01	-0.08	-0.13	0.15	-0.07
Dissatisfied	-0.20	-0.07	-0.15	-0.23	-0.15	-0.01	-0.02
Distractible	-0.03	0.01	0.10	0.03	**-0.25**	0.04	-0.13
Distrustful	**-0.26**	**-0.27**	-0.09	**-0.34**	-0.10	-0.02	0.08
Dominant	-0.11	0.08	0.15	-0.25	-0.13	0.14	0.03
Dreamy	-0.02	-0.12	0.11	0.07	-0.07	-0.04	-0.03

	ADJ	AMB	SOC	INP	PRU	INQ	LRN
Dull	0.14	0.11	-0.19	-0.01	-0.04	0.01	0.07
Easy-going	**0.32**	0.00	0.03	**0.25**	0.14	-0.01	0.00
Effeminate	0.15	-0.05	0.14	0.04	-0.19	0.20	-0.01
Efficient	0.10	-0.03	-0.06	-0.03	0.22	-0.05	0.09
Egotistical	-0.03	0.19	0.12	-0.09	-0.04	0.12	0.05
Emotional	-0.11	-0.15	0.10	**0.25**	0.08	-0.08	-0.13
Energetic	**0.30**	**0.26**	**0.32**	**0.25**	0.11	0.11	-0.06
Enterprising	0.01	0.07	0.16	-0.13	0.03	**0.25**	0.07
Enthusiastic	0.20	0.19	0.22	0.21	0.07	0.02	0.01
Evasive	-0.06	-0.13	-0.15	-0.11	-0.04	0.08	0.12
Excitable	0.02	0.00	**0.29**	0.19	0.00	-0.01	-0.06
Fair-minded	0.08	-0.05	0.03	0.02	0.02	0.07	0.05
Fault-finding	-0.20	-0.06	0.11	**-0.30**	**-0.31**	-0.06	0.05
Fearful	-0.14	-0.14	-0.08	**-0.29**	-0.12	-0.11	0.11
Feminine	-0.21	**-0.30**	-0.06	0.17	0.13	-0.14	**-0.22**
Fickle	-0.16	-0.18	0.02	-0.21	-0.13	-0.10	-0.06
Flirtatious	0.16	0.13	**0.52**	0.28	0.04	**0.24**	0.11
Foolish	-0.03	-0.08	0.14	-0.19	**-0.23**	0.00	-0.18
Forceful	-0.03	0.07	0.12	**-0.34**	-0.08	0.15	0.15
Foresighted	0.02	0.06	-0.17	**-0.27**	0.20	0.08	0.19
Forgetful	0.09	0.06	0.12	0.09	-0.14	-0.06	-0.19
Forgiving	0.18	-0.06	0.20	**0.25**	0.07	-0.10	-0.08
Formal	0.13	-0.03	-0.17	0.00	0.11	-0.21	-0.09
Frank	0.08	0.14	0.03	-0.11	-0.05	0.17	0.12
Friendly	0.21	0.06	0.20	**0.42**	0.24	-0.03	-0.18
Frivolous	0.07	0.11	0.16	0.00	0.12	0.18	-0.04
Fussy	-0.17	0.00	-0.03	**-0.31**	-0.05	0.12	0.15
Generous	0.17	-0.11	0.15	**0.33**	0.18	-0.11	-0.19
Gentle	**0.25**	-0.04	0.09	**0.33**	0.30	-0.13	-0.11
Gloomy	-0.09	-0.09	-0.02	-0.14	-0.16	-0.12	-0.01
Good-looking	0.02	0.02	0.13	0.21	0.16	-0.04	-0.17
Good-natured	0.19	0.11	0.00	0.19	0.16	0.01	-0.07
Greedy	-0.08	0.03	0.04	-0.16	-0.12	0.06	-0.07
Handsome	**0.37**	**0.36**	**0.30**	0.12	-0.01	**0.22**	0.07
Hard-Headed	-0.12	0.03	0.03	-0.18	-0.21	-0.02	0.06
Hard-hearted	-0.03	-0.13	-0.03	**-0.33**	-0.11	0.00	0.06
Hasty	-0.22	-0.11	-0.10	**-0.33**	-0.09	0.08	0.08
Headstrong	0.01	0.14	0.20	-0.11	-0.12	0.04	0.16

	ADJ	AMB	SOC	INP	PRU	INQ	LRN
Healthy	0.24	0.13	0.29	0.18	0.01	0.10	-0.03
Helpful	0.07	0.06	0.07	0.21	0.21	-0.01	**-0.22**
High-strung	-0.01	0.07	0.10	-0.17	-0.11	0.10	0.13
Honest	0.16	0.00	0.10	0.10	0.21	0.01	0.12
Hostile	-0.10	0.11	0.07	**-0.23**	-0.07	0.13	0.19
Humorous	**0.31**	**0.24**	**0.31**	**0.24**	**0.22**	0.14	0.15
Hurried	-0.18	-0.12	0.01	**-0.23**	-0.20	-0.01	-0.02
Idealistic	0.00	0.01	0.06	0.08	0.13	0.14	0.01
Imaginative	0.17	0.09	**0.28**	0.19	0.04	0.20	**0.24**
Immature	-0.01	0.08	**0.24**	0.03	-0.19	0.19	-0.13
Impatient	-0.08	0.05	0.18	-0.16	-0.16	-0.02	-0.04
Impulsive	-0.09	-0.06	**0.31**	-0.09	-0.18	0.08	0.02
Independent	-0.02	0.02	0.07	-0.04	0.01	0.13	0.14
Indifferent	0.15	-0.09	-0.01	0.06	-0.04	-0.08	0.13
Individualistic	0.09	0.18	0.19	0.02	-0.02	0.16	0.20
Industrious	0.03	-0.08	**-0.29**	-0.21	0.12	0.12	**0.29**
Infantile	0.04	0.03	0.07	**-0.28**	**-0.26**	0.04	0.04
Informal	-0.05	0.05	0.10	**-0.23**	**-0.23**	0.03	0.16
Ingenious	-0.13	-0.17	-0.02	-0.10	-0.02	-0.07	**0.28**
Inhibited	0.05	-0.05	0.03	-0.10	-0.01	0.02	0.19
Initiative	0.04	0.00	-0.14	-0.12	0.02	-0.06	0.11
Insightful	0.18	0.05	-0.10	-0.02	0.08	-0.09	0.07
Intelligent	0.04	-0.02	0.07	0.20	0.13	-0.12	-0.14
Interests narrow	-0.12	-0.12	-0.07	-0.29	-0.21	-0.07	-0.21
Interests wide	0.11	0.03	**0.33**	0.19	-0.03	**0.29**	0.06
Intolerant	-0.08	0.07	0.06	**-0.30**	-0.13	0.09	0.06
Inventive	0.11	0.03	0.02	-0.05	0.14	0.22	**0.27**
Irresponsible	0.07	0.18	0.16	-0.06	**-0.24**	0.10	0.02
Irritable	-0.19	-0.05	-0.05	**-0.41**	-0.05	-0.04	0.04
Jolly	0.08	-0.05	**0.29**	0.26	-0.11	-0.01	-0.02
Kind	0.20	0.11	0.20	**0.26**	0.20	0.06	0.02
Lazy	-0.13	**-0.30**	-0.05	0.14	-0.05	-0.20	-0.09
Leisurely	0.10	-0.05	0.16	**0.22**	-0.13	0.00	-0.02
Logical	0.08	0.04	-0.21	-0.11	0.20	0.20	0.04
Loud	-0.03	0.15	0.29	-0.10	**-0.23**	0.11	-0.17
Loyal	0.02	-0.06	0.12	-0.02	-0.07	0.15	0.14
Mannerly	**0.22**	0.06	0.11	0.21	0.14	0.06	-0.04
Masculine	**0.35**	**0.37**	0.23	-0.06	-0.03	**0.25**	0.03
Mature	0.14	0.05	0.13	0.21	0.12	0.15	-0.04
Meek	0.12	-0.02	-0.20	-0.12	0.05	0.06	0.06

	ADJ	AMB	SOC	INP	PRU	INQ	LRN
Methodical	-0.03	-0.04	-0.05	-0.07	0.19	0.09	-0.01
Mild	0.10	**-0.26**	-0.12	0.14	**0.23**	0.13	0.05
Mischievous	-0.12	0.11	**0.23**	-0.06	-0.15	0.20	-0.01
Moderate	-0.05	**-0.29**	**-0.23**	0.05	0.07	0.02	-0.02
Modest	0.18	0.03	-0.05	-0.12	-0.02	0.14	**0.22**
Moody	**-0.31**	-0.06	0.16	0.01	-0.07	-0.04	-0.17
Nagging	**-0.23**	-0.12	-0.02	**-0.29**	-0.12	0.10	0.00
Natural	0.17	-0.05	0.10	0.14	0.09	0.10	0.05
Nervous	0.00	-0.10	0.01	0.03	-0.02	-0.05	-0.02
Noisy	0.10	-0.09	0.18	-0.09	-0.14	0.10	-0.07
Obliging	-0.01	-0.14	0.14	-0.03	-0.04	0.10	-0.08
Obnoxious	0.03	-0.06	0.10	-0.21	-0.17	0.12	-0.02
Opinionated	-0.06	0.11	-0.07	**-0.25**	-0.03	0.08	0.20
Opportunistic	0.00	0.06	0.10	0.02	0.11	-0.05	0.11
Optimistic	0.20	0.00	0.21	0.14	0.09	0.10	0.03
Organized	0.01	-0.11	-0.12	0.04	**0.22**	-0.20	-0.11
Original	0.14	0.02	0.04	0.12	0.03	0.15	0.08
Outgoing	0.11	0.14	**0.43**	**0.27**	0.12	0.05	-0.04
Outspoken	0.13	**0.29**	**0.37**	0.04	0.10	0.21	0.16
Painstaking	-0.11	**-0.25**	-0.17	**-0.27**	0.07	0.14	**0.25**
Patient	**0.25**	-0.04	-0.15	**0.23**	**0.31**	0.07	0.07
Peaceable	0.12	0.01	0.05	0.18	0.11	0.05	-0.01
Peculiar	0.18	-0.06	-0.06	0.07	-0.05	-0.05	0.09
Persevering	0.19	0.05	0.20	0.06	0.02	0.10	-0.06
Persistent	0.19	0.12	0.02	-0.03	0.07	0.06	0.12
Pessimistic	-0.29	-0.11	-0.05	**-0.25**	0.03	0.12	-0.02
Planful	-0.01	-0.02	-0.16	**-0.23**	0.07	0.01	0.19
Pleasant	0.02	-0.03	0.14	0.33	0.18	-0.05	-0.02
Pleasure-seeking	0.12	0.14	0.25	0.17	-0.01	0.02	0.08
Poised	0.15	0.07	-0.07	-0.03	**0.30**	0.06	0.01
Polished	**0.22**	-0.02	-0.05	0.13	**0.35**	-0.06	0.03
Practical	**0.28**	0.06	0.06	0.00	0.15	0.11	0.01
Praising	**0.23**	0.19	0.27	**0.34**	0.15	0.05	-0.11
Precise	0.18	0.03	-0.01	-0.02	0.20	0.06	0.16
Prejudiced	0.00	-0.16	0.06	**-0.26**	-0.09	0.09	-0.03
Preoccupied	0.04	-0.15	0.05	0.05	-0.04	0.05	-0.02
Progressive	0.13	0.07	-0.07	0.00	0.17	0.02	0.01
Prudish	-0.15	-0.16	-0.15	-0.19	**-0.25**	-0.09	-0.21
Quarrelsome	-0.30	-0.09	0.00	**-0.54**	-0.20	0.08	0.07

	ADJ	AMB	SOC	INP	PRU	INQ	LRN
Queer	-0.18	-0.31	0.01	-0.02	-0.18	-0.03	-0.04
Quick	0.11	0.17	0.15	-0.01	-0.02	0.03	-0.07
Quiet	0.04	**-0.28**	**-0.39**	0.00	0.05	-0.15	0.00
Quitting	-0.04	-0.01	0.02	-0.01	-0.06	-0.09	-0.06
Rational	0.09	0.09	0.06	-0.01	0.05	0.05	0.02
Rattlebrained	0.04	-0.03	0.03	0.00	0.02	0.16	-0.03
Realistic	**0.26**	0.08	-0.01	0.09	**0.22**	0.04	0.05
Reasonable	0.21	0.07	0.04	0.02	0.10	0.03	-0.12
Rebellious	-0.21	-0.01	0.02	**-0.30**	**-0.26**	-0.02	0.04
Reckless	-0.05	0.02	**0.23**	-0.13	**-0.34**	0.13	-0.01
Reflective	0.18	0.03	-0.05	0.07	-0.03	0.17	0.04
Relaxed	**0.27**	0.04	0.15	0.20	0.00	-0.08	-0.07
Reliable	0.21	0.19	0.06	0.07	0.13	0.08	0.05
Resentful	-0.03	0.06	0.04	**-0.22**	-0.05	0.09	0.11
Reserved	0.11	-0.18	-0.20	0.06	0.09	-0.10	-0.06
Resourceful	0.07	0.08	0.10	-0.08	0.00	0.16	0.13
Responsible	0.06	0.04	0.13	0.16	0.06	-0.11	-0.07
Restless	0.02	-0.08	0.00	-0.05	-0.01	0.18	0.17
Retiring	0.04	-0.14	-0.05	**-0.23**	-0.13	0.05	-0.02
Rigid	-0.14	-0.11	**-0.22**	**-0.31**	0.01	-0.03	**0.28**
Robust	-0.01	-0.09	-0.02	0.00	0.00	0.15	0.12
Rude	-0.13	-0.09	0.00	**-0.31**	-0.25	0.00	-0.11
Sarcastic	0.04	0.10	**0.26**	0.02	-0.04	**0.27**	0.16
Self-centered	0.00	0.12	0.13	-0.05	-0.19	0.17	0.06
Self-confident	**0.37**	**0.39**	0.12	-0.02	0.17	**0.22**	0.09
Self-controlled	0.19	0.15	0.03	-0.10	0.03	0.15	0.02
Self-denying	0.05	0.04	0.01	-0.11	-0.06	0.05	**0.25**
Self-pitying	-0.10	-0.12	-0.01	-0.13	-0.20	0.15	-0.02
Self-punishing	-0.24	-0.23	-0.04	-0.23	-0.04	0.07	0.01
Self-seeking	0.02	0.05	0.05	-0.11	-0.04	-0.07	0.06
Selfish	-0.09	-0.02	0.07	-0.16	**-0.25**	0.00	0.05
Sensitive	0.09	-0.09	0.16	**0.39**	0.21	-0.06	-0.16
Sentimental	0.01	-0.11	0.19	**0.31**	0.14	0.09	-0.13
Serious	-0.02	-0.08	-0.16	**-0.23**	0.09	-0.04	0.11
Severe	0.06	-0.13	-0.04	-0.15	-0.02	0.05	-0.08
Sexy	0.04	0.17	**0.22**	0.09	0.08	0.09	0.11
Shallow	0.17	0.16	0.15	-0.03	0.11	0.12	0.13
Sharp-witted	-0.01	0.04	0.07	0.01	0.05	0.07	0.12
Shiftless	0.12	-0.16	-0.10	0.05	-0.08	0.05	0.17

	ADJ	AMB	SOC	INP	PRU	INQ	LRN
Show-off	0.00	0.10	0.12	-0.07	0.00	0.20	-0.05
Shrewd	0.11	0.03	0.00	-0.10	0.09	0.10	**0.27**
Shy	-0.02	-0.16	-0.14	0.00	0.04	-0.03	0.07
Silent	-0.10	-0.24	-0.30	-0.27	-0.11	**-0.23**	-0.11
Simple	0.19	-0.03	-0.09	0.00	-0.02	0.02	-0.04
Sincere	0.08	0.07	-0.18	-0.16	0.09	0.03	0.03
Slipshod	0.17	0.15	0.06	-0.04	-0.03	0.13	0.10
Slow	-0.11	-0.20	-0.13	**-0.24**	-0.09	-0.13	-0.19
Sly	0.05	0.04	0.12	**-0.22**	-0.21	0.10	0.18
Smug	-0.01	-0.08	-0.04	**-0.28**	-0.17	0.09	0.06
Snobbish	0.06	0.07	0.01	-0.04	-0.18	0.17	-0.07
Sociable	0.17	0.08	0.41	0.26	0.13	0.14	-0.09
Soft-hearted	-0.08	-0.12	0.14	0.14	0.16	0.01	0.09
Sophisticated	0.08	0.00	-0.08	0.08	**0.25**	-0.09	0.03
Spendthrift	0.11	0.02	0.11	-0.06	-0.18	0.01	0.11
Spineless	0.00	-0.11	-0.03	-0.13	-0.01	0.08	-0.02
Spontaneous	0.01	-0.04	0.21	0.20	0.00	0.15	0.18
Spunky	-0.06	-0.17	0.14	0.03	-0.10	-0.06	0.07
Stable	0.18	0.01	-0.06	0.06	0.09	-0.04	0.12
Steady	0.15	-0.09	-0.04	0.03	0.11	0.04	0.10
Stern	0.02	0.07	-0.03	**-0.23**	-0.02	0.03	0.04
Stingy	0.01	-0.09	-0.15	**-0.33**	-0.19	0.07	0.11
Stolid	0.02	0.02	-0.10	-0.04	0.07	0.03	0.21
Strong	0.03	0.16	0.18	-0.06	-0.06	0.07	0.15
Stubborn	-0.12	0.02	0.11	-0.12	-0.15	0.07	0.11
Submissive	0.13	-0.02	-0.07	-0.09	**0.29**	0.19	**0.25**
Suggestible	0.09	-0.06	0.05	-0.02	0.08	0.05	0.00
Sulky	-0.01	0.00	-0.10	-0.16	-0.05	-0.01	0.09
Superstitious	-0.07	-0.10	0.17	0.03	-0.05	0.20	-0.18
Suspicious	-0.07	-0.13	0.02	-0.05	-0.16	-0.02	-0.08
Sympathetic	0.10	-0.14	0.17	**0.29**	0.18	0.12	-0.04
Tactful	0.08	0.06	-0.04	-0.07	0.12	0.17	0.00
Tactless	-0.11	-0.08	0.10	-0.18	**-0.31**	0.06	-0.14
Talkative	0.09	0.02	**0.38**	0.28	-0.04	0.16	-0.10
Temperamental	**-0.29**	-0.01	0.07	**-0.25**	-0.16	0.03	0.00
Tense	-0.12	0.09	-0.01	-0.21	-0.08	0.10	0.13
Thankless	-0.09	-0.10	-0.07	**-0.26**	-0.12	-0.05	-0.06
Thorough	0.03	0.08	-0.07	-0.15	0.09	0.06	**0.23**
Thoughtful	0.15	-0.02	0.14	0.22	0.15	0.10	-0.02
Thrifty	0.07	-0.05	-0.09	-0.05	0.08	0.10	0.11

	ADJ	AMB	SOC	INP	PRU	INQ	LRN
Timid	0.05	-0.05	-0.07	-0.01	0.01	-0.07	-0.05
Tolerant	0.09	-0.17	**0.22**	**0.25**	0.08	0.18	0.00
Touchy	-0.18	-0.05	0.19	-0.12	-0.27	-0.05	-0.03
Tough	-0.02	0.09	0.10	-0.01	-0.02	**0.30**	0.04
Trusting	0.18	-0.11	0.14	**0.33**	0.17	-0.19	**-0.25**
Unaffected	0.05	-0.16	**-0.30**	-0.05	-0.06	-0.07	-0.02
Unambitious	0.03	-0.04	0.02	-0.12	-0.16	0.18	0.02
Unassuming	0.11	-0.12	-0.07	-0.02	0.09	0.26	0.20
Unconventional	-0.12	0.00	0.01	-0.28	**-0.29**	0.07	0.12
Undependable	-0.06	0.02	0.06	-0.09	**-0.22**	0.01	-0.02
Understanding	0.05	-0.05	0.06	0.21	0.13	-0.03	-0.13
Unemotional	0.05	-0.14	-0.17	-0.12	-0.03	0.15	0.16
Unexcitable	-0.13	**-0.22**	-0.14	**-0.26**	-0.05	0.04	-0.04
Unfriendly	-0.06	-0.05	-0.14	-0.13	-0.10	-0.05	0.00
Uninhibited	0.16	0.12	0.15	-0.08	-0.04	0.09	0.12
Unintelligent	0.00	-0.12	-0.05	**-0.26**	-0.16	0.06	-0.02
Unkind	0.14	0.16	-0.07	-0.02	-0.06	0.09	0.09
Unrealistic	0.03	0.07	0.06	**-0.22**	-0.12	0.05	0.02
Unscrupulous	0.06	0.02	0.07	-0.17	-0.04	-0.12	0.07
Unselfish	0.07	-0.09	0.06	-0.03	0.01	-0.05	-0.15
Unstable	-0.16	-0.07	-0.11	**-0.35**	-0.09	0.03	0.15
Vindictive	-0.11	0.00	-0.02	**-0.27**	**-0.22**	0.00	0.16
Versatile	0.03	0.05	0.01	0.08	0.07	**0.25**	0.14
Warm	0.08	-0.13	0.04	**0.32**	0.18	-0.04	-0.08
Wary	-0.05	-0.10	-0.05	-0.19	0.00	0.12	0.14
Weak	0.07	0.02	0.02	-0.19	-0.10	0.09	0.12
Whiny	-0.11	0.05	-0.03	0.01	-0.03	0.07	0.09
Wholesome	0.11	-0.10	0.06	0.20	0.08	-0.04	-0.08
Wise	0.11	0.10	0.01	0.03	-0.03	0.03	0.00
Withdrawn	-0.03	-0.11	-0.07	-0.21	-0.12	0.11	0.05
Witty	0.09	0.03	**0.22**	0.07	-0.01	0.18	**0.25**
Worrying	-0.14	-0.13	0.03	0.00	-0.14	-0.02	0.04
Zany	-0.16	-0.16	0.02	-0.10	-0.09	0.01	0.06

Note: N = 84; ADJ = Adjustment; AMB = Ambition; SOC = Sociability; INP = Interpersonal Sensitivity; PRU = Prudence; INQ = Inquisitive; LRN = Learning Approach; Correlations in BOLD are significant at p < .05, two-tailed.

Table D.2
HPI Scale Correlations with Adjective Checklist Items

	ADJ	AMB	SOC	INP	PRU	INQ	LRN
Is critical, skeptical, not easily impressed.	-0.06	0.11	-0.03	**-0.43**	-0.13	0.21	**0.22**
Is a genuinely dependable and responsible person.	**0.26**	0.17	0.07	0.11	0.10	0.18	**0.22**
Has a wide range of interests.	0.10	0.17	0.37	0.19	-0.07	0.15	-0.02
Is a talkative individual.	0.04	0.21	0.39	**0.28**	-0.05	0.07	-0.12
Behaves in a giving way toward others.	-0.09	-0.05	0.06	**0.23**	**0.24**	-0.14	-0.02
Is fastidious. (Meticulous attention to detail)	-0.14	-0.06	-0.14	-0.08	0.10	-0.01	0.10
Favors conservative values in a variety of areas.	0.07	-0.12	-0.17	0.11	0.18	-0.07	-0.10
Appears to have a high degree of intellectual capacity.	0.08	**0.25**	0.02	0.05	0.20	0.08	0.21
Is comfortable with uncertainty and complexity.	**0.26**	**0.22**	0.05	0.01	0.01	-0.02	0.06
Anxiety and tension find outlet in bodily symptoms.	**-0.29**	**-0.33**	-0.02	0.04	-0.10	0.00	0.04
Is protective of those close to him or her.	0.01	-0.09	0.14	0.16	0.11	-0.16	-0.10
Tends to be self-defensive.	**-0.23**	-0.10	0.19	0.03	**-0.24**	0.06	-0.03
Is thin-skinned; sensitive to anything that can be construed as criticism or an interpersonal slight.	**-0.34**	**-0.30**	-0.04	-0.02	-0.18	**-0.22**	**-0.29**
Genuinely submissive; accepts domination comfortable.	0.16	-0.13	-0.10	0.19	0.24	-0.01	0.07
Is skilled in social techniques of imaginative play, pretending and humor.	-0.04	0.03	0.26	0.29	0.07	0.07	0.00
Is introspective and concerned with self as an object.	-0.06	0.05	-0.09	0.15	0.11	-0.04	0.10
Behaves in a sympathetic or considerate manner.	0.03	-0.13	0.05	0.30	**0.22**	-0.03	-0.20
Initiates humor.	-0.03	0.10	**0.32**	0.13	-0.04	0.12	-0.07
Seeks reassurance from others.	-0.20	-0.11	0.15	**0.33**	0.04	0.01	**-0.24**
Has a rapid personal tempo; behaves and acts quickly.	0.08	0.19	0.27	-0.01	0.06	0.04	0.14
Arouses nurturant feelings in others.	0.07	0.09	0.01	**0.30**	0.18	0.01	-0.11
Feels a lack of personal meaning in life.	**-0.25**	-0.14	-0.05	-0.18	-0.09	-0.01	0.04
Exprapunitive; tends to transfer or project blame.	**-0.32**	**-0.23**	-0.05	-0.24	**-0.22**	0.04	0.08
Prides self on being "objective," rational.	0.07	0.16	-0.11	0.01	**0.23**	0.16	0.07
Tends toward over-control of needs and impulses; binds tensions excessively; delays gratification unnecessarily.	-0.10	0.04	-0.02	-0.14	-0.04	**0.24**	0.19
Is productive; gets things done.	0.05	0.18	0.10	0.00	0.10	0.12	-0.05
Shows condescending behavior in relations with others.	-0.10	0.02	-0.04	**-0.26**	-0.10	0.13	0.05
Tends to arouse liking and acceptance in people.	0.11	0.00	**0.29**	**0.44**	**0.27**	0.00	-0.04
Is turned to for advice and reassurance.	0.11	0.13	0.12	0.15	**0.29**	-0.04	0.21
Gives up and withdraws where possible in the face of frustration and adversity.	-0.11	-0.11	-0.03	0.11	-0.09	-0.05	0.10
Regards self as physically attractive.	**0.32**	**0.41**	0.19	0.17	**0.29**	0.11	0.05
Seems to be aware of the impression he or she makes on others.	0.08	0.16	0.07	0.02	0.13	0.03	-0.02
Is calm, relaxed in manner.	**0.30**	0.08	-0.05	0.22	0.14	-0.01	0.02
Over-reactive to minor frustrations; irritable.	**-0.28**	-0.09	0.08	-0.13	-0.25	-0.03	-0.13

	ADJ	AMB	SOC	INP	PRU	INQ	LRN
Has warmth; has the capacity for close relationships; compassionate.	0.09	-0.02	**0.24**	**0.39**	0.18	0.10	-0.20
Is subtle negativistic; tends to undermine and obstruct or sabotage.	-0.12	-0.13	0.06	-0.20	**-0.24**	0.06	0.05
Is guileful and deceitful, manipulative, opportunistic.	-0.06	-0.07	0.01	**-0.25**	**-0.25**	-0.04	0.02
Has hostility towards others.	**-0.22**	-0.10	-0.07	**-0.37**	-0.05	0.07	0.06
Thinks and associates to ideas in unusual ways; has unconventional thought processes.	-0.07	0.10	-0.16	**-0.24**	-0.15	0.13	0.12
Is vulnerable to real or fancied threat, generally fearful.	-0.20	**-0.26**	-0.08	-0.09	-0.02	-0.17	-0.15
Is moralistic.	0.14	0.02	-0.05	0.15	0.11	0.01	-0.10
Reluctant to commit self to any definite course of action; tends to delay or avoid action.	**-0.24**	-0.19	**-0.23**	-0.19	-0.17	-0.18	-0.17
Is facially and/or gesturally expressive.	-0.08	0.01	**0.31**	**0.30**	-0.08	0.01	**-0.24**
Evaluates the motivation of others in interpreting situations.	0.11	0.10	-0.02	-0.07	0.06	0.00	0.15
Has a brittle ego-defense system; has a small reserve of integration; would be disorganized and maladaptive when under stress or trauma.	**-0.26**	**-0.30**	-0.05	-0.06	-0.08	-0.12	-0.13
Engages in personal fantasy and daydreams, fictional speculations.	0.12	0.00	0.22	0.21	-0.09	0.16	0.14
Has a readiness to feel guilty.	-0.21	-0.19	-0.01	0.11	0.07	-0.10	-0.09
Keeps people at a distance; avoids close interpersonal relationships.	-0.10	-0.07	**-0.23**	**-0.33**	-0.15	-0.07	0.13
Is basically distrustful of people in general; questions their motivations.	-0.21	-0.15	-0.13	**-0.37**	0.00	0.08	**0.24**
Is unpredictable and changeable in behavior and attitudes.	**-0.30**	-0.08	-0.05	**-0.28**	**-0.23**	-0.01	0.09
Genuinely values intellectual and cognitive matters.	0.09	0.10	0.04	0.03	0.10	-0.09	0.03
Behaves in an assertive fashion.	-0.15	0.14	0.05	-0.02	0.08	0.07	0.16
Various needs tend toward relatively direct and uncontrolled expression; unable to delay gratification.	0.06	0.10	0.02	0.03	-0.03	0.00	0.07
Emphasizes being with others; gregarious.	**0.33**	0.11	**0.45**	0.51	0.17	**0.24**	-0.01
Is self-defeating.	**-0.31**	-0.17	0.00	**-0.22**	-0.18	0.04	0.01
Responds to humor.	0.17	0.11	0.24	0.21	0.13	0.13	0.08
Is an interesting, arresting person.	0.09	0.09	0.21	0.14	**0.23**	-0.02	0.12
Is experience seeking.	0.07	0.11	0.19	0.07	0.05	**0.25**	0.11
Is concerned with own body and the adequacy of its physiological functioning.	0.18	0.18	0.03	0.09	0.05	0.02	-0.12
Has insight into own motives and behavior.	0.12	0.02	0.10	0.09	0.12	-0.03	-0.02
Creates and exploits dependency in people.	-0.06	0.04	-0.11	0.04	0.07	0.00	0.12
Tends to be rebellious and non-conforming.	**-0.23**	0.04	-0.05	**-0.25**	**-0.26**	0.01	-0.03
Judges self and others in conventional terms like "popularity," "the correct thing to do," social pressures, etc.	**0.26**	**0.22**	0.07	0.16	0.00	0.08	-0.09
Is socially perceptive of a wide range of interpersonal cues.	0.11	0.14	0.22	0.04	0.13	0.09	0.08

	ADJ	AMB	SOC	INP	PRU	INQ	LRN
Characteristically pushes and tries to stretch limits; sees what he or she can get away with.	-0.05	0.14	0.08	**-0.22**	-0.20	**0.23**	0.18
Enjoys esthetic impressions; is esthetically reactive.	0.13	**0.23**	**0.23**	0.19	0.21	0.20	0.08
Is self-indulgent.	0.03	0.13	0.17	-0.01	-0.08	0.12	0.11
Is basically anxious.	**-0.30**	-0.11	-0.01	-0.10	-0.13	-0.10	0.02
Is sensitive to anything that can be construed as a demand.	**-0.31**	-0.17	-0.02	-0.07	-0.09	-0.07	-0.21
Behaves in an ethically consistent manner; is consistent with own personal standards.	0.16	0.03	0.05	**0.22**	**0.23**	0.04	-0.02
Has high aspiration level for self.	**0.30**	0.21	0.07	0.11	**0.32**	0.03	0.15
Concerned with own adequacy as a person, either at conscious or unconscious levels.	-0.10	-0.06	0.00	0.15	0.02	-0.10	0.22
Tends to perceive many different contexts inappropriately.	-0.21	-0.04	0.06	-0.11	**-0.24**	0.05	0.08
Is subjectively unaware of self-concern; feels satisfied with self.	**0.28**	0.22	-0.02	0.03	-0.04	0.11	0.12
Has a clear-cut, internally consistent personality.	**0.34**	**0.35**	0.12	0.21	0.13	0.17	0.09
Tends to project his or her own feelings and motivations onto others.	0.05	0.04	0.16	0.17	-0.08	-0.04	-0.03
Appears straightforward, forthright, and candid in dealing with others.	0.11	**0.27**	-0.05	-0.08	0.18	0.10	0.05
Feels cheated and victimized by life; self-pitying.	**-0.29**	0.02	-0.13	-0.10	-0.17	0.05	-0.14
Tends to ruminate and have persistent pre-occupying thoughts.	-0.14	-0.14	-0.06	0.05	-0.09	0.02	0.04
Interested in establishing relationships.	0.07	-0.03	**0.32**	**0.42**	0.08	0.10	-0.1
Is physically attractive; good looking.	0.09	0.13	0.03	0.12	0.17	-0.12	-0.03
Has fluctuating moods.	**-0.37**	-0.01	0.17	-0.08	-0.06	0.06	0.04
Able to see to the heart of important problems.	0.04	0.00	0.10	0.09	0.12	-0.06	0.10
Is cheerful.	0.14	0.15	**0.28**	**0.25**	0.20	0.08	0.06
Emphasizes communication through action and non-verbal behavior.	0.16	0.07	0.00	0.14	0.10	-0.07	0.04
Handles anxiety and conflicts by refusing to recognize their presence; repressive or dissociative tendencies.	-0.16	-0.08	-0.04	-0.03	-0.20	0.13	0.04
Interprets basically simple and clear-cut situations in complicated and particularizing ways.	-0.09	-0.06	-0.12	-0.04	0.03	0.02	-0.06
Is personally charming.	0.15	0.11	0.11	**0.35**	**0.28**	-0.02	0.01
Compares self to others. Is alert to real or fancied differences between self and other people.	0.11	0.07	0.18	**0.27**	0.14	-0.04	-0.03
Is concerned with philosophical problems; e.g., religious, values, the meaning of life, etc.	0.03	0.07	0.01	0.15	-0.05	0.02	-0.01
Is power oriented; values power in self or others.	0.01	**0.25**	**0.25**	-0.10	0.04	0.17	0.11
Has social poise and presence; appears socially at ease.	0.08	0.04	0.13	0.08	0.11	0.10	-0.06
Expresses hostile feelings directly.	-0.11	0.10	-0.11	**-0.31**	0.04	-0.08	0.10

	ADJ	AMB	SOC	INP	PRU	INQ	LRN
Behaves in a masculine style and manner/Behaves in a feminine style and manner.	0.04	0.12	-0.04	0.04	0.17	0.05	-0.12
Tends to pro-offer advice.	0.07	-0.01	0.06	0.15	0.15	**0.26**	0.18
Values own independence and autonomy.	0.09	**0.28**	0.09	0.17	-0.05	**0.24**	0.13
Is emotionally bland; has flattened affect.	-0.20	-0.21	-0.16	-0.22	-0.18	-0.05	0.03
Is verbally fluent; can express ideas well.	0.05	0.20	0.06	0.01	-0.06	0.05	0.11
Is self-dramatizing; histrionic.	0.13	0.11	0.05	0.02	-0.07	0.14	-0.10
Does not vary roles; relates to everyone in the same way.	0.04	-0.13	-0.22	0.09	0.07	-0.16	-0.07

Note: N = 84; ADJ = Adjustment; AMB = Ambition; SOC = Sociability; INP = Interpersonal Sensitivity; PRU = Prudence; INQ = Inquisitive; LRN = Learning Approach; Correlations in BOLD are significant at p < .05, two-tailed.